Notes on St. Martin's church and parish

T. H. Baker

Alpha Editions

This edition published in 2019

ISBN : 9789353606749

Design and Setting By
Alpha Editions
email - alphaedis@gmail.com

NOTES

ON

St. Martin's Church and Parish

COMPILED BY

T. H. BAKER.

SALISBURY:
BROWN & CO., BOOKSELLERS, CANAL.

SALISBURY:
BENNETT BROTHERS, PRINTERS, JOURNAL OFFICE.

1906.

ST. MARTIN'S CHURCH, NORTH WEST VIEW, 1906.

PREFACE.

These Notes on St. Martin's Church and Parish make no pretension to be a history of the same. Nothing is known of the foundation of the Church, and very little relating to it before the 16th Century, beyond the fact that it was in existence before the transference of the City from Old Sarum. This, doubtless, is the reason why it has not been so fully noticed by any writers as the more recently-erected churches of St. Thomas and St. Edmund.

Therefore, the information contained in these pages has been collected in order to bring to light such facts as have been hitherto unpublished, or were not available to the public in general. It consists of copies of documents in the Parish Chests, some of which, although in a damaged condition, are sufficiently intelligible to show their purport. Extracts from the Churchwardens' Accounts and Vestry Books, Notes from Hatcher's History of Salisbury, St. Martin's Parish Magazine, the Gentleman's Magazine, besides much valuable information given by the Rev. C. N. Wyld, who was Rector at the period of the last Restoration; the Rev. Canon Myers, the present Rector; and lastly, by Mr. W. C. Pearce, the Parish Clerk, who has communicated details known to no one else. Thanks are also due to Mrs. Cheesman for kindly giving permission to use the photograph of the Church as a frontispiece, and to Mr. Ponting for his opinion on some of the architectural details.

T. H. BAKER.

1906.

INTRODUCTION.

My friend, Mr. Baker, has asked me to write a few words of introduction to the Notes which he has compiled on St. Martin's Church. The Book owes its origin to a small cause. A few years ago a sermon was preached at St. Martin's, in which some account was given of the history of the Church and its ornaments. It aroused considerable interest, and as some members of the congregation expressed a desire to see the information in print, Mr. Baker kindly undertook the publication of a leaflet, which should serve as a guide for visitors, containing a brief summary of the different points to be noticed in the fabric of the Church, &c. It was felt, however, that there was so much more to be said on the subject, and so much interesting material to draw from in the Churchwardens' Accounts, Vestry Books, and documents in the Church Chests, that Mr. Baker consented to do a further service, and collect and record all that he thought would be of value to those who desired to know more of the history which gathered round their Parish Church. The result is now given to the reader in the following pages. To the writer, the Book, which is the outcome of many hours of research, has been a labour of love, but he would not wish it to be regarded as more than a collection of Notes. As such, however, it is a veritable mine of wealth, from which a great deal of interesting and valuable information can be drawn. Mr. Baker deserves our warmest thanks for placing so many facts within our reach, and helping us to realise something of the part which our old Church and Parish have played in the history of this City and Country.

CHARLES MYERS.

Epiphany, 1906.

INDEX.

ST. MARTIN'S CHURCH, NORTH WEST VIEW, circa 1820.

SOME HISTORICAL NOTES

ON

THE CHURCH OF SAINT MARTIN, SALISBURY.

A.D. 1217—1904.

The earliest mention we find of St. Martin's Church is in a document relating to Bishop Richard Poore (circa A.D. 1217), where it is stated "It chanced that after a rogation procession to St. Martin's the Canons returned to Old Sarum and found the gates of the Castle precincts closed for fear of the Germans, and were thus excluded all night from their lodgings. Such inconveniences as this, and the scarcity and hardness of the water on the hill, determined the Bishop and his colleagues to use all diligence to found a cathedral church and a new city independent of Old Sarum and of the immediate influence of the Castle." Now from this it is certain that a Church dedicated to St. Martin existed, somewhere near, before the Cathedral and City of New Sarum were built; and certain portions of the present edifice testify to the fact that they are of a period anterior to this date.

On the authority of Leland, who visited Salisbury in 1542, it has been asserted that the ancient Church of St. Martin stood near St. Nicholas' Hospital. There may have been a Chapel dedicated to that Saint there, but it does not upset the theory that it was not identical with the parish church under consideration. At this time St. Martin appears to have been a popular Saint. In the parish of Mere alone there were two Chapels dedicated to St. Martin. Leland's words are "And on the North side of the Hospitale is an old Barne wher in tyme past was a paroch Chirch of St. Martine." "This Chirch was prophanyd and a nother new made in Saresbyri for it bearing yet the name of St. Martine. The cause of the translation was by cause it exceeding low and colde and the Ryver at rages cam into it. The Chirch of St. Martine and the Hammelet or Village of Harnham stode or ever any part of New Saresbyri was builded"; and again Holinshead, who wrote about 1570, says "Harnham was sometime a pretie village before the erection of New Salisburie and had a church of St. Martine belonging vnto it, but now in steed of this church there is onelie a barne standing in a verie low mead, on the north side of St.

Michael's hospitale. The cause of the relinquishing of it was the moistness of the soile, verie oft ouerflowne." With regard to this latter assertion the Rev. Mr. Letwich (who wrote 1769) remarks in "Antiquitates Sarisburienses," page 90, "This account is very inaccurate, yet corrects itself. St. Martin's Church was never altered, as to situation, from its first erection, but continued where it at present is; it is to the North, or rather north-east of St. Nicholas's Hospital, improperly called St. Michael's. In like manner, when Harnham is called in the MS. part of the City, it must mean either the suburbs of the City or else that it extended to both sides of the river, as it does at this day." Leland only quotes from tradition, Holinshead probably took his remarks from Leland.

An inspection of the present building discloses the fact that a low Norman South Aisle of a previous Church existed before the Tower and Spire were erected, by the traces of weather moulding which projected over its steep roof being still extant. Against this West wall of the South Aisle the Tower and Spire were erected in the early part of the 14th Century, probably in 1318, as in that year Reginald de Tudeworth bequeathed by his will two shillings to the work of the Church of St. Martin in Sarum.* Mr. Ponting, the Diocesan Architect, remarks:—"I take it that on the advent of Richard Poore† the Eastern and Western parts of the Norman Church were re-built, but the Nave and Aisles remained until the 15th Century. You will see that a stone with Norman Star on it is built into the 14th Century Tower at the West end of the South Aisle; this was doubtless in the Norman work then demolished."

In 1228 Bishop Poore bestowed on a priest named Harvey, who was probably a Canon of the Cathedral, a church *recently erected*, and dedicated to St. Martin.‡ Why Hatcher says *recently erected* I cannot conceive, as such is not mentioned in the original document, the words in which are "Scire volumus universos nos intuitu caritatis contulisse dilecto magistro Herveo ecclesiam Sci.' Martini de manerio nostro Sarum cum Capella de Stratford, &c."

From the above it is evident that there was a Church of St. Martin existing at the beginning of the 13th Century, and probably about this time the present Chancel was built. Mr. Ponting assigns to it the date of 1230 to 1240. Again there are evidences of its having been constructed from materials which had formed part of another building, some of the stones in the East end show signs of having been exposed to fire. And although there may be different opinions on this matter, there are indications of there having been at some former period a Central Tower, another token of its being a Norman foundation. If so, this probably was removed when the 14th Century Tower and Spire were built. The

* Hatcher, p. 90. † A.D. 1217. ‡ Hatcher, p. 44.

Arch at the East end of the Nave was inserted in previously existing work. In the 15th Century the whole of the remains of the original Norman Church was demolished and the building put into its present form.

In a deed in the Cartulary of St. Nicholas' Hospital, dated 17th February $126\frac{8}{9}$ relating to the foundation of the House of St. Edmund, Sarum, the bounds of each of the Salisbury Parishes are defined, St. Edmund being then severed from the older parishes of St. Martin and St. Thomas, from which it appears that the original parish of St. Martin extended from St. Nicholas' Hospital to Winterborne Ford, including Milford, and as St. Thomas' parish was certainly not defined till after the City was founded, we may safely conclude that previous to that time St. Martin's parish included the whole tract of land situated between the Avon and the Bourne from Harnham to the limits of Old Sarum.

Again in later days when the West Porch and the Chapel of Corpus Christi were built, the Stoup on the outside of the door was placed on the South side, showing that from that direction the majority of the congregation was accustomed to come to worship.

A writer in the Gentleman's Magazine in 1830 says of St. Martin's Church:—

"The steeple is evidently coeval with the cathedral and was probably erected by the same architect. The ascent to the top stone is affected by the same means as in the cathedral spire—internally to about three-fourths of the height, where a small door opens, and the remainder is ascended by means of iron handles fixed into the stone work. The columns dividing the nave and aisles are clustered and surmounted by pointed arches: and between the nave and chancel is a low segmental arch. Over this is the decalogue, and the arms of Queen Elizabeth and Charles I. At the altar, in conformity with the modern practice, the decalogue is again repeated.

"In the chancel are some old seats. The ceiling is oak, being a pointed vault, ribbed and panelled, with bosses at the intersections, and sustained on corbels, ornamented with figures of angels. The three aisles are alike in height and decoration. The font is elevated on a platform in the south aisle; it is of an octagonal form, of large dimensions, and the basin is sustained on eight columns. The pews are old, probably about the period of the Reformation.

"In a dark corner of the church stands a curious brass reading desk, sustained on an eagle, now tastelessly thrown by as useless.

"The church has a western gallery, in which is the organ.

"In the churchyard, southward of the church, are two stone coffins, one of which is represented in the accompanying woodcut. [Here follows some remarks on the engraving on the coffin.]

"On the north side of the church is the base and shaft of a stone cross.

"On a gravestone in this churchyard was chalked the lines indicating the old game of "The Nine Men's Morris," showing that this ancient pastime is still in common use in this part of the country."

From the foregoing notes some idea may be gathered of the state of the church at that time (1830).

The Chancel arch has been removed. It was only a modern erection of lath and plaster.

The seats in the Chancel have disappeared.

The font has been removed to its present position.

The oak pews were sold in 1849, when the Church was reseated.

The Eagle has been restored, and is now used as a lectern.

The Western Gallery built in 1700 has been taken away.

Two stone coffins in the Churchyard are nowhere to be found.

The old game of "Nine Men's Morris" is forgotten.

There is no record of the work done in the Church in the 15th Century, when the great restoration took place.

The Churchwardens' accounts go back as far as 1567, but many years are missing. The annexed extracts from them and from the Old Vestry Books, which are complete since 1637, give all particulars of interest relating to the Church from their commencement.

From the extracts from the Parish books hereto annexed we are able to gather a record of the principal works which have taken place in and about the Church since the year 1567. The Church was then covered with wooden shingles, for which tiles were substituted in or about 1598. The Churchyard was enclosed with a thorn hedge till about 1594, when a mud wall was erected in its place, which entailed an annual outlay in repairs till 1667, when a brick wall took its place, which cost about £50.

In 1700 Mr. Richard Fry, a baker, then "Head Churchwarden for the second time," built a new Gallery at the West end of the Church.

1778.—A Gallery was erected on the screen leading into the Chancel, and the Organ then introduced, placed on it. Previous to this there had been no Organ since 1653, when it was demolished and sold.

1824.—A new Organ, purchased of Mr. Blyth, of Isleworth, which cost 185 guineas, was set up in the West Gallery.

"1838.—The old elliptical arch of wood between the chancel and the church has been removed, and a Gothic arch with pillars in exact accordance with the style of the church erected in its stead. The plain, heavy, curved ceiling of the chancel has been also taken down, and replaced by one of the same character as that of the church, with ribs and flowers at the intersections. The last, but not the least, improvement we have to notice is the opening of the East window, which had been obscured for many years by being walled up. Its fine proportions and elegant tracery are thus again brought into view, and the effect is much heightened by its being filled with neat stained glass from the manufactory of Messrs. Fisher and Mackrell, of this city, whose endeavours in the restoration of this most useful art will, it is hoped, be rewarded by a more general use of so ornamental and pleasing an embellishment. If the present wretched and inappropriate pews in this church were but removed, and their places supplied with open seats, fine specimens of which may be collected from parts of the old ones still remaining, St. Martin's, Salisbury, would, in our opinion, be rendered one of the most pleasing sacred edifices in this county."—(*Salisbury and Winchester Journal*, May 21, 1838.)

"1849.—The Restoration of St. Martin's Church having been at length completed, the interesting ceremonial of its re-opening for the purposes of Divine Worship took place yesterday. The whole of the interior has been uniformly re-seated, the sittings being all open according to the practice now in vogue and agreeable to the usages of the primitive Church. The galleries, which stretched their unwieldy bulk along the east end of the church, have been demolished, and the organ removed to the west end of the south aisle.* The instrument itself has undergone a thorough "setting to rights," and upwards of £100 have been expended in its improvement. The walls and ceilings of the sacred edifice have been cleansed and coloured, and the ribs and bosses of the latter have been grained a dark oak colour. A neat and appropriate lectern has been substituted for the defunct reading desk, and the ancient carving of the former pulpit has been imposed upon some new panels, and the pulpit now forms a very pleasing feature of the edifice. The venerable eagle has undergone a diligent polish, and like a phœnix, has renewed its youth. The font has been removed to a site near the east (? west) door, an appropriate position for it when its symbolical reference is taken into consideration. In the chancel the work of restoration and improvement is especially visible. The old nondescript monstrosity which formerly went by the name of a west (? east) window has been replaced by a three-light lancet window, filled with stained glass, on which are depicted the Last Supper, the sacred monograms, and the emblems of the four evangelists. Beneath is a superbly illuminated altar-piece—a dainty work of art—designed and executed by Mr. Wm. Osmond, of this city.† It is divided into three compartments. On the outer ones, the Decalogue has been

* Query. To east end of North aisle.—(T. H. B.)

† This was made of Slate with Wooden Frame. It was removed about 1884.—(C. N. W.)

written in black letter, with illuminated capitals and a rich border of a very chaste and beautiful character. In the central compartment occurs the emblem of our Faith, with the sacred monogram at the intersection of the arms, surrounded by a scroll bearing the inscription:—"He was wounded for our transgressions." The border of this compartment is likewise richly illuminated, the sacred monogram being repeated at intervals, while at each corner occur monograms of the sacred name and the Divine attributes. Both the design and execution of this interesting work of pictorial art are worthy of the pencil of the gentleman from whom it proceeds. We must devote a passing tribute of praise to the liberality and skill of those citizenesses whose contributions supplied, and whose fair fingers embroidered, the crimson velvet altar-cloth, which now so admirably harmonises with the emblazoned window and illuminated altar-piece which have rendered the chancel of St. Martin's Church one of the prettiest in the city."—(*Salisbury and Winchester Journal*, December 15, 1849.)

From *Hatcher* (circa 1840).

The Church of St. Martin is situated at the eastern extremity of the city, a short distance beyond the line of the antient rampart. It consists of a nave with two aisles, a chancel without aisles, and a tower, surmounted with a steeple, adjoining the western termination of the south aisle. On the southern side of the west door is a small receptacle, apparently for the vessel containing holy water, and on the north side a triangular headed niche, which once contained an image, probably of the patron saint. On the north side of the entrance porch is a building, originally the chapel of Corpus Christi, and now used as a vestry room. In the wall is an altar tomb, of the style of the latter end of the 13th or beginning of the 14th century, but without inscription or armorial bearings, or any other indication to whom it may have belonged. The length of the nave to the entrance of the chancel is 82 feet 9 inches, and the depth of the chancel 38. There is a piscina on the right side of the altar; and a door on the south side, in the angle at the junction of the chancel with the church, forms an entrance into this division of the building. The nave is separated from its aisles by five arches, four of which are each 15 feet wide. These are supported on square piers, deeply fluted, and each adorned with four shafts. The two arches next to the chancel are narrow, and in a style something different from the rest. The capitals are not uniform. The roof is ceiled, and the intersections of the ribs are ornamented with bosses. On the south side these ribs spring from corbel heads. The architecture of the church is in the perpendicular style used in the beginning of the fifteenth century; but the chancel may be considered as little more modern than the cathedral.

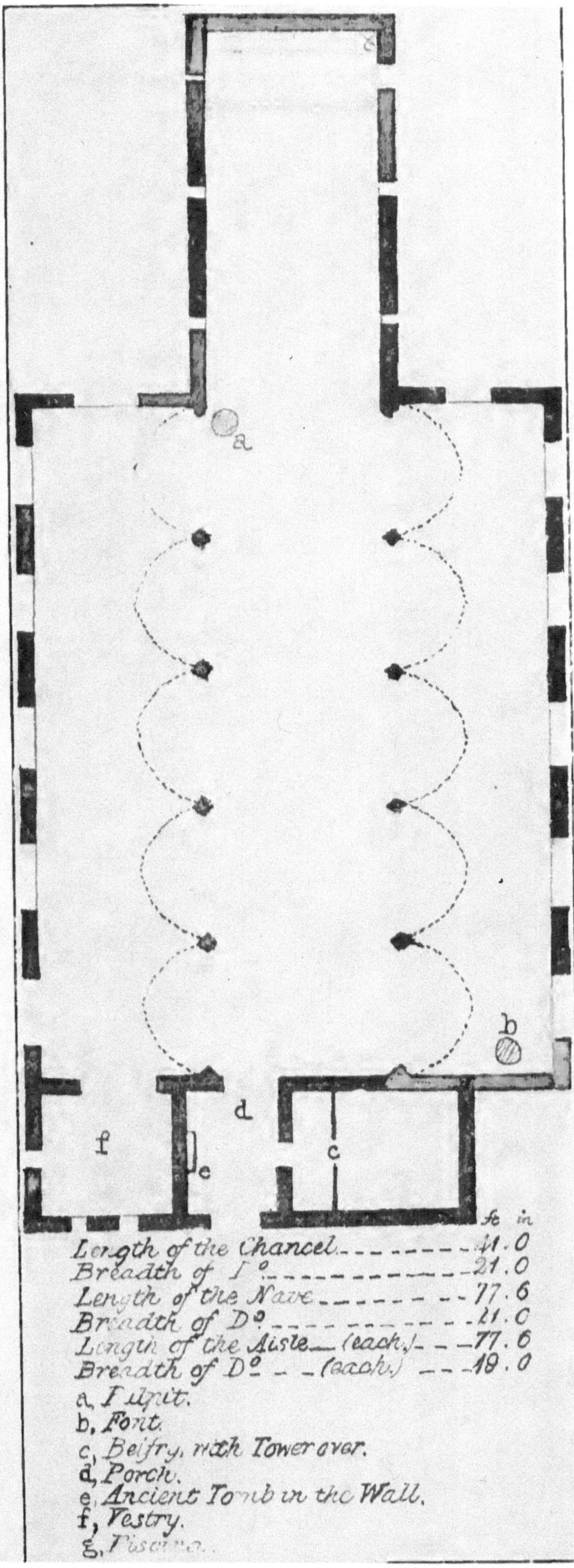

ST. MARTIN'S CHURCH, circa 1836. (from *Hatcher*).

On the north side of the chancel is a monument to the memory of Bennet Swayne, of Milford, who died on the 10th of July, 1748, aged 52. He was the last descendant of a family, several generations of which occupied the mansion at the foot of the hill. The monument commemorates his grandfather and father, who both bore the name of Bennet Swayne, and Thomas his brother. On a brass plate against the pillar on the north side is a Latin inscription to the memory of John Sebastian Carpenter, a native of Devonshire, who is lauded for his knowledge of the Italian, French, and Spanish languages; and is described as not unacquainted with the Latin, Greek, and Hebrew. In the course of travel, according to the words of Homer, as applied to Ulysses,

Πολλῶν δ' ἀνθρωπων ἴδεν ἄστεα καὶ νοόν ἔγνω.

At length returning to his native land, after many dangers past, he, for five lustres, discharged the ministerial duties of the Divine Word, and died peaceably in his grand climacteric in 1632. He gave to the hospitals in Salisbury an hundred pounds for ever, to the Trinity forty, and to the Carpenters twenty-four.

On a slab in the floor of the south aisle is an inscription in memory of Edward Wendover, gentleman, who died April 1, 1645; and a second to William Wendover, merchant and draper, of London, his son, who died February 25, 1632. In the four corners are shields, which were originally charged with armorial bearings, and underneath the inscriptions, which are introduced round his portrait, described in page 342, as follows:—

A portrait once belonging to the Bakers' company was for several years in the possession of the late Mr. Dennis, baker. It bore this inscription: "Mr. William Windever, merchant, in Newe Sarum, deceased ye xxix of January 1632, hath geven to the Company of Bakers ye some of fifty pounds, to be ynjoyd five pounds to a man yerely, for ever. Amen."

At the corners are four coats of arms, inscribed respectively:— *I bred him. But I fedd him. I made him free. Yet known by me.* The first is his family coat, viz., Sable, two bars argent, in chief three demi-lions of the second; the second is the arms of the Merchant Adventurers; the third, the Salters' Company; the fourth, his Merchant's mark $\substack{16\ *\ 34 \\ x\ x\ x}$ with the date 1634. Below are the names

JOHN ODELL	}	Wardens
WILLIAM WEBB	}	1634.

By the address on a letter in his hand, this person appears to have been a Hamburgh merchant. The family was long settled in Salisbury.

Among the other sepulchral memorials are those of the family of Baker, Hinxman, Goldwyer, Rolfe and Blake.

Over the small door on the north side of the church, a coarse painting of St. Christopher was found some years ago, when the whitewash was removed. There were also traces of inscriptions, but the words were illegible. It seems to have covered an earlier and coarser painting of the same saint, and probably belonged to one of the confraternities established in the church.

We cannot conclude our description without a tribute of commendation to the taste displayed in some recent alterations. A false ceiling was removed from the chancel, which was thus opened to the body of the church, and the east window adorned with mosaic stained glass. A new organ has also been fitted up with great neatness. On the whole, this church exhibits a gratifying contrast to that of St. Thomas, where a far more beautiful structure has been injured and disfigured by ill-judged and unskilful attempts at improvement "—(*Hatcher*.)

The Rev. C. N. Wyld, Rector from 1879 to 1894, has left the following notes which he made on the Church :—

"The Fabric of St. Martin's Church.

It is situated the extreme East End of the City, a short distance beyond the line of the Ancient Rampart.

It is situated in the City, though several houses in the Street on each side are in Milford.

It consists of a Nave, 2 Aisles, a Chancel, Tower, Spire, a Porch, a Room now used as a Vestry, once a Chapel of Corpus Christi. There was a porch outside the North door.

The Church has certain peculiarities, viz. :—

The Chancel being purely Early English, the Door to the Porch and Tower being the same, and yet the orientation of the Chancel does not agree with the line of the West Wall, which slopes aside.

It is a nice point whether this Chancel and Tower were erected before the Choir of the Cathedral.

Bishop Poore instituted one Harvey to a New dedicated Church of St. Martin's in 1228, so probably the original Church here was built before the Choir of the Cathedral.

There is in the East wall of the Tower, inside, the Tabling of the former Roof, which fixes the position of some part of this Church previous to the structure of the 15th Century.

Nothing is known of the Church up to the Reformation, historically. About 1560 I have seen it reported that the Chancel was in a disgraceful state, holes in the Roof, &c. In the Church everything* connecting its history with the time previous to this date is obliterated—with the exception of the Fabric itself, and at the Restoration in 1886, though everything was examined carefully, nothing was found except the Niche in South Aisle, and

* i.e., all points of interest.—(C. N. W.)

the remains of a Piscina in East Wall, North Aisle, and traces (quite unfit for Restoration) of painting on the North Wall, North Aisle.

All that can be gathered of alterations or state of the Church previous to this is (subsequent to the Reformation) as follows:—

About 1810 (A) Chancel had a flat Ceiling.

(B) A Gallery across Chancel Arch for Organ West Gallery.

At a subsequent date A & B were removed.* 1849. A Restoration took place, but nothing was done to the Fabric or Floor. It was re-seated, coloured, West Gallery removed, Screens put up between Choir and Aisles. There was much pre-Reformation oak work left, and this was sold by auction in the Church.

1869.—The earth was removed from outside of the Church about 2 or 3 feet, and a new Organ was erected.

1871.—The Ecclesiastical Commissioners improved the Chancel by putting down some tiles, re-arranging the Steps. The Altar was enlarged.

The Churchyard Cross was also restored.

1880.—Railings were placed along the Churchyard, as it was a playground for the Children from the School.

1881.—The Porch inside, and basement of Tower was restored.

The chief points of interest in the Church are as follows:—

Chancel.—A large Tomb, Classical Style, to the Swayne family, once at Manor House, Milford.

A curious monument over Chancel door. The Piscina.

The Nave.—The Corbels in Roof very good. The Font. A Holy water Stoup.

South Aisle.—Piscina. Niche with restored Alabaster figures of Annunciation, part of these were found in Tower, part in Niche. The rest is new.

The Tabling in the East wall of Tower.

The Royal Arms, dating back to Queen Elizabeth.

The Consecration Cross (13th Century) in the wall of the South aisle was found in the Church and placed in its present position in 1886."

The Tomb in the Porch was shifted in 1848. It stood before this where the present door to the Vestry is.

The vestry door was previous to this period in the same wall at the west side of the tomb immediately inside the door of the Porch.

There was an ordinary roof over the Vestry and Porch, the form of which may still be traced on the Tower.

* This arch, being lath and plaister, was removed at the Restoration in 1886, and an oak wooden one put in its place, resting on stone Corbels. These Corbels were carved by Harry Hems, of Exeter.

From the Parish Magazine for November, 1886 :—

The plastering with which the walls were covered has been hacked off, the defective portions taken out and rebuilt, and the whole pointed. The Tower and Spire has been carefully restored, the defective stone work taken out, new crosses have been put on the West Gable of Nave, and the East Gable of South Aisle. The West Window of Nave, which was found to be in a bad state, has been entirely renewed.

The whole of the stonework, which was previously painted or whitewashed, has been cleaned down, the defective parts cut out, the splays to the windows cleaned down, and flint work inserted between the dressed stonework, new stone sills fixed, the sills being previously of plaster.

The roofs, which were very much out of shape, and which, through want of proper ties, were thrusting the walls out, have been taken off, the defective rafters replaced with new ones, proper ties inserted, diagonal firring pieces put on the top and well bolted to rafters to strengthen the roof. It has been retiled with the old tiles. The old oak ribs showing in the ceiling have been brought as near as possible to their original form and refixed, and the panels plastered as before, excepting that they have been slightly tinted, and the whole of the oak in the roofs, which was covered with paint, has been cleaned off. The roof over the South Aisle is entirely new, with the exception of the old oak ribs and wall-plates, which have been re-used ; the old oak rafters where sound, having been used in place of defective ones in the Nave and North Aisle. The stone corbels supporting principals to roof over North Aisle, which were painted the same as the oak, have also been cleaned. The Chancel Arch, which was discovered upon examination to be of lath and plaster and of recent construction, has been removed, and an oak rib on stone corbels has been put to hide the difference in height between the roof of the Chancel and that of the Choir. This alteration throws open the Chancel, which was before very dark, brings into view the very nice Early English doorway, and the window on the other side. It also allows of the Choir stalls being lengthened, which were before very much cramped.

The whole of the floor of Nave, Aisles and Choir has been taken up, a layer of concrete nine inches thick placed over the whole area of the Church, which was absolutely necessary from a sanitary point of view. The piers to Choir Arch have been underpinned, and concrete has been put around the foundations of all the piers of Arcading to Nave to strengthen the foundations, which were found to be very poor indeed. The old stone paving relayed in the passages, and the floor has been formed of solid wood blocks. The old seats are refixed. In 1849 several old seat and bench ends, sad to relate, were sold and lost to the church for ever. The whole of the walls inside have also been replastered.

The stove has been pushed back into the corner, the stove pipe being carried into the chimney, instead of as before, through the ceiling into the roof, which was at once unsightly and unsafe. Chairs now occupy the space vacated by the stove. The West window of the North Aisle, the lower part of which was bricked up, has been opened to its proper depth, and stone panels inserted between the mullions.

A little recess in the East wall of this Aisle is all that was found of an old piscina. A stone frame has been put around it, otherwise it remains untouched. Above this, in a hole in the wall, may be seen the cap of a Norman pier, which is one of several pieces of Norman work found in the walls of the Church, which points to a Norman building having originally stood on the site. At the East end of the South Aisle, where were previously the children's seats, a small Communion Table has been put. The chapel has been restored. The doors of the staircase to the Rood Loft have been taken away,* and one or two steps inserted, although owing to the space having some years ago been partially bricked up, it could not be made complete. Under the doorway is a curious and valuable brass, never noticed before† being out of sight in the chancel. It is to the memory of a former Rector of St. Martin's. Close to this will be seen an elegant little niche disclosed when the plaster was removed, and in it was found the remains of two figures, supposed to be a representation of the Annunciation. An offer has been made to restore these figures, and the work will be executed by Mr. Osmond in accordance with the designs submitted. The East wall of the Tower, which was no doubt the West wall of the original church, and on which the Tower and spire were raised, was found to be in a very bad state; the Tower and spire were therefore shored up, and the greater portion of this wall taken out and rebuilt, large tie stones being inserted inside the wall to tie it together;‡ this wall has not been plastered as previously, but neatly pointed, so as to show the dressed stonework on the upper part.

The Charity boards have not been replaced.

The font has been slightly moved, being very inconvenient before.

In the West window four lights of stained glass will be noticed, two are to the memory of a dear friend of St. Martin's, Mr. Lloyd, one put up by the Children, and the remaining one by those confirmed by Bishop Moberly to his memory. The window

* These were sham doors of deal put up in 1848.—(C. N. W.)

† This brass in memory of John Sebastian Carpenter was copied by Mr. Kite and described in "The Monumental Brasses of Wiltshire," 1860.

‡ It was only rebuilt below the Tabling and Freestone.—(C. N. W.)

eventually is to represent our Blessed Lord, the Twelve Apostles, and St. Martin.

The decoration of the Chancel has added greatly to the appearance of the Chancel and Church.

The hangings on the East wall are new and have been given by the small contributions from poor members of the Congregation.

The bells have been hung in a new frame by Mr. Blackbourn and two new bells will be put up, making eight in all, one a gift anonymously, the other by a general subscription, being a condition of the gift of the former.

The inside of the Tower remains as it was. Outside a lightning conductor has been placed.

The roof of the Chancel has been stripped and retiled at the expense of the Commissioners.

The above work was carried out by Messrs. Young from the designs and under the superintendence of the Architects, Messrs. Crickmay and Son.

The gifts to the Church have been as follows :—

An offering towards painting Chancel Roof.

Two new Bells.

Restoration of figures in niche in South Aisle.

Four lights in West Window.

The Morning Chapel restoration.

A Prayer Desk for same.

A beautiful fair Linen cloth for the Altar in the Chancel.

Entire remaking of white Altar Cloth.

The repair of all the Brass.

Folio Bible 170 years old, for the Lectern, well bound.

Standards in Chancel refitted on new Pedestals.

New Hanging in Church.

1884.—A New pulpit was erected, the gift of the Rev. Claud Brown, Vicar of Verwood, Dorset.

1897, July 21st.—Foundation Stone of the Clergy Vestry laid by the Mayoress, Mrs. Whitehead.

1897.—Screen erected in South Aisle ; the large oak beam on the top was brought from an old barn at Stockton, the rest was taken out of the Church at the restoration, 1886.

1898.—The Vestry opened on Palm Sunday by the Bishop of Salisbury.

1898.—The Organ was raised and the Choir Vestry formed beneath.

1903.—The Hatchments were restored and placed in their present positions in the Church, having been removed from the Nave, at the restoration in 1886. They commemorate the following persons :—

In the North Aisle.

No. 1. (West) Baker. Henry Baker died 1794.
2. (Middle) ? Inglish impaling ? or ? Multon imp. ?
3. (East) Mary Thomas died 1783.

The Royal Arms James I. are on the West Wall.

In the South Aisle.

No. 1. (West) Batt impaling ? John Batt died 1723.
2. — ? *Wendover* quartering ?
3 & 4. Baker impaling Phipps.

Edward Baker died 1796. Jane (Phipps) his wife died 1800.
Royal Arms. Elizabeth.

Notes.

(1.) The West Gallery erected in 1700 extended the whole width of the Nave and North Aisle. The Staircase to it was in the South Aisle. The Entrance near the Belfry door entered the Gallery by the Westernmost pillar between the South Aisle and the Nave. The Trinity Hospital men sat on the North Side of the Organ. The West window was blocked and covered with lath and plaster.

(2.) The Gallery over the Chancel Screen where the Organ stood from 1777 to 1823 was situated between the two pillars at the entrance to the Chancel. The screen was solid, with doorway in the centre, the doors of which, when closed, shut off the Chancel from the other part of the Church. The ceiling of the Chancel was flat, cutting off the upper part of the East window and the top parts of the side windows. The Singers sat on the floor, the Chancel side of the Organ.

(3.) The West gallery was panelled deal with the list of Charities written on the front.

(4.) 1552, July. At a visitation held by Bishop Capon. The Chancel of St. Martin is described as being in great decay, and as having been so for 14 or 15 years, that the ministers cannot abide there in any tempest. (*Hatcher*, p. 265).

The Chapels.

Although there is no record of the endowment of a Chantry in St. Martin's Church, there is existing evidence of there having been two Chantry Chapels, one at the East end of both North and South Aisles, each having remains of a piscina.

In a letter in the parish chest referring to a bequest of Richard Vesey, dated 8, Henry VII. (1492) is the following paragraph, from which it may be concluded that one of them was the Chapel of the Holy Ghost. "8. H. 7. iiij tenements in Culver Street assured to the Church Wardens by the executors of Richard Vesey to certain persons of St. Martyns in Sarum to bestowe yerely therof iij[s] iiij[d] vppon an obbit. Note y[t] yt apprethe not by that dede that the lands weare gevyn to kepe that obbyt for ever & therefore not within the Statute of I Ed. 6.

"Of the iiij tenements next the Churche yarde of St. Martyns ther is orderyd to be bestowed of the rents therof yerely for ever v.[s] for an obbytt &c. & the rest of the rents therof after the quit rent & reparacons payed, shalbe yerely delyvered to the use of the exhibycon of the Holy Gost preest there praying dayly & yerely for the donor for ever."

From the record of a visitation of the parochial churches by Bishop Waltham in 1394 we find there were three Chantry chaplains belonging to St. Martin's. (*Hatcher*, p. 191.)

Thomas Veseye's obit was founded Michaelmas 5. Edw. III. (1332) owte of a tenement in Winchester Street viij[s]. (*Wilts Magazine, Vol. xii., p. 381.*)

1391 Nicholas Baker was buried in St. Martin's. He leaves to the fraternity of St. John there 12 pence. (*Hatcher*, p. 97.)

Incumbents.

The only ancient record extant as to the Rectors of St. Martin's is—

1228. Master Harvey

The duties were carried out by the Provosts of St. Edmund's from the date of the annexation to that College till its dissolution in 1544, of whom we give a list.

Provosts of St. Edmund's.

		Patrons.
1313.	Richard de Hertyngg	Episcopus.
1316.	Thomas de Ilvestone	
1321.	William de Boyton	
1322.	John de Pateney	
1326.	Michael de Roffa	
	Peter de Wymborne	
1335.	Adam de Northova, exch. with P. W.	
1351.	John de Arnale	
1360.	Adam Charles	
1395.	Robert Ragenhil	
1416.	John Conge	
1428.	William Spaldyngton, exch. with J. C.	
1445.	John Pyville, p. m. W. Spaldyngton	
1454.	William Osgodby, p. res. J. P.	
1458.	John Sax, p. r. W. O.	
1464.	Peter Courtenay	
1500.	William Elliot	
1506.	Christopher Twyneho	

		Patrons.
1509.	Edward Powell, p. m. C. T.	
1534.	Thomas Thurlby ...	Thomas Benett, Vic. gen. in loco episcopi
1537.	John Gough	Episcopus

After this period St. Martin's had its own Rectors, who have been as follows :—

1555.	William Mantell ...	The Bishop, by lapse
1577.	Edward Clarke ...	The Bishop, by lapse
1606.	John Odell, p. m. Clarke	The Vestry*
	(Sebastian Carpenter officiated)	John Bailey
1632.	Anthony Hillery, first designated as Rector ...	The King
1661.	Thomas Henchman	
1661.	John Sedgewick ...	Robert Bailey
1662.	Thomas Rawbone ...	Francis Hill
1664.	Francis Horton ...	Francis Hill
1670.	Timothy Morton, by res. of Francis Horton ...	Francis Hill
1687.	Nathaniel Spinckes, by res. of T. Morton ...	Francis Hill
1698.	Peter Terry	
1727.	William Greenaway, by death of Peter Terry ...	Edward Hearst
1734.	John Lumby, by death of Wm. Greenaway ...	Alexander Head, pro hac vice
1754.	John Lumby, by cess. of the said John Lumby ...	Edward Hearst
1757.	James Lewis, by res. of John Lumby ...	Edward Hearst
1763.	William Hearst, by res. of James Lewis ...	Edward Hearst
1767.	John Baker, by res. of William Hearst ...	Robert Cooper
1809.	Thomas Davis, by resig. of John Baker ...	Henry Penruddocke Wyndham
1830.	William Wyndham Tatum	Wadham Wyndham
1870.	John Vodin Walters, p. m. W. W. T. ...	Mrs. King Wyndham
1873.	Samuel Waring Mangin ...	Mrs. King Wyndham
1879.	Calcraft Neeld Wyld ...	Mrs. King Wyndham
1894.	Charles Myers ...	Bishop of Salisbury

* Edward Wendover, Gent., John and Thomas Batt, Charles Jacob, Gent., John Harding and Henry Newman.

CHURCHWARDENS OF ST. MARTIN'S.

1567. Wyllm. Syms
1568. Alexander Carthard
1579. Richard Gauntlett
1580. John West
1581. John Mychell alias Woddsheade
1583. John Wade
1584. Thomas Lyttle
1585. Richard Charles
1586. Xpofer Player
1588. Edward Hide
1589. ffrancis Vermon
1590. Richard Parsons
1592. Charles Jacob ye Elder
1593. Xpofer Player
1597. John Baylie
1598. Lancelot Davis
1599. Lancelott Davis
John Baylie
1602. Lenerd Russell
1603. Edward Odwell
1604. Richard Wolford
1605. William ffry
1606. William ffry
1607. ffrancis Vermon
1610. William Arte
1611. William Sommers
1614. Raph Hurd
1618. Henry Castell gent
1619. Willm Woolbrigge
1620. Thomas Chiffinch
1621. Xpofer Horte
1622. Henry Jacob
1624. John Batt
1626. Edmund Snow
1627. William Windover
Raphe Hurde
1628. Edward Whatlie
1629. Thomas Snowe
1630. Edward Knight
1631. Thomas Snowe
1632. John Russell
1633. Richard Heely
1635. Christopher New
1636. Christopher Batt, Jr.
1637. Christopher Batt, Sr.

1638. Daniel Hales
1639. Simon Rolfe.
1640. Thomas Raindle & Samuel Bell
1641. Samuel Bell & John Payne
1642. John Payne & George Antrum
1643. George Antrum & John Windover
1644. John Windover & Christopher Horte
1645. Christopher Horte & Christopher New
1646. Christopher New & Christopher Batt
1647. Christopher Batt & Thomas Jacob
1648. Thomas Jacob & John ffloud
1649. Thomas Jacob & Symon Rolfe
1650. Symon Rolfe & Tho : Rands
1651. Thos. Rands & William Antram
1652. William Antram & Richard Heely
1653. Richard Heely & Symon Ranger
1654. Symon Ranger & John Payne
1655. John Payne & John Godfry
1656. John Godfry & Nicholas Beach
1657. Nicholas Beach & William Jeneway
1658. William Geneway & Andrew Crane
1659. Andrew Crane & William Woodrolfe
1660. William Woodroffe & Moses White
1661. Moses White & Giles Nash
1662. Giles Naish & Willm. Smyth
1663. Willm. Smyth & Thomas Phillips
1664. Thomas Phillips & Henry ffricker
1665. Henry ffricker & James Strete
1666. James Streete & John Nash
1667. John Naish & John Munday
1668. John Munday & Jno. Gilbert
1669. John Gilbert & Wm. Antram
1670. William Antram & Wm. Jeneway
1671. William Jeneway & Jno. ffricker
1672. John Fricker & William Penny
1673. William Penny & ffrancis Shergold
1674. Roger Hill & Thomas Harris
1675. William Smith & Walter Pope
1676. Walter Pope & William Antram, Jr.
1677. William Antram & Richard Durnford
1678. Richard Durnford & Josiah Rolph
1679. John Smith, Senr., & John Payne
1680. John Payne & Robert Sutton
1681. Robert Sutton & Richard ffry
1682. Richard ffry & Christopher Bat
1683. Christopher Batt & Edward Hall

1684. Edward Hall & Richard Jeneway
1685. Richard Jenaway & Edward Cox
1686. Edward Cox & Josiah Rolfe
1687. Josiah Rolfe & Richard Marsh
1688. Richard Marsh, Junr., & Jno. Lawrence, Junr.
1689. John Lawrence, Junr., & Nicholas Blake
1690. Nicholas Blake & James Street
1691. James Street & William Windser
1692. William Winsor & Edward Edmonds
1693. Edward Edmonds & Christopher Willmott
1694. Christopher Willmott & Jonathan Nueman
1695. Jonathan Newman & Moses Staples
1696. Moses Staples & Stephen Copland
1697. Stephen Copland & John Hall
1698. John Hall & Joseph Jennings
1699. Joseph Jennings & Richard ffry
1700. Richard ffry & Peter Tinham
1701. Peter Tinham & James Bartlett
1702. James Bartlett & John Willis
1703. John Willis & Richard Rumsey
1704. Richard Rumsey & Thomas Studdart
1705. Thomas Stoddart & John Blackmore
1706. John Blackmore & Daniel ffloyd
1707. Daniel ffloyde & Thomas Jatt
1708. Thomas Jatt & Thomas Hall
1709. Thomas Hall & John Duke
1710. John Duke & John Davis
1711. John Davis & Thomas Batchilor
1712. Thomas Batchelor & Richard Rumsey
1713. Richard Rumsey & Richard Payn
1714. Richard Payne & James Sammells
1715. James Sammells & Samuell Rolfe
1716. Samuell Rolfe & Robert Speggs
1717. Robert Spaggs & Richard Marsh
1718. Richard Marsh & Thomas Bryne
1719. John Davis & Edward Blake
1720. Edward Blake & Richard Rogers
1721. Richard Rogers & Thomas Shergold
1722. Thomas Shergold & John Woodward
1723. Thomas Shergold & William Tapper
1724. William Tapper & Thomas Martin
1725. Thomas Martin & James Bartlett
1726. James Bartlett, Jr., & . . . . . Martyn
1727. Joell Sanger & Richard Mortermer
1728. Richard Mortimer & Edmund White
1729. William Bowles & Samnel Andrews

1730. Samuel Andrews & John Waters
1731. John Waters & Alexander Head
1732. Alexander Head & Roger White
1733. Roger White & Edmund Heath
1734. Edmund Heath and George Baverstock
1735. George Baverstock & Wm. Freemantle
1736. Wm. Freemantle & Thos. Dyke
1737. Wm. Newman & Thomas Thomas
1738. Thomas Thomas & Daniel Collis
1739. Daniel Colles & John Safe
1740. John Safe & John Chafy
1741. Richard Payne & John Marsh
1742. James Bartlett & Austin Wheeler
1743. Augustine Wheeler & William Pasby
1744. William Pasby & William Freemantle
1745. William Freemantle & Daniel Floyd
1746. Richard Floyd & John State
1747. Augustine Wheeler & Wm. Newman
1748. William Newman & Robert Spaggs, Jr.
1749. Robert Spaggs & Edmond Roberts
1750. Edmond Roberts & William Whitchurch
1751. John Page
1752. John Page & John Bond
1753. John Page
1754. John Rolfe
1755. Thomas Lake & Jeffery Gowan
1756. Geoffry Gowan & Josiah Rolfe
1757. Jeffery Gowan & Josiah Rolfe
1758. John Gawen & Joseph Willis
1759. Joseph Willis & Edmund White
1760. John Thorpe & Robert Cooper, Jr. John Rolfe paid fine
1761. Richard Floyd & Thomas Lake
1762. Roger White & Austin Wheeler
1763. Roger White & Wm. Whitchurch
1764. Henry Dew & Thomas Spratt
1765. Whitfield Bourn Biggs & John Goodfellow
1766. John Goodfellow & John Rolfe
1767. John Rolfe & Robert Cooper
1768. Robert Cooper, Junr. & Thomas Lake
1769. Thomas Lake & Jeffery Gowan
1770. Jeffry Gawen & Joseph Willis
1771. Joseph Willis & Richard Floyd
1772. Richard Floyd & Thomas Cooksey
1773. Thomas Cooksey & Joseph Corfe
1774. Joseph Corfe & Charles Othen, Senr.

1775. Charles Othen & Samuel Smith
1776. Samuel Smith & Thomas Gibbs
1777. Thomas Gibbs & Edward Baker
1778. Edward Baker & William Hutchence
1779. William Hutchence & James Coombs
1780. James Coombs & John Tanner, Junr.
1781. John Tanner, Junr., & Charles Othen, Junr.
1782. Charles Othen, J^r., & Thomas Cooksey
1783. Thomas Cooksey & George Young. Mr. Crouch paid the fine
1784. George Young & Joseph Rogers
1785. Joseph Rogers & Samuel Emly, Junr.
1786. Samuel Emly & William Woolfryes. Thos. Lake paid fine
1787. William Woolfreyes & Robert Woods
1788. Robert Woods & James Turner
1789. James Chubb & Robert Carey Corfe
1790. Robert Carey Corfe & Thomas Adams
1791. Thomas Adams & John Young
1792. John Young & William Tinney
1793. William Tinney & John Spencer
1794. John Spencer & Richard Sutton
1795. Richard Sutton & Robert Hutchence. Isaac Young paid fine
1796. Isaac Young & James Sutton
1797. James Sutton & William Coy
1798. William Coy & Henry Sutton
1799. Henry Sutton & John Lander
1800. John Lander & William Ellis
1801. William Elliss & William Ghost
1802. William Ghost & John Blatch. Mr. Iremonger paid fine
1803. John Blatch & Thos. Wilkie. Edward Baker paid fine
1804. Thomas Wilkie & John Rumbold
1805. John Rumbold & Thos. Whitmarsh. Benjamin Charles Collins & George Baker paid fines
1806. Thos. Whitmarsh & Edward Pearce
1807. Edward Pearce & John Webb
1808. John Pern Tinney & William Watson
1809. William Watson & Joseph Williams
1810. Joseph Williams & George Short, J^r.
1811. George Short & George Baker. Richard Webb paid the fine
1812. George Baker & James Foot
1813. James Foot & John Woolfryes

1814. John Woolfryes & Charles George Brodie
1815. Charles George Brodie & William Woolfryes, Junr.
1816. William Woolfryes, Junr. & Thomas Cusse
1817. Thomas Cusse & John Atkinson
1818. John Atkinson & Joseph Saunders
1819. Joseph Saunders & Henry White
1820. Henry White & Richard Sutton
1821. Richard Sutton & George Atkinson
1822. George Atkinson & George Sutton
1823. George Sutton & James Cobb
1824. James Cobb & Henry Finley
1825. Henry Finley & William Osmond
1826. William Osmond & William Wheeler
1827. William Wheeler & John Cother.
1828. John Cother & Samuel Webb
1829. Samuel Webb & William Hiscock
1830. William Hiscock & James George Coombs
1831. James George Coombs & John Toovey
1832. John Toovey & James George Coombs
1833. James George Coombs & Henry Everett
1834. Henry Everett & William Prangley
1835. William Prangley & James Bonnett. James Ainsworth paid fine
1836. J. W. Finch Noyes, of Milford, & Thomas Hobbs, publican, of St. Ann Street
1837. Richard Read and Richard Cooe
1838. Joseph Saunders & Thos. Norton Wyndham
1839. Henry James Bracher & Walter Goddard
1840. Samuel Cusse Keynes & Samuel Noke Wilmot
1841. Samuel Noke Wilmot & Giles Emly
1842. Thos. John Holloway & Robert Coney, of Milford.
1843. Robert Coney & Patrick Gregson Cunningham
1844. Patrick Gregson Cunningham & Joseph Snow
1845. Joseph Snow & William Windsor
1846. William Windsor & George Beckingsale
1847. George Beckingsale & John Blake, of Ford
1848. John Blake & John Waters
1849. John Waters & George Pothecary, of Milford
1850. George Pothecary & Henry William Cobb
1851. Henry William Cobb & John Large
1852. John Large & William Higgins
1853. William Higgins & Edward Thomas Stevens
1854. Edward Thomas Stevens & Thomas Pain
1855. Thomas Pain & Edmund Walter Brodie
1856. Edmund Walter Brodie & Frederick Roe
1857. Frederick Roe & Samuel Cusse
1858. Samuel Cusse & William Osmond, J^r^.

1859. William Osmond, Junr., & Samuel Noke Wilmot
1860. Samuel Noke Wilmot & Henry Blackmore
1861. Henry Blackmore & William Woodlands, of Milford
1862. William Woodlands & Thomas Pay Howe
1863. Thomas Pay Howe & George Richardson
1864. George Richardson & Thomas Pay Howe
1865. Thomas Pay Howe & George Richardson
1866. George Richardson & Richard Lloyd
1867. Richard Lloyd & Herbert Holloway, of Milford
1868. Herbert Holloway & John Squire
1869. John Squire & Nathaniel Harding
1870. Nathaniel Harding & Richard Munkhouse Wilson
1871. R. M. Wilson & George Gerrish
1872. George Gerrish & William Pinckney
1873. William Pinckney & George Newman
1874. George Newman & W. H. Foot
1875. W. H. Foot & John Harding
1876. John Harding & Jack Robert Yelf
1877. Jack Robert Yelf & James Wilton
1878. James Wilton & William Beach
1879. William Beach & Henry Dilly
1880. Henry Dilly & Henry George Vincent
1881. Henry George Vincent & Henry Hawkes Mallandaine
1882. Henry Hawkes Mallandaine & Charles Holmes Notley
1883. Charles Holmes Notley & James Hollis
1884. James Hollis & Edward Frederick Kelsey
1885. Caleb William Gater & Joseph Williams Lovibond
1886. Joseph Williams Lovibond & Ambrose Tucker
1887. Ambrose Tucker & William Thomas Webb
1888. William Thomas Webb & Robert Stokes
1889. Robert Stokes & John Dyer
1890. John Dyer & Arthur Whitehead
1891. Arthur Whitehead & Arthur Russell Malden
1892. Arthur Russell Malden & Trayton Cheeseman
1893. Trayton Cheeseman & Hamilton Fulton
1894. Hamilton Fulton & Henry Elliott Fox
1895. Henry Elliott Fox & Charles G. Wyatt
1896. Charles G. Wyatt & E. C. Boyle
1897. E. C. Boyle & William B. Canning
1898. William B. Canning & Ambrose Tucker
1899. Ambrose Tucker & Walter Goddard
1900. Walter Goddard & Henry Goulding Parry
1901. Henry G. Parry & Sir Reginald Francis Douce Palgrave, K.C.B.

1902. Sir Reginald F. D. Palgrave, K.C.B., & Thomas Awdry
1903. Thomas Awdry & Thomas Henry Baker
1904. Thomas Henry Baker & Alfred D'Angibau.

PARISH CLERKS.

1568. John gryge
1580. Richard Dawson
1599. Thomas Smith
1632. John Odwell, died 1655
1655. Richard Hill
1691. Thomas Holmes
1694. John Bradford
1724. William Holmes. died 1730
1746. - - Creed
1765. Richard Langley
1799. John Burch
1844. George W. Burch
Samuel Burch
1857. William C. Pearce

SEXTONS.

1619. Jordan
Henry Lake
1620. John Tucker
1627. John Cook
1632. Thomas Rumsey
1660. William Rumsey
1681. Thomas Wheeler
1724.—1780. Robert Summers
1780. George Lake
1795—1841. William Burch, ob. æt. 87
1841. William Burch, ob. 1847, æt. 71
1847. George Podger
1893. George Sanger

ORGANISTS.

1567. Laweys
1611—1620. John Atkins
1637. Edmond Tucker
1777. Samuel Smith
1783. Jane Smith
1822. Miss Biddlecombe
1827. William Henry Biddlecombe
1843. John Richardson, Junr.
1847. William Pryce Aylward
1871. Charles William Pearce
1873. Thomas Herbert Spinney

1875. W. F. Newton
1877. William Hatch
1878. Charles B. Shuttleworth
1879. Walter Barnett
1880. Charles B. Shuttleworth
1882. Charles Rogers
1887. George W. Blake

EXTRACTS FROM THE CHURCHWARDEN'S BOOK.

The Bells.

1567.	Probably only 4 bells	
1580.	Many entries of repairs to the bells	
1581.	Charges about the new Bell	
	It. for unhanging of him	$xviij^{d}$
	for drawing him to the Bellfonders house	$xj^{d.}$
	for bringinge the Bell to church ...	$xvij^{d}$
	for getting of her up and hanging of hir ...	iij^{s} vj^{d}
	for a new cheeke for the wheel	$viij^{d}$
	for a new strappe	v^{d}
	for shutting ij dubble strapes	iij^{d}
	for nailes	iij^{d}
	for shutting a single strappe	j^{d}
	for wrytinge the Band for the Bellfoundes	x^{d}
	for casting the bell to John Wallis ...	iij^{l} vj^{s} $viij^{d}$
	to his srvants	vj^{d}
	for nailes to hang the Bell & for an Iron pin	v^{d}
	for Drawing the Bell & carrying home of the slyde	xj^{d}
	for taking downe the Bell the last tyme ...	ij^{s}
	for mending the whele	xx^{d}
	for mending the clipper of the new bell ...	vij^{s}
	for new Roundinge the Bell and shutting the sofit of the second bell to Wm Pride	$xiij^{s}$ iv^{d}
	the whole sum aboute the new bell	v^{l} ij^{s}

		£	s.	d.
1774.	Edmund Lush's new frame for the Bells ...	40	0	0
	His Bill for repairing the Bell Loft ...	5	6	8
	Buckets Bill for his Plan & Estimate which he gave Mr. Willis for hanging the Bells	1	1	0
1843.	James Bridgman for Bells as p^{r} Contract ...	63	0	0
	Sep. 29 Paid for ringing the New Bells twice	1	2	0
	Salary to Ringers	6	0	0
1847.	Feby 16. John Wilkes for altering and repairing the hanging of the Bells by Messrs Mears Men	3	10	0
1851.	Job Dibsdale for repairing Bells ...	12	0	0

		£	s.	d.
1881.	Jerram and Blackburne, re-hanging Bells and repairing frame	38	5	0
1884.	Blackburne, repairs to Belfry, Tuning Bells	5	0	0

THE BELLS, as described by Mr. Lukis.

1, 2 } Thomas Mears, Founder, London, 1842.

3, 4 } William Smith, Walter Pope, Churchwardens, 1675.
R.F.†

5. Be mee and loly to heare the Word of God. 1582. I.W.*
6. Call a soleme assemblie, gather the people I.W. 1628 I.D.‡ (between the Canons) G.L. I.P.

The above is from the Rev. W. C. Lukis' Wiltshire Bells. *W. Arch. Mag., Vol. II., p. 206.*

THE BELLS as at present.

Treble.—" Mears et Stainbank Londini fecerunt Th : Blackbourn erexit" 1886.
C. N. WYLD, Rector : J. G. LOVIBOND. A. TUCKER.
Custodientes Ecclesiæ.
Cum voco venite."

Second.—" Mears et Stainbank Londini fecerunt Th : Blackbourn erexit" 1886.
" JOHANNES WORDSWORTH. S.T.P. Episcopus Sarum
GULIELMVS. M. HAMMICK Prætor Urbanus
1886. Laudate Dominum."

Third.—THOMAS MEARS Founder London 1842.

Fourth.—THOMAS MEARS Founder London 1843.

Fifth.—WILLIAM SMITH. WALTER POPE Churchwardens 1675.
R.F.

Sixth.—WILLIAM SMITH. WALTER POPE Churchwardens 1675.
R.F.†

Seventh.—" BE MEC AND LOLY TO HEARE THE WORD OF GOD."
I.W. 1582.

Tenor.—" CALL · A · SOLEMME · ASSEMBLIE." " GATHER : THE PEOPLE." I.W. 1624.
G.I. Figure of a Bishop with Pastoral Staff. I.P. I.D.

BOOKS.

1580.	for a booke that manoes bought ...	iiij[d]
	for a paper & a forrell for the Register booke	xij[d]
1581.	It. for a boke for the church set on[t] to preay to god for the houerthro' of the Quene M[tis] enymeayes	iiij[d]
1598.	To Sim tichborne for makinge of a booke for the water works	ij[s]

† R. F. = Richard Flory. ‡ I.D. = John Danton.
* I.W. = John Wallis.

1603.	for mending of o^{r} Bible & for clapsing ...	xviij^{d}
	Layed out for the Boke called the "Paraphrase of Erasmus vpon the Newe Testament"	xiij^{s} iiij^{d}
	Item laied out for makinge a Desk and A chayne for this Booke	xviij^{d}
	paid for ij prier Bookes the 4th day of September	viij^{s}
1604.	Laied out for a comnnion Booke ...	viij^{s}
1605.	for a Neue booke of prayers for ye kinge...	vj^{d}
1618.	pd. for the newe booke	xxij^{s} vj^{d}
1627.	pd. for a service booke for the Clarke ...	4s. 6d.
	pd. for a booke of Articles at the bishop's Citation	4d.
	pd. for a booke sent against the fast daye ...	10d.
1632.	payd for a servis book for Mr. Carpenter	8s.
	payd for a booke of the 39 articles for him	2s.
1637.	paid for a booke to bee read the 5th of Nouember	6d.
		s. d.
	It. paid for 2 bookes for the fasting wensdaies	02 04
1640.	It. for two bookes of the fast	02 00
	for a booke of prayer for the King ...	00 03
	payd to Glide for a booke of the fast ...	00 04
1643.	pd. for ffaste bookes	3 00
1658.	for the Act for the better observance of the Lords Day	0 6
1660.	It. to the Booke binder for a service booke	10 0
	payd for a proclamation	0 5
1661.	ffor 2 service books for the Kings birthday	1 2
	ffor 2 service books for the fast the 19th of June	1 4
	to John Bennet for Ten Acts	0 6
	to Mr. Ringwood for the grand bond ...	1 0
	To John Nash for making out and ruling the seat book	0 6
	To John Bennet for 2 bookes for the fast...	1 4
	To the Clerke for wrighting the seat booke	0 6
1662.	for a new Comon Prayer Book ...	6 6
1663.	for the Act concerning fire Hearths ...	0 6
	It. a Common Prayer Book for the Church with Claspes to itt and a Regester ...	13 0
1671.	for bringing the Carnis book for the fast ...	1 0
1681.	pd. for a Common prayer book	12 6
	10^{ber} 10 pd. for ye proclamation & ye Service book for ye fast on 10^{ber} 22th ...	1 0

		£	s.	d.
1683.	pd. Rob. Browne for a thanksgiving book		1	0
	ffor the Booke of Homilyes		11	0
1686.	pd. for ye proclamation & book of thanksgiving		1	0
	pd. for Altering the book of Common prayer		2	6
	pd. Robert brown for the book fasting & thanksgiving on the 30 of January & on ye 6 of ffebruary		1	6
1687.	pd. for altering and new binding the Comon prayer book		4	0
1690.	Pd. the Apparitor for a booke of injunctions		1	0
	Pd. for a Form of prayer		0	6
	Pd. for a proclamation and for a forme of prayer for ye 19th of October ...		1	6
	Pd. for a forme of prayer for the 5th of November		1	0
1691.	Ap. 29. Pd. for Proclamation & Prayer book for ye Monthly Fast		1	6
	Nov. 21. Pd. ye Apparitor for proclamation & Prayer book for ye Thanksgiveing day		1	6
1693.	Ap. 28. Pd. ye Apparitor for proclamation & prayer book for ye 10th May ...		1	6
	June 14. Pd. ye Apparitor for a forme of prayer		1	0
	9ber 18. Pd. ye Apparitor for proclamation & prayer book ye 26th inst. for ye Thanksgiving		1	6
1699.	Paid for a New Psalm Book		1	0
1700.	Paid for a proclamation to suppress Profaneness		1	0
1714.	pd. for 2 prayer books, a proclamation and an Injuncion for ye Clergy ...		3	0
1715.	Paid for two Books of Thanksgiving ...		2	0
1741.	Paid Mr. Farr for a ffast Book and Proclamation		2	0
1742.	Jan. 9. Paid Mr. Easton for a Comon P. Book & Alm. ...		6	0
1750.	A Prayer Book for the Minnister ...		14	0
1751.	Mr. Collins a Church Book		16	0
	Mar. 2. Mr. Farr Fast book		2	0
1767.	Paid Mr. Easton for 2 Folio Com. Prayer Books	1	10	0
1774.	Mr. Seallys Bill for a common Prayer Book	0	17	0
	Deduct for light Gold Recd of late Church Warden Cooksey	1	5	9

		£	s.	d.
1788.	Mr. Turner A prayer for the Kings recovery	0	2	6
1819.	New Prayer book & Bible for reading desk	2	2	0

The Churchyard.

1585 & following years. Pd. for a load of thornes to fence the Churchyard 4s.

1594. Last entry of repairing the hedge, therefore it is probable a mud wall was erected in its place shortly after, as in 1603 and following years up to 1667 there are entries for repairing the mud wall.

1653. The Cross demolished. The Stones sold to Christopher Batt for £1.

1667. A new brick wall was erected at a cost of about £50,
For looking to ye Churchyard in ye time of ye Contagion.

1709. For Grubing up the Ealming Tree
For Cuting off the more.

		£	s.	d.
1720.	paid for Trees and planting them ...	1	2	6
1726.	paid for 38 Elms and Carriage	1	19	6
	paid for 12 Elms		12	0
	paid for planting the trees and levelling ye Walks		11	0
1751.	making the Churchyard Walks			
1758.	Cleansing ye Well in ye Churchyard			
1784.	Bank and Ditch thrown up in the Lower part of the Church Yeard			
	And for Furz plant 16 Hundred			
1792.	The Avenue of Lime Trees planted			
1872.	Paid on acc^t. of repairs of Churchyard & alterations	69	17	9
1881.	Wilton Bro^s. 192 Yards Hurdle Fencing ...	40	16	0
	Ditto Making new pr. Gates & wicket Wrought Iron Hanging Posts ...	19	18	6
1880.	Keynes & Co. Ornamental Shrubs ...	4	12	6
	Trees per Rev. C. N. Wyld	1	16	0
1879.	6 large cast Iron Gratings and Frames ...	8	5	0
1883.	Osmond for repairs to Stonework of tombs	11	1	6
1903.	Wilton Bro^s. Fence E. side of Churchyard	39	14	6

Furniture and other Ornaments, &c.

1568. The Dexte
Church goods sold.
One Cope valor
one blewe vestm^t val.
One grene sylk stremer val.
the best banner
one blewe vestment
ij Corprasses, ij frontlatts, iiij Keyrchers & iij buttons

1568.	One payer of Sersters and the fote of the Crosse	viij^{d}
	one vestment xx^{d}	
	A great Payer of Canstickes and also Clothes of the Pashion	
	iij Canstickes of bras xviij^{d}	
	One blewe vestm^{t} x^{s}	
	A blak vestm^{t}	
	A white deacen ij^{s} vj^{d}	
1580.	for iiij matts to lay about the formes for the communicants to knell on	ij^{s} iiij^{d}
	for turned candlesticks	vj^{d}
	for ij tapers	ij^{s} iiij^{d}
	for a pound of systes	xiij^{d}
1585.	ffor j^{lb} of sises*	xvj^{d}
	ffor a new surples in clothe viij els ...	xxj^{s} iiij^{s}
	rings ij^{s} iiij^{d} in washinge iiij^{d}. Som. tot.	xxv^{s}
1588.	for the making of the cover over the polpit to the goiner	xj^{s}
	paid to the painter in wrytinge the quene's m^{tis} name in letres of gould wth a posy	iiij^{s}
	It. for the Iron worke to hold the tremer	xviij^{d}
1590.	for the new Dext to Read the Litanye at ...	vj^{s} viij^{d}
	the Dext on the Comunion table ...	vj^{d}
	It. paid to a somner for the warninge for to kepe holyday for the trynmpe of the victory oner oure enymyes	iiij^{d}
1594.	For ye staple of ye Vante	j^{d}
	To Trowe for new casting ye Vante & for xvj^{li} of zoder	xiiij^{s}
	for 9 ells of Holland at ij^{s} viij^{d} per ell to make a new Surplus	xxiiij^{s}
	for making	iij^{s} iiij^{d}
1594.	layed out to the Joyn^{r} for the perryment ...	ix^{s} ix^{d}
	for the triminge up of Mr. Maior's Pewe ...	xviij^{s} j^{d}
1595.	Layed owt for v yards & a halfe of fyne grace grene at xij^{s} the yard ...	iij^{li} vj^{s}
	Layed owt for iij yards of damask tabling at viij^{s} vj^{d} the yarde	xxv^{s} vj^{d}
	Layed owt for xiij ownes & qr of grene silk at ij^{s} vj^{d} the ownce	xxxij^{s} x^{d}
	Layed owt for Buckrom	x^{s}
	Layed owt for the making of bothe of the Communyon Clothes	v^{s} j^{d}
	Layed owt for the Carriage of them home	vj^{d}
	Sm vj^{li} xix^{s} xj^{d}	

* Sises = wax tapers.

1599.	for one ell of hollonde to make ij napkins for the comunion tabell	iij^{s} iiij^{d}
	Itm to misteris Clarke for making of them	vj^{d}
1602.	Laide out for a board for the communion table	iij^{d}
	Laide out for laces and tassels and making the cushing	iij^{s}
	Gave to the sexton of saint Edmans for bringing the pulpet cloth	iiij^{d}
	Laide out for a Desk for the communion table	vj^{d}
	Laide out for painting the Dext for the communion table	vj^{d}
	for makinge of iiij fformes vnto two carpenters	xxij^{d}
	Bought xij yeardes of Diaper cloth the price therof is	xij^{s} ix^{d}
1605.	for the Kings Armes	iij^{li} xv^{d}
	For New Clothe by the sides of the Armes	ij^{s} vj^{d}
	ffor the Payntters Worke about the Armes	xxx^{s}
	ffor the Joyners worke	vij^{s}
	for helpers aboute the Armes	iiij^{d}
	ffor the Table of Degrees of Mariage ...	xiiij^{d}
	for the Joyners worke for ye Comandements and for makeing the newe Pewes ...	xvj^{d}
	for the Joyners worke for the tables by ye Kings Armes	xij^{s}
	for the paynters Worke	xix^{s}
	for the Pulpitt Clothe and Cushins ...	iiij^{li} xvj^{s}
1607.	for a box to keepe the Com'union bread ...	v^{d}
	for 12 yeards of Elle Broode saye for ye p(ewes) at ij^{s} iiij^{d} the yearde, the some is	xxviij^{s}
	for 5 Dossen of Lace & halfe at viij^{d} the Dossen	iij^{s} viij^{d}
	for two Thousand of Copper nailes ...	ij^{s}
	for Iron nailes about the same work ...	ix^{d}
	for two yards of Matt	iiij^{d}
	for Goodwife Jordanes help	iiij^{d}
	for a Carpenters help	iiij^{d}
	for the Embroiderer to doe the worke ...	v^{s} viij^{d}
	for the Embrotherers man	ij^{s}
	for one Gimell for the pewe Dore ...	ij^{d}
1610.	for 20 yeards of matt for the quire ...	xx^{d}
	ffor a Butt for the minister at ye table ...	iij^{d}

Layd out for the Lampe.

1610.	The prise of the Lampe at London	lv^{s}
	ffor William Creeds paynes that bought it and for the Carriage of it Downe	ij^{s}
	ffor a pulley	vj^{d}
	ffor the Lyne to hange it wth all	xviij^{d}
	ffor two Iron Crookes and nayles	vj^{d}
	ffor his paynes that hanged it up	v^{d}
1612.	for the stole & the Lyones to the Joyner	15s.
	for giltinge & painting the Lyones and the stolle	12s.
	for a Communion Knellinge forme	j^{s} iij^{d}
	for Six Cussions	ix^{s} vj^{d}
1618.	pd. for a Doore to the pulpett	vij^{s} iiij^{d}
	pd. for Jemelles for the same	vij^{d}
	pd. for the Deske for the newe booke	ij^{s}
	pd. for the Chaine of the newe booke	viij^{d}
1620.	pd. the Joyner for movinge ye commandments & for board	vij^{s} vj^{d}
	pd. for painting & making cleane the armes	vj^{s}
	pd. for 4 yeards of greene sarge at 2^{s} 2^{d} ye yearde	viij^{s} viij^{d}
	pd. for 2 thousand of sadlers nayles	ij^{s} iiij^{d}
	pd. for other nayles	v^{d}
	pd. the workeman & for a Desk & hooks	v^{s} iij^{d}
	pd. for a red skinne	x^{d}

		s.	d.
1629.	pd. for a newe iron for the hower glasse	2	6
1632	payd for a ladder for the Churche	10	0
	payd for mending five of the brass candlestiks	2	6
	payd for a small brass Candlestik for the priste	2	0
	payd for anne Iron for the hower glasse	2	6
	payd for a quart of sack for Mr. Carpenter	1	4
1633.	For 2 oure glasses	1	4
	for refreshing ye Kings arms	8	0
	for newe writtinge the commandments	3	0
	for the Desk before Mr. Mayor for to sett the Candells	2	0
	for new Diaper for the new forms at the Communion table	5	0
	for payntinge & triminge of the chest in the vestrie	3	0
	for payntinge 4 panes of the ministers pue	4	6
	for a lock to Timothie parfitt & for the key to the chest in the vestrie	2	6

		£	s.	d.
1633.	Paid for a Lock for ye pullputt		0	2
1636.	Many new seats were made.			
1637.	paid for a collection box		1	0
1639.	The Clerk's Desk and the reading desk were added to the pulpit.			
1640.	for 9 ells of holland for a surplice for the minister	1	16	0
	It. payd for lace for the necke of the surplice	0	8	0
	for making thereof	0	8	0
	payd for an houre glasse	0	0	8
	for 2 waiters at ye Church doore ...	0	0	8
	payd to Umphry Beckham for 22 foote of square timber for ye stile	0	4	6
1642.	Payd for an houre glase and standish ...	0	2	4
1643.	pd. Jo. Beckam for Winscott	10	5	10
1655.	pd. to the Joyner for mending the Seats & nails & a Hingell & other stuffe with his labour		3	6.
1655.	It. for a yard of Tabby		10	0
	It. pd. for 1 yard of Callimanka ...		3	0
	It. for Gold. ha. an ownce		3	0
	It. for Silke		1	0
	It. for Ribbon		0	6
	It. for making the Cushin & mending the other Cushin and Cloath		6	0
1657.	Pd. for a locke for the maiestrates pew ...		0	8
1659.	Itt. pd. the Smith for making a frame for the Mase and Sword	0	10	6
	Itt. pd. for painting the frame for ye sword and mase		8	0
1662.	for Hollon for A surplus 10 Eles Att 6s. 9d.	3	7	0
	for making the surplus	0	8	0
	ffor painting the ffont	1	0	0
	Pd. the freemason for 2 Window att the west end of the Church	3	3	0
	for scouring the Lampe, the Eagle, & the Candle sticks		1	6
	for a Key for the Christening seat ...		0	4
1663.	It. pd. Mr. Legge for fower paire of snight bittles	0	4	2
	Itt. to John Persivall for wrighting the $\text{commnd}^{\text{mts}}$	1	6	8
	To Rich. Rowden for mending the brazen Deske	0	8	0
	Payd Will. Crouch for y^e Rayle Round the Communion table And Cutting y^e table —& for 2 Benches to Kneel on ...	5	16	00

		£	s.	d.
1664.	It. pd. Mr. Legge for fower paire of Snuight bottles		4	2
1669.	ffor feathers for the pulpit Cushion and for a bottom lyneing & the worke		6	10
	ffor an houre glasse		0	8
1683.	for A Houre Glas		0	8
	ffor the frame of the mape of Mariges		1	0
	It. pd. for the Letters for the King's Evill & pd. for the frames		0	6
1685.	Many new seats			
1704.	Pd. Mr. Silby for painting the Vaunt & mending		16	6
1705.	Pd. for ye board for ye Eagle & lineing, tape and nailes		5	3
	Paid for Ingraving a brass plate and ye Cross on ye new Bible		6	0
1707.	Paid *Tilby for Setting ye Gold letters on ye Gallery		10	0
1709.	Paid Mr. White for Painting ye King's Armes	1	0	0
	New Seats			
	Paid Robert Baden for making the Sun Diall	1	10	0
1713.	Pd. John Ward for 2 Seat doors for the new Cockpit Seats		12	0
1717.	Paid James Thrasher for mend 3 Sockets for the Branch of ye Sconce		1	0
1725.	pd. for the Mayors Cushion		7	0
	pd. for tossells and makeing the Cushion & mending the Pulpitt Cloath		8	6
1732.	Paid Mr. White for the Pulpit Cloath and Cushion	20	0	0
1736.	Octob. 25. To Mr. Robt. Cooper for a Surplace	2	15	0
	Decbr. 8. pd. for making ye Minister Surplace	0	10	0
1737.	March 27. Pd. for Makeing ye Ministers Scarfe	0	2	6
	April 13. Pd. Mr. Froud for ye Ministers Scarfe	1	10	8
1739.	Jan. 30. pd. for A looking glace	0	0	6
1747.	Ap. 16. Pd. for Ten yards Holland at 9s. pr yard	4	10	0
	Pd. for making Surplice	0	10	0
1748.	May 18. Mending the Pulpit Cushion	0	3	0

* Query Silby *or* Tilby.

		£	s.	d.
1748.	Aug. 12. To Mr. Sanger for repairing the Church buckets	0	14	0
1750.	A Looking Glass for the Vestry ...	0	1	0
	May 11. Pd. Mr. Eason for a Ink Stand	0	5	0
	Aug. 14. For hooks and eyes for ye Pulput Cloath	0	0	4
1751.	Brooks mending the Mayors Seat ...	0	19	7
1756.	Paid for the New Branch Cash 29 3 11 } By old Brass &c. as ꝑ Bill ... 2 6 1 }	31	10	0
	Paid Brooks for putting up the Branch & Nails &c.	0	4	0
1764.	Mr. Robt. Coopers Bill ꝑ 12 Ells Holland for ye ministers Surpalis	4	7	0
	For makeing Do.	0	10	6
	Harry White for Crying the Church Windows	0	1	0
1765.	Dec. 30. Candles for Innocents Night ...		8	4
1767.	The Dial		11	6
1768.	the Ministers Tent		18	4
1773.	½ y^d^green bayes to ye Docters reading pew			9
1774.	Edmund Lush new frame for the Bells ...	40	0	0
	His Bill for repairing the Bell Loft ...	5	6	8
1779.	New Seats			
1780.	12¼^yds^ of Green Cloth at 3s. 6d. ꝑ y^d^ for Lineing ye pulpit pew &c.	2	2	9
	48yds. Binding for ye pulpit pew &c. at 1d. ꝑ y^d^	0	4	0
	Pd. for 2 pound Flocks for ye pulpit ...	0	0	10
	6½^yds^ of Green Kersey Cloth for ye Communion Table @ 4s. 6d. ꝑ y^d^ ...	1	9	3
	Pd. Mr. Simmons for making ye Communion Table Cloth		2	0
	Pd. Mr. Jebboult for Painting & Repair^g^ ye alter piece	4	10	0
1781.	25yds ½ Lace Thred & making ye Cushins & Cloaths		6	3
1791.	17 yards of silk for curtains for the Corporation and Churchwar^s^ Seats at 3s. ꝑ yard	2	11	0
	14 Do. ferret at 2d. ꝑ yard		2	4
	Nails 10d. Making 3s.		3	10
	5 dozen of rings and silk		2	0
	Heavy expenses this year in repairs.			
1807.	March 25. Paid Mr. Henbests bill for the Iron Gates at the Entrance of the Church Y^d^	13	2	6

		£ s. d.
1813.	Paid for an Iron Chest	8 11 6
1825.	Paid Mr. Beare Painters Bill for writing Extract of Charities in Gold Letters on Organ Gallery	14 8 $1\frac{1}{2}$
	March 12. Paid Mr. Beare Bill for painting Galleries, Pulpit, Organ, Chancel, &c.	18 14 10
	Paid Mr. Beare Bill for repairing Windows broken by the late Storm	3 12 $9\frac{1}{2}$
1827.	for taking a large stone out of the Water at the end of the Church-yard ...	10 0
	Paid Mr. Osmond's Bill for removing Monuments, repairing Windows, &c. ...	3 12 9
	Paid Mr. Salmons Bill for New Chairs &c. for the Communion table	3 16 11
1826.	Sextons Bill for lowering and wheeling away earth from the North side of the Chancel	11 0
1827.	To Singers by Order of Vestry	5 0 0
	A Stove	
1840.	Mr. Fawcett a Surplice	1 13 3
1844.	June 6. Paid Messrs Stevens & Blackmore for Black Cloth to cover the Pulpit and for Pulpit Tassels	4 2 4
	Paid Messrs Keynes for Matting ...	7 13 0
1849.	Church entirely reseated and much old oak sold by auction in South Aisle	
1870.	Wilton and Sons New Stove	47 0 0

THE ORGAN.

1567.	for ye repayryng of ye organs	xij^{s} v^{d}
1581.	to thomas Raindole ij^{d} per quarter (organ blower)	
1603.	Paied for the makinge of the Orgains ...	iij^{li} vj^{s} viij^{d}
	Paied for a littell Iron Bare & ij Staples & a locke	xvj^{d}
	Paied for two bordes for to make up the Casse of the Orgains	x^{d}
	Paied for paintinge of the Orgains ...	viij^{s}
	for a locke & a stapell for the Orgains and gimoles for the same casse to cover the Keyes	ij^{s} v^{d}
1611—12.	Mr. Champingtonne for kipinge the organes	v^{s}
1612.	John Atkins the Organist	
1637.	paid Mr. Hayward for mending the Orginns	10s.
	Edmound Tucker organist salary ...	£2 0 0

1639.	Mr. Tooker the Organists salary £2 per annum			
	Thos. Ball for blowing 4s. per annum			
1653.	The Organ demolished			
	Recd. of Mr. Anthony Wilkinson for the Organ Case			10s.
1778.	A new Organ erected by Mr. Samnel Smith at a cost of	£100	0	0
		£	s.	d.
1779.	Ap. 19. Paid Mr. Smith his Salary as organist	6	0	0
	Paid him for an Iron pot	0	6	0
1780.	Jan. 13. Pd. Mr. Green for Wainscoting ye Organ	2	0	0
	Ap. 27. Pd. Mr. Smith his Salary as Organist	5	0	0
1781.	June. Paid Mr. Smith as Salary as Organist	6	1	0
1785.	April 30. Paid Jane Smith Salary for the organ one year	5	0	0
	And Salary to keep the Organ in Repair for the same time (yearly) (T. H. B.) ...	1	0	0
1822.	Miss Biddlecombe's Salary	5	0	0
1824.	A new Organ by Mr. Blyth, of Isleworth, for 185 guineas			
1827.	Miss Biddlecombe's Salary	15	0	0
1835.	Mr. William Biddlecombe			
1843.	„ Richardson			
1847.	„ W. P. Aylward			
1871.	„ C. W. Pearce			
1873.	„ Spinney			
1875.	„ W. F. Newton			
1877.	„ W. Hatch			
1878.	„ Shuttleworth			
1879.	„ W. Barnett			
1880.	„ Shuttleworth			
1882.	„ Rogers			
1887.	„ G. W. Blake			

Payments to Ringers.

1568.	for ringing of the beles for the quene ...	xxj^{d}
1580.	for vj Ringers	viij^{s}
1588.	It. for vj Ringers for the crownation Day (yearly)	viij^{s}
	It. for vj Ringers on ye xix Day of November being the Trynmphant Daye ...	vj^{s}

1594.	Layed owt to the Ringers on her Maties byrthe Daye	xvj^{d}
	Layed owt more to the Ringers on the trynmfe Day	ij^{s}
1599.	Payd to the Ringers on the day of the overthrowe of the Spanierds on ow^{r} coste	iij^{s} vj^{d}
	for Ringinge for my Lady markis ...	xij^{s}
1602.	Laide out to the Ringers for Ringing for the King	v^{s}
	for the Ringers at the byrth Day ...	iij^{s} iiij^{d}
	for the Ringers at the Coronation (yearly)	viij^{d}
	The Ringers at the triumphe Day ...	iij^{s} iiij^{d}
1603.	paid to the Ringers the xxiiijth day of marche being the beginninge of the Raigne of Oure King	viij^{s}
	Paid to the Ringers the xixth Day of June being the Birth Day of o^{r} maj^{ti} ...	xiiij^{d}
	Paid to the ringers upon the Triumphe Day for the King, being the vth day of August	viij^{s}
	Paid to the Ringers the xxth of October when the Queen came in	iij^{s}
	Paid to the Ringers the xxjth of October when the King & the Prince came in ...	iij^{s}
	Paid to the Ringers upon Allhalorne day when the King & Queene came to o^{r} lady church	iij^{s}
	Paid to the Ringers when the Queene went away from Wilton being the ixth day of December	iij^{s}
	Paid to the Ringers when the King & the prince went away being the xij of December	iij^{s}
1605.	ffor the Ringers the Tryhuph day ...	viij^{s}
	for ye Ringers on the tryumph the 5 of November	iij^{s} iiij^{d}
1606.	for the Ringers at the Birth of the Kinge	v^{s}
	for the Ringers the Trynmph being the fifth of Agust (*yearly*) ...	viij^{s}
	for the Ringers when the Kinge was in this Countrye	x^{s}
	for the Ringers at the Buriall of Mr. Clarke	ij^{s} vj^{d}
	for the Ringers the Tryumphe the fifth of November (*yearly*)	viij^{s}
	for the Ringers on the Coronation day (*yearly*)	ix^{s} iiij^{d}

1607.	for the Ringers at the Cominge of the Kinge and Queene & at the Coortes Remoovinge	x^{s}
1620.	pd. for Ringers at the Cominge on of the Bishopp	v^{s}
	pd. for Ringers at the Cominge and goinge of the Kinge	vj^{s} viij^{d}
	pd. for ringing for the birth of the yonge lord of penbrooke	v^{s}
1622.	pd. for Ringinge in of the Bishop ...	j^{s} viij^{d}
1625.	for the Ringinge of the bells at the proclayminge of the Kinge	v^{s}
	paid the Ringers for Mr. Eires guift ...	v^{s}
1628.	Novem. 5. pd. the Ringers for ringing the powder treson daye	8s.
	March 27. pd. the Ringers for Ringing thes day	s. d. 9 4
	paid them quarteridge for Ringing ...	5 0
1633.	paid the ringers for ye prograce of the King	7 8
1643.	Ringing the Prince & the Marquisse into Towne	2 6
1644.	ffor not ringen the Lord Goren ...	10 0
	for candles to ring the 8 Clock bell	
1659.	Itt. pd. for Ringing the Bells when his Highnes the lord protector was proclaimed	06 06
1660.	for Ringing for the Bishop	2 6
	payd to the Ringers for Ringing 2 thanksgiving dayes	10 0
	Itt. to the Ringers att ye proclaiming of the King	8 0
1661.	to the Ringers at the precession ...	0 6
	to the Ringers for the Kings birthday ...	8 0
1667.	for Ringing the day the peace was proclaimed w^{t} ye Dutch and gunpowder treson day	8 0
1671.	for Ringing his maiesty throw the town ...	8 0
1683.	St. Jorges daye for the Bells	8 0
	for prosession day ringing	1 6
1686.	pd. for ringing on news of ye Kings speech	
	pd. for Ringing upon the News of taking Argile	8 0
	pd. for Ringing for Munmouths defeatte	4 0
	pd. for Ringing for the taking of Munmouth	8 0
1687.	pd. for Ringing St. georges day ...	8 0

		s. d.
1687.	pd. for Ringing King Charles birthday and return	8 0
	18th August pd. for Ringing when the King rode through the towne	8 0
	pd. for Ringing all hollanday (yearly) ...	1 0
	pd. for Ringing a thanksgiving day. Queen being with child	8 0
1690.	Paid for Ringing the bells at the news of King Williams victory in Ireland ...	8 0
	Paid for Ringing the Bells at the returning of King William from Ireland ...	6 0
1691.	Aprill 20. Pd. for half a days Ringing for ye Kings return from Holland ...	5 0
	July 20. Pd. for Ringing for ye Victory in Ireland	10 0
	Oct. 10. Pd. for Ringing for taking of Limerick	6 0
	Oct. 22. pd. for Ringing for ye Kings comeing from Holland	10 8
1693.	9^{br} 2. To caish pd. for Ringing ye Kings returne fro: fflanders	6s.
	27. To caish pd. for Ringing ye thanke-giveing day	10s.
1699.	May 29. Paid for Ringing Kg. Charles Restoration	10s.
	Paid for Ringing All Saints day (*yearly*) ...	1s.
	Dec. 7. Paid for Ringing the Kings coming home	10s.
1700.	Oct. 21. Paid to the Ringers for ye Kings coming home	10s.
1702.	Paid for Ringing the Queens Proclamation	10s.
1704.	pd. the Ringers the 11th and 12th August being the Victory by ye Duke of Malborough	15s.
1705.	July 16. Paid ye Ringers for ye victory at Hogstet	10s.
	Oct. 29. Paid for Ringing on the news of takeing Barcelona	6s.
1706.	Pd. ye Ringers for ye victory obtayned by ye Earll of Galloway oner ye Duke of Berwick	10s.
	Pd. ye Ringers at ye News of taking Madrid	10s.
	Pd. ye Ringers for ye Victory obtayned by ye Duke of Marlborough at Ramelies ...	10s.
	Sep. ye 16. Pd. ye Ringers for ye Victory obtayned by Prince Euguen over ye french in Italy	10s.

1707.	May 1. Paid for Ringing ye Union Day	10s.
1708.	Paid for Ringing at the Takeing of Lile	10s.
	Decem^r 6. Paid the Ringers for the news of takeing the Castle of Lile ...	10s.
1710.	April 17. Paid the Ringers for ye news of fforceing the ffrench lines	10s.
	Paid ye Ringers for ye news of Takeing Doway June ye 20th	10s.
	Paid the Ringers for Good news ye 28th of Aug^t	10s.
1712.	Paid the Ringers for ye news of the Surrend^r of Dunkirk	10s.
1713.	pd. the Ringers being the day y^t peace was proclaim'd	10s.
	July 7. pd. the Ringers ye Thanksgiving day	10s.
1714.	pd. for Ringing Proclaiming the King ...	10s.
	pd. for Ringing the King's arrival ...	10s.
1715.	July 9. Paid ye Ringers when ye Bishop came Downe	10s.
	Augt 2. Paid ye Ringers the Kings Succession to ye Crowne	10s.
	Sepr 19. Paid ye Ringers vpon the Kings Landing	10s.
	Paid for Ringing for ye victory at Preston	10s.
	Paid for Ringing for ye victory in Scotland	10s.
1717.	May ye 28. Paid the Ringers King Georges Birth Day (*yearly*)	10s.
	Oct. ye 30. Paid the Ringers the Princes Birth Day	10s.
	Nov. ye 4. Paid the Ringers the Young Princes Birth day	10s.
1718.	Aug. 25. Paid ye Ringers for ye Victory obtained on the Spannish Fleet ...	10s.
1723.	Paid the Ringers when King George Landed	10s.
1724.	Paid the Ringers at the coming of ye Bishop	10s.
1732.	Sept. 28. Paid the Ringers for the Kings returne	10s.
		£ s. d.
1736.	May 29. pd. for Ringing ye Prince of Wales Marriage	10 0
	Jan. pd. for Ringing when ye King Landed	10 0
	20. pd. for Ringing ye Prince of Wales Birth Day	10 0
1739.	March 17. pd. for Ringing for Taking of port o billow	10 0

		£	s.	d.
1740.	July 20. Paid for Ringing at ye Taking Shagre		10	0
	May 21. Paid for Ringing for Taking Cartegen	1	0	0
1741.	Oct. 22. Paid for Ringing the King's return		10	0
1743.	Nov. 5. Ringing when the King came home		10	0
1746.	July 19. Ringing when the Duke came home		10	0
1747.	Ap. 15. Ringing Duke Wm Birth Day		10	0
1747.	May 18. pd. Ringing Victory at Sea		16	0
1748.	Feb. 9. Ringing when Peace was proclaim'd		10	0
1750.	Nov. 20. Paid for Ringing when the King came home		10	0
1751.	May. pd Ringing for the Hessians		10	0
1754.	June 11. pd. for Ringing the King's inocalation		10	0
1757.	May 23. Paid the Ringers for the King's Prussia Success		10	0
	King Prussia Birth Day		10	0
1758.	Aug. 19. Ringing & putting ye Flag on ye Tower on ye Taking of Cape Bretoon		12	6
1760.	June 4. Ringing Prince Wales		10	0
	22. Ringing Kings		10	0
	30. Ringing Quebeck		10	0
	Augt 2. Ringing Duke of York		10	0
	Octr 9. Ringing Montreal		10	0
	22. Ringing Coronation		10	0
	31. Ringing Kings		10	0
	Nov. 17. Tolling Bell Kings Funeral		4	0
1762.	Oct. 1. Ringing for Taking the Havanna		10	0
1763.	May 5. Ringing on the Proclamation of Peace		10	0
	Augt 18. Prince Born. Ringing		10	0
1765.	June 29. To the Ringers on the Birth of another Prince		10	0
	July 27 & 28. To the Ringers for the Dukes of York & Gloster, &c.	1	0	0
1778.	Paid ringing for their Majesty, Sep. 30 & Oct. 1	1	0	0
	Paid for the use of a Flag, &c.	0	8	0
1780.	March 1. Pd. the Ringers on ye arrival of ye news from Sir George Rodney	0	10	0

		£	s.	d.
1780.	June 17. Paid the Ringers at the News of Taking Charles Town		10	0
1780.	Putting up the Flag & Pole	0	2	0
	Oct. 11. Paid the Ringers on the News from America	0	10	0
1781.	Mar. 9. Paid the Ringers at the News of Taking Eustatia	0	10	0
1782.	May 20. Paid the Ringers for extra News from Adm^l Rodney		10	0
1783.	Jany 2. Paid the Ringers for the arrival of Sir Rog^r Curtis		10	0
1784.	July 29. Paid for Ringing for the peace & for put out the Banner	1	0	6
1787.	Ordered that the ringers be no longer paid for ringing on the 29th of May, 25th October, or 5th November.			
1792.	Oct. 1. Ringing when the King ret. from Weym^o.		10s.	
1794.	May 3. Paid the Ringers News ye Victory Over ye French		10s.	
	27. Paid to Ringers on News of Victory Over the French fleet		10s.	
	June 4. Paid the Ringers Victory over ye French Fleet		10s.	
	Aug. 15. Paid the Ringers Kings Coming and Flag		13s.	
	Sept. 29. Paid the Ringers and Kings Coming and Flag		13s.	
1796.	Aug. 1. Ringing when the King went to Weymouth		10s.	
			s.	d.
	Puting up the Flag		2	6
	Sep. 16. Ringing on the Kings Return to Weymouth		10	0
	Nov. 4. Ringing for Good News ...		10	0
1797.	July 31. Ringing when the King went to Weymouth		10	0
	Sep. 10. Ringing on the Kings return from Weymouth		10	0
1798.	Sep. 1. Ringing when the King went to Weymouth		10	0
	Dec. 5. Ringing for Good News 3 Octo^{br}		10	0
	Ringing for the Kings return from Weymouth 22^d Oct.		10	0
1799.	Sept. 4. Ringing for a Glorious Victory ...		10	0
	The Flag on the Spier		5	0

		£	s.	d.
1799.	Oct. 3. Ringing Good News taking Dutch Fleet		10	0
	Oct. 4. Ringing on the Kings return from Weymouth		10	0
1801.	May 1. Paid William Birch for Ringers on the arrival of the news of the Victory obtained by our Fleet, off Copenhagen		10	0
1802.	April 1st. paid William Birch for Ringg on the arrival of the news of the Signing of the preliminaries of Peace between England and France		10	0
1804.	Sep. 28. For ringing on the return of Salisy Volrs from permanent duty in May—also in 1805		10	0
	for do. on the return of Salsy Cavalry from do.		10	0
	Dec. 1. For ringing on the King's going thro' Salisbury Aug. 24 & 25 ...		10	0
1805.	June 4 for ringing on acct of H.R.H. the Duke of Cumberland being at Salisbury		10	0
	for ringing on Acct of the Royal Family passing thro' S.		10	0
	Oct. 24. Do. Do.			
	Nov. 19. for ringing on acct of the decisive Victory obtained over the combined Fleets of France & Spain in which the Immortal Nelson fell		10	0
1806.	for ringing on Acct of a general Thanksgiving		10	0
	9 Jan. for 2 Hours Knell on Acct of the Funeral of the ever to be lamented Lord Nelson		4	0
1809.	March. Ringing for Gen. Slade ...		10	0
1814.	Ringing for the Peace with America ...		10	0
	Ringing for the Princess Charlotte of Wales 15 & 16 Decr	1	0	0
1815.	Aug. 7. W. Burch for ringing for the Glorious battle of Waterloo ...	1	0	0
	Nov. pd. W. Burch for ringing for the Princess Charlotte of Wales ...		10	0
1806.	Mar. 29. for ringing on acct of the Victory obtained over the French Fleet by the British Squadron under the Commd of Adml. Duckworth		10s.	

1818.	March 25. Ringing for Cavalry ...	5s.
1821.	Tolling for y[e] Duch. York (1 June) ...	8s.
	Aug. 8. By 3 Hours Tolling Bell for the Queen	6s.
1830.	July 12. Tolling the bell at the King's Death & Burial	12s.
	Ringing for the Duchess of Kent ...	10s.
1837.	Tolling the Bell for Bishop	2s.
	Ringing Princess Victoria's Birthday ...	10s.
	June. P[d] tolling Bell for the death of the late King	2s.
	Ringing Bells for the Queen's Accession ...	10s.
	tolling Bell late King's Funeral ...	8s.
1840.	Ap[l] 8. Ringing the Bells at Queen's Marriage	10s.
		£ s. d.
1844.	Paid Ringers as pr bill for ringing on Festivals	4 11 0
1845.	Paid Salary to the Ringers yearly (to 1866)	6 0 0
1849.	Paid Ringers on reopening Church ...	1 10 0
1852.	Nov. Ringers Duke Wellington's Funeral	0 13 0
1856.	May 24. For Ringing the Bells on the Proclamation of Peace	0 12 0
	May 29. For Ringing on the Celebration of the Peace	0 18 0
1862.	Jan[y] 6. Tolling Bell for Prince Consort, Dec. 14	6s.
1870.	April 12. Ringers for muffled Peal Funeral late Rev. W. W. Tatum	5s.
		£ s. d.
1895.	Ringing on the Bishop's return, 18—5—95	1 1 0
1897.	Jubilee ringing	3 3 0
1901.	Bells on Mafeking Day	1 1 0
	Queen's Funeral	1 1 0
	Queen's Birthday	1 1 0
	Declaration Day	1 1 0

Sundry Payments.

1568.	Mr. Godfry for hys yers waygys ...	xx[s]
	John gryge for hys yers waygys. (Clerk)	iiij[li]
	To the Shyngulmen for hewyng of a XI thowsen of Shyngell	iij[li] vj[s]
	To ower lady cherche for Smoke verthyngs	iij[s] iiij[d]
	for mersement to my lord busshope ...	vj[d]
	for makyng of wex agaynste Crystmas ...	iiij[d]
	for Skoryng of the Dexte iiij tyms ...	xvj[d]

1568.	for the leying of a xj thowsen of Shyngull at vj^{s} p. thowsen	iij^{li} vj^{s}
1580.	for leying of a thowsen of old Shingull ...	vj^{s}
	for Tho : warren for a dayes worke to carry the stones & the rubble out of the Church	vij^{d}
	To Ryc. Dawson x^{s} for midsom. quarter for morning prayer v^{s} quarterly charge (*yearly*)	
1581.	for mending the Church hedge xij^{d} (yearly charge)	
	to thomas Raindoll ij^{d} per quarter (organ blower)	
1584—5.	for singing bread	iiij^{s}
1588.	It. to a poure man that whipped the dogges	iiij^{d}
1589.	for making of a plate for the whirligog ..	xviij^{d}
	for two tapers of two poundes and a pound of scises	iij^{s} vj^{d}
1590.	for ij wex tapers containing ij^{li} weight ...	ij^{s} iiij^{d}
	for one pounde of Syzes	xiij^{d}
	to goodman Arnall for making a new brazen snoffell to sett the wex taper on ...	iij^{d}
1591.	for the hier of an horse to Downton to appere before the comission^{rs} for vew of the water course	x^{d}
	To William Purnell ye carpenter for mending ye who^{r}lyegog & Mr. Newmans seat and others	xviij^{d}
1594.	To John Sparkes for penticost money ...	iij^{s} iiij^{d}
	for the Dog whipper	ij^{d}
1597.	Layd out for a Irone for the making of whaffers	iiij^{s}
1603.	paied to the Aparator for the subconner the xxvjth day of August for sealinge of the churche Dore	vj^{s} viij^{d}
	It. paid to the Ringers the same day ...	ij^{s}
1606.	for horse hire to Ringwood about the p^{r}sentm^{t} of the water	xvj^{d}
	for the horse meate and my own Charges ...	xij^{d}
	for a Bootte to vewe the Water	vj^{d}
	for Vewing the River	iiij^{d}
1607.	for the Orgin players wages (quarterly) ...	vj^{s} viij^{d}
1610.	for Henry Lake (Blower) quarterly ...	xij^{d}
	(Last entry of Smoke farthings this year)	
1618.	pd. for a Dinner for the minister, Churchwardens and sidesmen	iij^{s} viij^{d}

1619.	for makinge a Bridge to vue the Ryver for the presession	iiij^{d}
1620.	pd. the Workeman for the Slattes ...	iij^{li} vj^{s} viij^{d}
1620.	pd. the Workeman about the Slattes ...	xx^{s}
	pd. for mattinge for the Channcell ...	iiij^{s}
		£ s. d.
1622.	pd. the Plumer 517 pound of new lead ...	2 6 4
	pd. for the Casting of 1032^{li} of leade ...	xxxiiij^{s} viij^{d}
1624.	pd. to Gyles Jeffries for the hyer of his horse to Cawne	ij^{s} vj^{d}
	Itm more for the hyer of Rob^{te} Holds horse to Cawne	ij^{s} vj^{d}
1628.	ffeb. 12. pd. goodman beckam for a frame for bowes and arrowes	4d.
		£ s. d.
1627.	Aprill 21. pd. for ffrankincense for the Churche	1 6
	June 24. pd. for making 12 graves at 3d. ꝑ grave	3 0
	„ 30. pd. for making 13 graves at 3d. ꝑ grave	3 3
	August 12. for frankincence for the Churche	1 0
	„ for making 12 graves at 3d. ꝑ grave	3 0
	Septem. 24. pd. for making 20 graves at 3d. ꝑ grave	5 0
	Novem. 17. for making 20 graves to Cooke	5 0
1628.	pd. for amending the lock at Church stile	0 4
1632.	payd for Rosemarie & bayes at Alholland tide	1 4
	payd for Rosemarie & bayes at Christmas	0 4
1633.	for clensinge the diche in the Churchyard	1 0
	paied John Cooke for digging up the Corps for the Crowner	0 6
1637.	paid for 35 yards and 3 quarters of Winscott at 2s. the yd.	3 11 6
	for moueing and fiting up the partition ...	0 5 0
	157 foot of ynch board	0 16 6
	paid for the caureing of the winscott ...	0 3 4
	paid for 21 paire of Gemelles	0 13 6
	paid for 34 yards of winscott at 2s. the yard	3 8 0
	paid for 200 of ynch board	1 4 0
	paid for the raille and peicing the Pullpit Staires	0 5 6
	paid for moveing and fiting up the particion	0 6 8

Sundry payments on the peater house.

		£	s.	d.
1642.—	It. for 2 wardens at ye Church Doore 8d.—(Two entries T.H.B.)	0	1	4
1643.	Wines. Muscadine & sacke payments for			
1649.	pd. for getting on a lock to ye ministers seate doore		0	6
1649.	pd. for 2 locks, one for ye ministers, ye other for his wives seate door		2	8
	for a board to make a bench at Capt. Ludlowes seat doore		1	0
1649.	pd. for making 2 lett^{rs} of Attorney from Mr. Payne and Mr. Antram to my selfe, to put some bonds in execution ...		1	0
	pd. Mr. Geo. Hooper a message (from the Comittee for removing obstructions in sale Bishops lands), ye quitt rent for ye church land due michaellmas 1647		10	0
1649.	pd. Mr. Geo. Hooper, as a fee to take off the apparence at ye s^{d} committee ...		3	0
	Payd Christopher Legg Coll^{r} for ye monethly assessm^{t} for the Army, for 3 moneths for the Church Land in Meadeward		4	0
1653.	To Mr. Bowles for making a Centist to be sent to London		2	0
1655.	Itm for Mr. Hill's Fees concerninge the Ministers		2	0
1657.	The great bell for Mr. Anthonie Hillary (Received)			
1660.	To Willm Rumsey for cleering the King's armes	0	2	0
1661.	To Richd Rowden for mending the brazen Deske		8	0
1663.	It. Rosemarie and Bayes for the Church att Chrismas		1	0
1667.	A bottle of Sack for the Chancellor ...		2	0
	for monys layd out of purse & for looking to ye Churchyard in ye time of ye Contagion		10	0
	Jon. Naish his Account for what monys hee Disburst for ye Brick wall made in the Churchyard of St. Martains in Sarume in the yeare 1667	49	6	8
1669.	ffor a bottle of Sack when Mr. Sanford preach'd in Mr. Horton's absence ...		2	0

		£	s.	d.
1663.	It. the entertaynement of the Minister (*Mr. Horton*) according to the order of the vestrie			
	It. for a pigge	0	3	0
	It. a Brest of Veale and a Legg of Mutton	0	5	3
	It. a Barrell of Ale	0	6	0
	It. 2 Bottells of Sacke	0	4	0
1669.	for going the procession two days and for ringing and other expenses		19	6
1679.	payd on our preambolation day		10	0
	payd Thomas Colier for kiling a fox ...		1	0
	payd John Bauden for bere & tobacko ...		1	0
	Layd out for one bottel of wine when Mr. Gilbard precht		2	0
	Mr. Thiselthwayt when precht in wine ...		2	0
	when Mr. Horton precht wine		2	0
	Rosemery and bais			
1681.	Paid for beer & Tobacco at ye vestry (*yearly*)		1	4
	Rosemery and bayes			
	Paid for a ffox Head		1	0
1669.	ffor Rosemery and Bayes at Christmas ...		1	0
1672.	Rosemary			
1677.	Rosemary and bayes			
	One bottle of wine at Church for a Stranger which priesht		2	0
	(This is a frequent entry for many years.—T. H. B.)			
1681.	for a hood for Mr. Morton		6	0
	Paid for Painting y^e stann		12	2
	Paid for tin of y^e stann		8	6
	Paid for hanging up y^e Candlestick ...		2	4
1683.	June y^e 13. Laide out att the Blue bore vpon y^e Churches account		1	4
	Spent vpon p^rambulacon (*annual expense*)		12	0
	Pd. $Rich^d$ Pile for 1 doz. of Buskes & Chokes &c.			
1686.	Expence when I Received y^e platte ...		3	0
1687.	pd. for the hood for the minister ...		17	0
	pd. for 7 bottles of wine when strangers ministers preached		14	0
	pd. half years chimny mony		1	0
1691.	Spent at y^e Visitation		12	0
	$Decemb^r$ 1. Pd. for Drink & Fire at Choosing Surveyors of y^e Highways ...		1	0
	Pd. for Carrying y^e Snow out of Church ...		1	6
1693.	Spent going y^e Perambulation y^e whole bounds, Clarendon, Fourd & y^e towne	1	7	6

		£	s.	d.
1693.	pd. Tho. Wheeler for Drinke, pipes & Tobacco County Day		1	7
	July 24. pd. Jo[n] Silcox for a Stote & Polecatts head		0	8
	pd. John Silcock for a grey's head ...		1	0
	pd. John Harris for polecatts heads ...		0	8
	pd. John Harris for a polecatts head ...		0	4
1699.	Paid for new hanging the Church bucketts		4	0
	Paid Edward Leake for Whitening and mending the Church	2	2	0
	Paid for Painting the Pillers in the Church	0	15	0
	Ap. 11. Paid for the Board & Workmanshipp for the tables of the Creed & Lords prayer		14	2
1701.	Paid Robert Baden for Sealing the Church	31	0	0
	Paid Mr. White for Painting the Church	12	3	0
	Paid Mr. White for Lackering y[e] Gallery ...	1	5	0
1709.	Paid for Grubing up the Ealming Tree ...		6	0
	For Cuting off the moore		2	0
	For ffilling vp the ground where the Ealm stood		1	0
1710.	Paid for mend y[e] Tyleing and mortar, to fill up the Spare place in y[e] Screen that was Guilded		2	6
	Paid Mr. Tilby for painting & Guilding y[e] Church	6	5	0
1714.	Pd. Mr. Williams for an Order for amending the Common prayer		1	0
1720.	Paid for trees and planting them ...	1	2	6
1726.	Paid for 38 Elms & Carriage	1	19	6
	paid for 12 Elms	0	12	0
	paid for planting the trees & binding and Levelling y[e] Walks	0	11	0
1727.	Paid Mr. Thresher for a Rope to Hang up the Sconces in y[e] Church ...		7	4
	Paid for the Vmbrella	1	2	0
	When Mr. Grenaway took possession of the Church a pint (of wine)	0	1	0
1731.	Pd. for Painting y[e] Skreen	0	9	0
1734.	Pd. W[m] Goodfellow for Painting y[e] Kings Arms & y[e] Dial	0	9	6
1736.	Disbursment for y[e] Vestry	36	17	11
	pd. for Crooks to Hang up Hatts ...	0	1	0
	For mending y[e] Whoreley Gogg ...	0	0	3

Year	Item	£	s.	d.
1740.	Dec. 21. Paid Iock: Lee for Crying ye Church Wind(ows) ?	0	1	0
1742.	Paid for Watering ye Ingen	0	5	4
1743.	Pd. the Widows at Perambulation ...	0	1	0
	Jan. 20. Langley for Crying	0	1	0
1748.	June 2. Pd. Mr. Farr for laying 5 Orders for the Horn'd Cattle wch Mr. Wheeler was to pay	0	10	0
1757.	Robt Summers for making the first Church Yard Walk	1	10	0
	Nov. 1. Robt Summers 2^d Church Yard Walk	1	12	0
	Robin 3^d Church Yard Walk	1	15	0
	Paid for Gravel	14	7	6
1758.	Cleansing ye Well in ye Churchyard ...	0	1	0
	making a Walk to ye Well in ye Churchyard	0	1	0
	Robt Summers for repairing ye Well ...	0	1	6
1758.	For an Otter	0	2	6
1758.	Sep. ye 16. for a Hedghog	0	0	2
1763.	Sep. 3. For Laying a form of Prayer for the Safe Delivery of the Queen ...	0	2	0
1764.	Ap. 5. Pd. Wm. Sanger ℘ 2 young Otters	0	2	0
	May 7. Jonathn. Harvey ℘ Keeping the Gallery Dore	0	1	0
1765.	June 29. Mr. Wride for 8 New Fire Buckets & repairing Old Wones ...	4	2	0
	for Cleaning the Well & opening the drain in ye Churchyard	0	2	6
	Dec. 30. Mr. Barbers Bill for Candles Innocents Night	0	8	4
1766.	1st Jan. for an Oxford Almanack (yearly)	0	1	2
	To Jno. Hill for an Otter	0	2	0
	Oct. 6. paid for Cleaning the Engine after the Fire at Mr. Matons	0	5	0
1767.	Sermon on Good Friday	0	10	6
	Nov. 9. Pd. Seal for Killing 6 Hedge-hoggs	0	2	0
1772.	March 4. Paid Doctor Baker for a Sermon (yearly)	0	10	6
1774.	paid Docter Baker for Good Friday Sermon	0	10	6
1775.	Robt. Summers for Keeping Gallery Door (yearly)	0	2	0
1778.	Paid Mr. Jeboult for painting & gilding the Kings Arms in the Front of the New Gallery	2	0	0

		£	s.	d.
1778.	Paid Do. for other Work	1	1	0
1780.	Nov. 16. Paid the Clening the Engin after the Fire at the Counsel Chamber ...	0	5	0
1784.	Nov. 9. Paid for an advertisement for Orphan Girls	0	5	0
1784.	Nov. 16. Paid Solomon Clarke for the Bank and Ditch thrown up the Lower part of the Church yeard	1	1	0
	And for Furz plant 16 Hund. ...	0	16	0
1785.	July 1. For Cleaning the Engin at Mr. Gillo's Fire	0	5	0
1789.	Roof out of repair & reported dangerous by Edm^{d}. Lush.			
1791.	Curtis for 5 Stoats	0	1	8
Total £ s. d. 15 1 2	Mr. Rogers's bill on acct. of the procession	12	11	2
	Mr. Seymour for Cakes	0	15	0
	At Smarts for Beer, &c.	0	8	6
	At the Bell for Do.	0	12	6
	Ringers	0	10	0
	Hayter and Hyman as Guides ...	0	4	0
1795.	Jan. 31. Paid Mr. Rogers For Trees and Workman	0	19	4
1797.	Jan. 6. W^{m}. Burch for taking up a Soldier in Order that Inquest may be taken ...	0	7	0
	Dr. Stevens for Cur^{s}. Vestry Chimney ...	1	6	0
1810.	July 7. Paid Watchman and Man for taking a Casualty to Blind Hole ...	0	2	0
1817.	Expenses of Perambulation	17	4	1
1826.	Ditto ditto	18	8	2
1818.	Paid Rev^{d}. Mr. Davis on Sunday School acct.	4	4	0
1819.	Qualification Cakes (Augt. 12) ...	0	2	0

1819 is a note on Marsh's Charity.

This Charity is given away in Bread in 6 3^{d}. Loaves to 6 poor women after service on Sundays, who inhabit the Alms Houses in Culver Street.

1830. July 8. Paid Vestry Clerk an Acct. collected on last Church rate to be retained by him and applied in payment of Costs under the Agreement entered into with Milford as this Vestry shall hereafter order, £151 4s. 11d.

		£	s.	d.
1831.	Febr. 3. Paid Mr. Coombs in part payment of the Costs incurred by the Action	20	0	0
	Paid Messrs. Wheeler & Cother, Defts., in part payment of the costs incurred in the Action	20	0	0
	June 23rd. Paid Mr. Coombs, Plff., in part payment of the costs incurred by the action	70	0	0
	Paid Messrs. Wheeler & Cother, Defts., in part payment of the costs incurred in the Action according to agreement ...	70	0	0
1832.	Sept. 27. Pd. the Sexton for carring the Church Chest to & from the White Hart when the Commissrs of Charities were there	0	2	0
1837.	John Redway fixing mourning	0	5	6
	The Choir paid £10 annually.			
1842.	Amount allowed towards rebuilding the Almshouses in Culver Street, Salisbury	100	0	0
1850.	New grate to Vestry	1	5	0
	The Restoration & Repairs cost	280	0	0
1866.	Burch, Bricklayer	66	19	11
1883.	Repairs to Porch (by Kite)	30	5	1
	,, Roof (Burch)	14	2	4
	,, Church (Hale)	17	12	0
1893.	R. Pepperell, Ventilator &c.	26	1	0
1895.	New Ventilator	8	5	0
1897.	E. Hale, New Clergy Vestry £270 / Extras £83 19 10	353	19	10
	Trask & Son, Stone Organ Screen, oak Chancel Screen & new Choir Vestry ...	291	0	0
	Hill & Son, taking down Organ, re-erecting and adding Stops	90	0	0
	Doran Webb, Architect, Fee for Designs Cost of Trowel &c.	36	15	0
	Macdonald & Malden, Faculty to erect Vestry	5	15	6
1900.	National Electric Wiring Co.	117	9	0
	Fitting Switches, New Lamps, &c. (Salisbury Electric Light Co.)	18	0	4
1903.	Gent & Hurley, Rewiring Electric Light, &c.	14	15	6
	Williams, Scaffolding, new door to Vestry, &c.	24	10	1

Receipts.

1567.	At hocktyde (*yearly*) … …	xl^{s}
	of ij men of fford for ye holy lofe …	xij^{d}
	Yearly entries for the holy lofe till	
1580.	for Dauncing mony … … …	iij^{s} iiij^{d}
1581.	Dauncing at Whitsontyde	
	for half pence (Easter yearly) … …	xxvij^{s} j^{d}
1588.	Rec^{d} of Mr. Thiselwyt for a stone that was in the church liten wolle … …	viij^{s}
	gather^{d} at the Whitson Daunce … …	xiij^{s} iiij^{d}
1594.	Receaved for groates … …	xxxiiij^{s} iij^{d}
1605.	Receved of the Widow fielde by her husbands Will one ladder	
1606.	Receaved of George White for his way to the water … … …	j^{d}
1632.	For a tree sold to Morgan morsse …	10s.
		£ s. d.
1653.	Rec^{d} of Mr. Xp'ofer Batt for the Stones of the Crosse … … …	1 0 0
	of Mr. Anthony Wilkinson for the Organ Case	0 10 0
1658.	for the great bell for Mr. Anthonie Hillary	0 2 10
1677.	for the Burial of The osler of the whit bears Child … … …	4
1691.	for the Burial of a Soldier from ye Pot & Lymbick … … …	0
1709.	Rec^{d} for ye Ealming Tree … …	6 6 0
1712.	Rec^{d} of Morrice Grace for two Ealmes …	2 10 0
	Rec^{d} for the Walnut tree … …	1 15 0
1729.	Rec^{d} for an Umbrella of the Church Warden of St Edmunds … … …	1 0 0
1744.	Recd of Mr. State a Servants place in ye Cockpitt South Isle … …	4s.
1786.	April 17. Rec^{d} of Mr. Lake The fine to Excuse him from Being Church Warden	10 0 0
1802.	April 18. To Cash receiv'd of Joshua Iremonger Esqr to exonerate him from serving the Office of Church warden in the parish of St Martins in the City of Sarum … … …	20 0 0
1811.	May 5. Received of Mr. I. Webb, Exeter Street the Fine for excusing his serving the Office of Churchwarden …	20 0 0

The Tower and Spire.

1318.	Probably built	
1589.	The reparation of the tower cost ...	iiij^{li} iiij^{d}
1603.	paid to the carpenter for seting up ij wyndoes in the south side of the belfry	v^{d}
1620.	pd. Thomas Snooke for his yeares ffee for keeping the steeple (annual to 1628) ...	ij^{s}
1622.	pd. for a labourer to make cleane the Tower and beer house	viij^{d}
1624.	paid the Carpenter for himself and ij men about the stayres and other worke about the Tower	xvj^{s}
	Itm. for one hundred and an halfe of bords & plancks for the staires, windowes & loft of the Tower	xv^{s}
	Itm. paid Thom's Snooke for xiij dayes and an halfe worcke about the Tower ...	xij^{s} vj^{d}
	Itm. paid his labourer for the lyke ...	viij^{s} iiij^{d}
	Itm. for one barrow of Lyme slopp ...	viij^{d}
	Itm. for ij bushells of lyme	viij^{d}
	Itm. for lathes and nailes to plaister the belfrie	ij^{s} iiij^{d}
	Itm. paid Kittle for leade and for mending of the Tower	iiij^{s}
	Itm. paid Henry Reynolls for nailes and other worcke about the Tower ...	xj^{s} viij^{d}
1633.	for mendinge the Whether Dore in the stipell	6^{d}
1687.	mendin the Steeple	
1703.	New lead and sundry repairs to the tower	

		£	s.	d.
1734.	P^{d} Robt Wapshar for Work about ye Spire & ye Church	3	4	11
	Paid for Lime & other Meterells used about ye Spire	0	16	0
1741.	Dec. Paid Mr. Clement Tozier for a new Vann	0	14	0
	Paid Mr. Kent for Gilding the same ...	0	6	3
1742.	Paid for mending ye Van	0	0	2
1774.	Mr. Lush's Bill for putting a new Floor in the Tower, &c.	8	9	7
1791.	Mr. Jeboult Gilding the Van	0	10	6
1865—67 & 69.	I. Matthews for Oiling the Van	0	10	0
	Cleaning Do ...	0	7	6
1883.	E. Hale repairs to Tower	20	9	8
1901.	V. G. Morris, London, Pointing Spire, &c.	43	0	0
	Lightning Conductor	12	0	0

Expenses of a Perambulation, 1817.

		£	s.	d.
June 25.	Paid Lawrence for going the boundaries	0	6	0
	Paid Bracher for Cheese	0	6	6
	Paid Bonnett for Cakes	0	9	0
	Paid Sutton for Bread	0	17	0
	Paid I. Wheeler for ribbon	0	6	0
	Paid Mr. Cusse for Horse & Cart ...	0	10	0
	Paid Sworn for a Ham	0	10	6
	Paid Blake	0	12	11
	Paid Small	0	5	0
	Paid Pepperell	0	8	4
	Paid the little boys	0	6	0
	Paid Mess[rs] Woolfreys for beer ...	3	12	0
	Paid Will Holloways bill	8	14	10
		£17	4	1

Expenses attending the Perambulation, 1826.

		£	s.	d.
May 6.	Paid for Ribbons and Rods for the boys	0	7	0
	„ for Carriage of Beer &c. ...	0	1	6
	„ Mr. Kain's Bill for Beer ...	0	7	6
	„ Mr. Burch for money thrown away	0	3	6
	„ 8 boys for their attendance ...	0	8	0
	„ Mr. Holloways Bill for dinners &c.	11	11	9
	„ Mr. Higgins for provisions ...	0	15	5
	„ Mr. Sutton Bill for bread ...	0	8	0
	„ Mr. Chinn for Beer &c. ...	3	7	0
	„ Mr. Cusse for Horse & Cart ...	0	10	0
	„ Boy for going through the water ...	0	1	6
	„ Halfpence thrown away ...	0	2	0
	„ Jn[o] Small attending as waiter ...	0	5	0
		£18	8	2

1766.

	£	s.	d.
May 7th. Expences of Processioning ...	10	3	3

AT THE WELL.

	£	s.	d.
To 14 Gallons of Ale	0	14	0
To Pipes and Tobacco	0	1	0
To Punch	0	7	6
To two Bottles of Mountain	0	4	0
To two Bottles of Port	0	4	0
To Cheese	0	5	0
To Butter	0	0	7
	£1	16	1

DINNER AT HOME.

	£	s.	d.
To 23 Persons at 18[d]. ℘ Head	1	14	6
To Port, 23 Bottles	2	6	0
To Punch	0	17	0
To Beer in the Parlor	0	14	6
To Beer gave to the Men	0	10	4
To Tobacco	0	1	0
To Fire	0	0	6
To Supper for 5 Persons	0	2	6
To the Cart	0	1	6
	£6	7	10
	1	16	1
	£8	3	11

Received the contents of the above
in full,

℘ me RICHARD PERYER.

Assistant Curates.

1827—1829.	Frederick Parry Hodges
1830 —	Henry Livius.
1841—1844.	John Melvile Glenie.
1845—1848.	R. Nicholson Wood.
1849—1856.	John G. Orger.
1854—1868.	Lloyd B. Walrond.
1856—1858.	Stanley Leathes.
1858—1861.	Edgar Hoskins.
1866—1870.	C. N. Wyld.
1868—1870.	J. F. Falwasser.
1872—1879.	Francis Raikes.
1873—1879.	Sidney E. Davies.
1878—1879.	H. P. Sketchley.
1879—1891.	C. W. Sherard.
1879—1881.	J. Howe Jenkins.
1880—1881.	Wm. Wynn Lloyd.
1881—1885.	Wilson Highmoor.
1882—1886 1891—1893	G. W. R. C. Kent.
1884—1885.	Arthur Krauss.
1885—1889.	H. W. North.
1886—1888.	M. D. Fletcher.
1889—1891.	S. Dugdale.
1888—1891.	C. F. Benthall.
1889—1894.	H. A. Hartley.
1893—1896.	V. A. Busbridge.
1894—1895.	Alfred C. Bridge.
1894—1896.	David R. Evans, Master at Salisbury School.
1894—1899.	Henry J. Trueman in charge of St. Mark's.
1894—1897.	P. A. Constable Ellis.
1894—1897.	G. W. Otton.
1894—1900.	W. R. S. Majendie.
1895—1898.	H. E. Hadow.
1897—1901.	W. L. Waugh.
1898—	J. M. Fisher.
1898—	L. W. Greenstreet.
1901—	F. R. Edmonds.
1904—	W. L. Cooper.

THE OLD VESTRY BOOK.

This Booke was given to the Church of St. Martin within the Citie of New Sarum by Mr. John Paine, Brewer and Inhabitant of the said Parishe A^{no} do^{ni} 1637.

		£	s.	d.
	The Names of those who have bin Benefactors to the Church of St. Martin wthin the Cittie of New Sarum or else to the Poor of that Parish. Gomminge gaue the ppetuall Inheritance of severall Tennements lyenge or beinge in Milford Streete & parte in Culver Streete wthin the City of New Sarum to ye use of the Poore of this parish wch Tenements are leased forth vnto Henry ffricker at the yeerely Rent of Five pounds & Tenne shillings	5	10	0
1618.	Edward Windover Alderman of this Cittie gaue an Annuity of One pounde thirteene shillings & fower pence to bee paid by the Deane & Chapiter of the Cathedrall Church of Sarum vnto the Churchwardens of this Parish yeerely for ever towards the bindinge of poor Children Apprentices	1	13	4
	John Windover Alderman of this Cittie gaue the sum of five poundes the Interest thereof to bee distributed yeerely for ever amongst the poore of this parish...	5	00	00
	—— Hurde gent. gave the sum of five powndes the Interest thereof to be distributed yeerely for ever amongst ye poore of this parish	5	00	00
	John Harding of this parish Tallow Chandler gaue Tenne powndes the Interest thereof to be distributed on St. John the Evangelistes day yeerely for ever amongst ye poore of this parish ...	10	00	00
	Giles Jeffery of this parish gave five powndes the Interest thereof to be distributed yeerley for ever amongst ye poore of this pish	5	00	00
1632.	William Windover of this Citty, Marchante gaue the sum of fifety powndes to the			

		£	s.	d.
	ffabrique of this Church for the reparation thereof as neede shall require	50	00	00
1636.	Leonard Russell of this parish, Tanner gave Twentie shillinges to the fabrique of this Church	01	00	00
1643.	Robert Wareham of this parish, Tanner gave Tenne shillings to the ffabriques of Church &c.	00	10	00
1644.	Isaac Girdler of this parish, Weavour gaue Tenne shillings to the ffabrique of this Church	00	10	00

1678. April 10th. This day the Accompt for the pish Church of St. Martin's being past by Wm. Antrum, Churchwarden the Vestrie men then psent at taken the same accompt doe order the taken of an inventorie of all the Goods belonging to the sd. pish Church as followeth.

Imprimus one silver flagon cost Thirteen pounds or thereabout.

It. one silver Cup with a cover of silver to it.

It. Too silver plates ffor to serve the bred.

It. Three pewter fflagons one biger then the other.

It. one peawter bason.

It. peawter plate to sett the fflagons on.

It. one pare of Greate brass Candlesticks.

It. one other pare of brass Candlesticks, south highhill.

It. one brass Candlestick more of the same size.

It. Too Greate brasses with severall sockets hanging in the boddy of ye Church.

It. one Greate brass Eagle, Caled a desk to Reade the bible on.

It. one Green Cloth on the Com'union table —one Screen.

It. one hollond Cloath ffor the Com'union Table.

It. 4 long diaper Cloaths to bee laied on the fformes & one napkin.

It. one silke Cloath for the pulpitt & Too larg Cushons.

It. in the Vesterie Roome one Table bord, one Greene Carpet, 6 greene Cushons & j silk Cushin.

£ s. d.

1632. It. to Joynt ffurmes one long wooden Chest & one other standing by the ffont.

It. one Iron Chest, Given by Mr. Windover, Gent., deceased.

6 Greeene Cushins added in ye yeare 1684.

It. Twelve black Leather buckets.

It. one book of Homilies—one furme more 1694.

The 29th of March 1686. Given had presented a Silver Salver waighing 62 ounces & a 6d. waight—One Velvet Pulpit Cloth.

One velvett Communion Table Cloth.

One black Cloth Tippett Given by me Richard ffry.

Aprill ye 11th 1726 Mr. Richd Marsh Gave a Green Table Cloth for the Vestry Table.

One Silver Salver cost £5 13s. 6d.

The 29th day of March 1656. A peice of Plate called a Salver weighing Sixety two ounces and Six pennyweight was given to the Parish Church of St. Martin's wi^th^in the City of new Sarum to be vsed att the Com'union Service their. Being presented the Same day at the Vestery of the said Church to Richard Jenneway & Edward Cox Churchwardens for the tyme being. Being the gift of Mrs. Alse Denham Widd. of this Parish 20 03 06

In the yeare of Our Lord 1700. Mr. Richard ffry, Baker then Head Church Warden of this pish the Second time did of his owne ffree and Voluntary Motion and at his owne pper Cost and Charges Build a New Gallery within this Church over the West Doore.

He then Like wise Gave a new Green Velvett Cloth with a Silk fringe round it for the Communion Table.

In ye yeare of our Lord 1705 Mr. Richard ffry and Mr. John Naish Gaue the Greate Bible on the Eagle.

Signatures, 1637.

The twelfth of April, 1637. The names of such as are present at the auditing of the account of Christopher Batt, gentleman, Churchwarden of the parish of St. Martin's :—

Anthony Hillary, Rector ibidem

John Batt, gentm.	John Paine
Edward Odwell	George Antrum
Robert R. H. Hole	Edmond Snowe
Richard Lyme	William Moulton
George Godfrey	John Rusell
Thomas Snowe	Isaak Girdler
Christopher Hort	John Windover, gentlm.
Thomas Chiffinch	Christopher Newe
Edward Whattlie	

1678. Aprill 10th. It is further ordered by the now Vestrymen that whoever shall for time to Com shall be eleckted and Chosen Church warden by the Vesterie men of the prish of St. Martins according to the Antient Custom That in case hee doth Refuse to take vpon him the s[d] office & to perform all Costoms beelonging to the s[d] offis hee shall in nowise bee discharged vntell hee paye a ffine of ffiue pownds.

It is further ordered ffor time to Com that the Churchwarden or wardens shall not exceede the expence of Ten shillings in Goen the p[r]ambulation.

It is ffurther ordered that the Churchwardens shall not exceede the expence of six shillings at one Vissitation.

Memorand that the three & twentyeth day of July 1645 Wee the Minister Churchwardens & other of the Vestry of the parish of St. Martins w[th]in the Citty of New Sarn whose names are here underwritten being assembled in the Church of St. Martins aforsd to advise & consult about matters belonginge to y[e] said Church did elect ordayne & apoint John Payne the elder of the Citty abouesaid Brewer & George Antrum of the same Citty Parchment maker as ffeoffees in trust to stand & be seised of the som of sixety & two powndes five shillings & nine pence of lawfull English mony beinge the stocke of the said Church to the intents & purposes in & by these presents mentioned limited expressed & declared viz[t] to lend or lett out the said money till the 25th day of March next ensuinge the date hereof in such severall som'es & vnto such severall psons as the Maior pt of the Vestry aforesaid shall nominate vpon good security by bond or bondes to bee made vnto them the said John Payne & George Antrum their heires executors adm[rs] &c. for the sole & proper vse & benefite of the parish Church of St. Martin aforesaid. And y[t] the said bondes soe made & sealed shalbee kept in the Iron Chest belonginge to the said Church till there shalbee iust occasion to produce them Provided alwaies that this Trust or Enfrofm[t] is to endure & hold untill the Wensday in Easter weeke next ensuinge & no longer. In witness whereof wee have hereunto set o[r] handes the day & yeare first aboue written.

Antho : Hillary Rect[r] S[ti] Martin Saru
Jo : Windover

Xpofer Horte
Christophur N. Newe } Churchwardens

Thomæ (signed) Chiffinch — Symon Rolfe
Willm Moulton
John Russell — Samuell Bell.

1735. It was agreed to pay Mr. White the sum of £12 10s., being the remaining part of the sum for the Pulpit Cloth.

1755. Order'd that the Keys of the Trunk sh[d] be lodg'd in the hands of the two eldest Vestrymen & the junior Churchwarden.

1756. Resolv'd that all the Seats which have been deem'd at any time to be Corporation Seats shall for the future be consider'd as such ; & whereas Mr. Bartlett when he was Churchwarden sold one of those seats to himself being the seat he usually sits in, it is likewise unanimously resolv'd that he shall quietly enjoy it for his life, but that after his decease the said Seat shall revert to the use of the Corporation, never to be sold more.

J. Lumby Rector, Roger White, Jn[o]. Staite, Rich[d]. Floyd, John Rolfe, Tho[s]. Lake, Jeffery Gawen, R[d]. Roberts, W[m]. Whitchurch, Aug. Wheeler, Rob[t]. Spaggs, Jn[o]. Page.

1755. Four Committeemen appointed by the Vestry in addition to the Churchwardens & Sidesmen viz. Mr. John Rolfe, Mr. William Newman, Mr. Whitchurch & Mr. White.

It was agreed that the sum of forty shillings be allow'd to be spent by the Churchwarden at the Visitation.

1756. Committeemen John Rolfe, Roger White, William Whitchurch & Tho[s]. Lake.

1758. Josiah Rolfe, Mr. White, Mr. Spaggs & Mr. Lake.
1759. Mr. Wheeler, Mr. Lake, Mr. Floyd & Mr. Roger White.
1760. Mr. Jos. Willis, Mr. R. Floyd, Mr. R. White & Mr. A. Wheeler.
1761. Mr. Rog^r. White, Mr. Will Whitchurch, Mr. Austin Wheeler & Mr. J^s. Spratt.
1764. Mr. Whitchurch, Mr. Wheeler, Mr. Floyd & Mr. Hutchins.
1765. Mr. Dew, Mr. Wheeler, Mr. Spratt & Mr. Floyd.
1766. Mr. Wheeler, Mr. Willis, Mr. Floyd & Mr. Spratt.
1767. Mr. Floyd, Mr. Wheeler, Mr. Spratt & John Goodfellow.
1768. Mr. Floyd, Mr. Wheeler, Mr. Spratt & Mr. Goodfellow & 1769.
1760. Mr. John Rolf is Chosen Churchwarden in the room of Mr. Robt. Cooper who paid his fine the Sum of £10. At a Vestry held on the 9th June 1760 upon looking over the Book the order for the fine of Ten pound for refusing to Serve the office of Churchwarden do not appear to have been enter'd, it is now agreed that Mr. Robert Cooper shall have Five pound of the Ten pound he pay'd for refusing the office return'd to him. At the same time it was unanimously agreed that for the future any Person who shall be Chose Churchwarden and shall refuse serving the office shall pay the sum of Ten pound.

John Thorpe
Thos. Lake
Joseph Willis
Roger White
Robt. Spaggs
Aug^s. Wheeler

March 21st, 1768. At a Vestry held this day it was agreed that half a Guinea should be paid by the Churchwarden to the Rector of this Parish for Preaching a Sermon on Good Friday morning annually. John Rolfe, Robt. Cooper Junr., Robt. Spaggs, Rich^d. Floyd, Thos. Spratt, Aug^s. Wheeler.

16th July, 1771. At a Vestry held this day it was unanimously agreed that a New Vane be placed upon the Spire in the room of the old one & that it be put in a proper & durable manner.

28th Oct., 1771. It was unanimously agreed that as the present Bell frame is quite gone to decay there should be a New one erected in its room to receive Six Bells wth New Wheels & that proposals being delivered by Mr. Lush and Mr. Beckett it was farther unanimously agreed that Mr. Lush should execute the whole.

1772. Resolved to enlarge the Workhouse of the City.
Thos Spratt appointed Vestry Clerk.

1773. 24th Nov. It was ordered that Mr. Lush do immediately carry into execution the Agreement of the Vestry made with him for a New Bell frame for 6 Bells & New Wheels for 5 Bells with every necessary thereto belonging for £40 & that he compleat the same sometime in February 1774.

1775. 9th June. It was agree'd & resolv'd on that the Revd. Mr. Lewis of The Close, Mr. Charles Othen Churchwarden, Mr. Richd. Floyd & Mr. Wm. Whitchurch, against whom Writs were taken by Peter Bathurst of Clarendon Park Esq. be defended & indemnified against the Suit of the said Peter Bathurst & that Mr. Slater do retain Counsel on their behalf & defence.

1777. List of Burial Fees, &c., decided on.
Decided that 20s. instead of 40s. be expended for the Visitation Dinner.

1777. July 7th. It was agreed wth Saml Smith on his erecting an Organ of the value of £100 and of the dimensions following about 17 feet in heighth and 9 feet in breadth with the Pipes Guilt containing these Stops, Diapason, Principal, Flute, Fifteenth, Cornet, Sesqualter, Jane Daughter of the said Saml. Smith to play the same on every Sunday morning and evening at Divine Service, so long as she shall live and capable for the performance thereof, the Gentn. of the Vestry allowing her Five Pounds a year during her life or the due performance as aforesaid, the said Saml. Smith to find from time to time a Bellows Blower. The said Organ to be put up and fit for playing on or before Ladyday next, which day the said Jane Smith's pay to Commence or if built by Christmas or soon after.

1778. March 4th. It was agreed That a Gallery be erected where the Screen now stands leading into the Chancel, and the Organ to be placed on the said Gallery. Mr. Smith to be at the Charge of Building the Gallery & Stair Case, the Gentn. of the Vestry allowing him Six Pounds, and it is farther agreed for the Gallery and Organ to be erected and put up with all necessary speed.

It was agreed that Forty Shillings should be allowed at each Visitation, as it formerly were before it was reduced to Twenty, towards the Expences of the Dinner, &c.

1781. It was agreed to allow Jane Smith One Guinea ℘ ann. for keeping in repair and Tuneing the Organ—the Vestry to be at no further Expence about it : and she to pay the Organ Blower. The first payment to be made at Lady Day next.

It was further agreed to alter the rails round the Communion Table, and to add new rails and doors in the Front.

1782. Burial fees revised.

1783. Mr. Crouch paid his fine of Ten Pounds to be excused serving the office of Churchwarden.

Whereas John Edgar Junr. upon repeated application hath refused to pay the Fees due to this Church for the interment of his late Wife it is resolved at this Vestry that no Stone or Monument be erected by him in future, nor any Inscription added to the present Monument, until he hath discharged the said Fees, and tis farther resolved, at the said meeting, that the Corpse of the said Mr. Edgar be not permitted to be interr'd in this Church, or Church Yard, nor any future Wife or relative of his (being non Parishioners) till the Parish be fully satisfied for the Fees above mentioned. It is ordered likewise that Mr. Tinney be paid his Bill, incurr'd on the above Acct.

1784. Robt. Cooper Esqr, Mr. Rolfe, John Goodfellow and Mr. Dew were elected Feoffees in the Room of Mr. White, Mr. Wheeler, Mr. Spaggs and Mr. Lake Deceased, and at the same time it was agreed that the remaining Walks in the Church Yard should be new gravelled, ordered likewise that old Curtains be replaced.

1785. Ordered that a Bank and Ditch be thrown up at the lower part of the Church Yard at such convenient distance from the water, as to allow the planting of Furze hedge as a fence, this wth the concurrence of Dr. Baker.

1785. Ordered that the Ten Commandments be painted with a Black Letter on a White Ground on each side of the Organ.

27th June. It is agreed that the South Aisle shall be repair'd, with respect to the Tiling, under the Direction of the Churchwardens ; & also that the Steeple of the Church shall be repair'd, under the same Direction.

Octr 12th. At a Vestry held to Consider about Establishing of a Sunday School in this Parish the Revd Doctor Baker was unanimously Chosen Treasurer, Two Persons having Applied as School-Masters who agreed to Educate the Children on the following terms —for Twenty & under thirty One Shilling, from thirty & under forty Eighteen pence, from forty & upwards two Shillings, the choice of the Master & the Appointment of a Committee was refer'd to a future Vestry.

Oct[r] 15th. At a Vestry held this Day Abraham Scott was unanimously Chosen to be the Master of the Sunday School at the same time Robert Cooper Esq[r], Mr. Robert Cooper in Milford Street, Mr. Jos[n]. Rolfe, Mr. Tho[s]. Cooksey Mr. Will. Hutchins Mr. Jos[h]. Rogers in Conjunction with the Rector were appointed a Committee for regulating the Business of this Charitable Institution.

1786. April 17th. It was agreed that the Alderman's Seats in the Middle Isle North Side be divided into two parts equally and Sold for the benefit of the Parish, and that each Seat be sold for 4 Guineas. And it was likewise agreed at the above time that two Sittings in the Seat now appropriated to the use of the Alderman's Wives shall be divided & sold, & that the Seat when thus divided be sold for 2 Guineas.

At this Vestry Mr. Lake having been unanimously chosen Churchwarden & paid his Fine of £10 to be exempted from serving that office, & Mr. W[m]. Woolfryes was unanimously chosen in his Stead.

1787. Resolved "That Seats may be built at the places fixed on by any Persons who are disposed to build, and that they be allowed to hold the Seats for 3 Lives, or on any better Terms which Mr. Emly (the Ch. Warden) may make with them: that Mr. Emly be authorised to purchase any Seats for the parish that are to be procured on eligible Terms."

Resolved "That there be no money allowed for ringing on the 29th May, the 5th Nov[r]. & the 25th October: and that there be no more Money allowed for Visitation Dinners."

1787. July 27th. Resolved unanimously "That the Corporation Seat in the Middle Aisle, North Side, which was directed to be divided & sold by a Vestry held 17th April, 1786, be not sold, & that the partition be taken down, and the Seat put in the same State as it was prior to the above Resolution of 17 April, 1786."

1788. Agreed that the Sextons Sallary for care of the Church should be increased to the Sum of £1 11s. 6d.

1789. 23rd July. It was agreed by a great Majority that the 40s. formerly allowed towards the Visitation Dinner be again allowed of, and paid as usually it used to have been.

1790. 5th April. Ordered that in future the Churchwardens for the Time being do sit in the Corporation Seat, on the left-hand of the middle Aisle with their wands, except when the Corporation shall have occasion for the use of it.

1791. April 8th. Agreed to add the Names of certain Persons as Feoffees in trust for Lands and Tenements belonging to the Parish of St. Martin's, Viz. Mr. Josiah Rolfe, Mr. Henry Dew, John Goodfellow, R^{t}. Cooper Esqr., Mr. Thos. Cooksey, Mr. Jo^{s}. Corfe, Mr. Edwd. Baker, Mr. W^{m}. Hutchence, Mr. James Coombs, Mr. John Tanner, Mr. Ch^{s}. Othin, Mr. Geo. Young. At the same time it was agreed that the Wicket leading from the Parchment Yards to the Church Yard should continue in its present situation, Provided that no Horse or Cart be ever permitted to enter the said Church Yard to serve the purpose of the said Parchment Yard.

1791. June 1st. It was agreed that a Preambulation take place according to antient usage on Thursday being assention day the 2^{d} June 1791.

9th September. It is unanimously agreed that the Steeple shall be repaired and that William Waters the person now employed for doing such work, hath undertaken to do the same at the rate of Eighteen shillings ꝑ week Beer included for his Labour, and the parish is to find all Materials necessary on this occasion and the Expence of two Labourers.

1792. Feby 10. It was agreed on that there should be immediately planted a Row of Lime Trees on each side the Walk leading from the Church down to the Turn Stile towards Peters Finger.

September 28th. It is unanimously agreed to repair the Tileing at the East end of the North Aisle at the least possible Expence it may be done so as to prevent the rains penetrating thro'.

1793. March 14. The Churchwardens & Robt. Cooper Esqr, Edwd. Baker, Esqr, Mr. Thos. Cooksey & Mr. W^{m}. Woolfryes, &c., instructed to look over and inspect the several Deeds and Writings belonging to the Vestry and report the same to a Vestry hereafter to be held for that purpose and if necessary to apply for any Professional assistance they are at Liberty to do it.

April 1st. Ordered that the Road from the Corner of St. Ann's Street to the Church be immediately repaired, likewise ordered that the offer of Mr. Coombs and Mr. Rogers to bring Gravel into the Church Yard be accepted.

Ordered that a Fair Copy of the Gentlemen of the Vestry be transcribed from this Book & be placed in some conspicuous part of the Vestry Room—John Baker, Rector, John Young, William Tinney, Ch. Wardens. Jeffry. Gawen, John Goodfellow, Rob. Cooper, Edwd. Baker, Wm. Hutchence, Jas. Coombs, John Tanner Junr, G. Young, Jos. Rogers, Thomas Lake, James Chubb, R. Cary Corfe.

1793. Octr 18th. Agreed that Mr. Wharton shall have the Liberty to stop up the Gate at the North east end of the Church Yard provided he reinstate the same in its antient form as a foot path whenever called upon so to do and that the Vestry do keep open the Ditch of 3 Feet wide on the East side of the wall as it antiently was kept open.

1794. Jany 24. At a Vestry held this day. Three Counsels Opinions were produced taken in consequence of the resolution of the last Vestry. And it is now agreed That the Churchwardens do conform wth the Executors and Mr. Cookseys Widow and Report the Result of such Conference at the next Vestry Meeting.

1795. April 2d. In pursuance of an Act of Parliament for raising Eleven Men for the Service of his Majestys Navy a Vestry was conveyn'd for that purpose for the Parish of St. Martin's in the City of New Sarum.

Mr. Robt Hutchence paid his fine to be excused serving the Office of Churchwarden.

Novr 25th. Resolved that the Bishop of Salisbury be applied to as Lord of the Waste to determine the Right & Propriety of having a Wall erected near the Entrance of the Church Yard of St. Martin's.

1796. March 23rd. It was agreed that Mr. Cooper and Mr. Woolfryes on behalf of the Vestry shod meet Mr. Bucher on behalf of the Bishop of Salisbury and Dr. Hancock on behalf of Mr. Greenfield. To settle and determine the Boundary of the Land in possession of Mr. Coombs and Report to the Vestry.

Agreed that the Sexton shall receive £1 10s. ℘ year for keeping the walks clean.

1797. Jany 26th. It was observ'd that many omissions of Entrys on the Vestry Book had occur'd in consequence of the very frequent non-attendance of the Clerk and Mr. Tinney was propos'd and unanimously Chosen Clerk to this Vestry, and the Churchwarden desir'd to signify to Mr. Goodfellow that the Vestry will have no further occassion for his Services.

April 12th. It was unanimously Resolv'd in consequence of the Encreas^{g} trouble and Expence attending the Office that no Person who is duly elected Churchwarden shall be excused serving that Office without paying the Sum of Twenty Pounds to the Vestry.

1798. April 7th. It is ordered "That any person or persons holding any Pew or Seat in the Church. By virtue of any Grant from the Vestry or otherwise. Such person or persons on leaving the Parish and going to reside in any other Parish or place Shall Forfeit and lose his or her right in or to any such pew or seat so quitted or vacated. And that from thence forth It shall be lawful For the Vestry to Grant such Vacated pew or seat to any other person or persons as they shall think proper.

August 15th. Account of Church Plate and Linnen Delivered to Mr. Coy (continued yearly).

A large Silver Flaggon	Linnen
A Challice Do.	Large Communion Cloth
large Salver Do.	Eight Small Cloths
Small Salver Do.	two Napkins
two Small Silver plates	

1799. March 24th. Ordered that the Lower part of the Church-Yard be filled up with the Rubbish of the City.

May 10th. Ordered that the tiling of the South Side of the Church be immediately repair'd.

It was also agreed that Mr. Hutchence may build a Wall at his own expence at the West end of the Church yard upon a strait line with his own Wall.

1799. July 4th. It is resolv'd that the Church Warden ought not to advance any Money to any person for Keeping in Repair the Engine of the parish.

December 18. It was ordered that the Church be forthwith compleatly repaired.

Ordered that Mr. Churchwarden Sutton do pay for the repair of the Engine of this parish the money now due for the same.

It is requested that the Churchwarden do wait on the agents of the several fire offices resident in this City to desire them to contribute in future to the keeping in Repair of the Engine of this parish.

1801. Mr. Hutchence having undertaken to build a new House for the use of the Sexton of this parish for the Time being on a piece of Land adjoining to the Engine House which belongs to the Lord Bishop of Sarum and it being represented that the said Lord Bishop is willing to grant a Lease for 21 years of such Land for such purpose to such persons as the Vestry might appoint to take the same with proper Covenants on their parts to be performed Mr. Churchwarden Lander, Mr. Hutchence and Mr. Coombes being present are requested to take the same and a Draft of the Lease being read they have consented thereto.

It being represented to the Vestry that the Register Books of this Parish have been very carelessly kept, and persons have had a very improper access to the same. The Churchwardens are requested to have a Lock affixed to the Box containing the same, and the Minister is requested to keep the key of the said Box with the Register Books always locked therein, except when they are in use.

The Church Wardens are requested to put in Repair the Church Yard Wall on the East side of the Churchyard. The Church-Wardens also are requested to put up a pair of cast-Iron gates at the Entrance of the Church yard extending on one side from the corner of Mr. Hutchence's House to the post now standing on the South Side of the Whirly-gig. The remainder of the present entrance to be stopped up.

1802. Mr. John Pern Tinney elected Vestry Clerk in the room of Mr. William Tinney deceased.

Seven new Feoffees were elected viz. Messrs. Samuel Emly, William Woolfryes, Robert Cary Corfe, Tho: Lake, W^{m}. Ellis, Richard Sutton, William Ghost.

April 19. Mr. Ghost unanimously elected Churchwarden.

Mr. Iremonger	was proposed		by Mr. Sutton,	12 votes.
Mr. Blatch	,,	,,	by Mr. Corfe,	5 ,,
Mr. Rumbold	,,	,,	by Mr. Young,	2 ,,
Mr. Pearce	,,	,,	by Mr. Goodfellow,	*nil.*

Mr. Iremonger paid £20 to be excused serving the office. Mr. Blatch was then elected.

May 24. A perambulation of the parish decided on, as it appeared that hereafter in the event of a necessity for making a rate for the repairs of the Church it may be very important to ascertain what Lands or property may be subject to assessment in such rate.

August 17. It was reported to the Vestry that a perambulation of the parish took place on the Ascension day and that no obstruction was made to the progress of the perambulators except at the entrance of Mr. Wyndham's Garden where a Wall was found erected in the Course usually taken by them on such occasions. And another wall was found erected at quitting that Garden which was also found an obstruction.

It was represented that Mr. Wyndham had expressed his regret for such obstructions and that in future the Boundary of the parish might not be doubtful he had undertaken to have engravings inserted in each of the walls signifying the points of division there between this parish and the parish of St. Edmond.

Mr. Tinney presented a Bill amounting to Sixteen pounds fifteen shillings and four pence. The same was examined and approved and Mr. Churchwarden Ghost is requested to discharge it.

1802. Novr 11th. It was unanimously agreed that the Seat appropiated to the use of the Mayor & Corporation of this City be new Lined and the Ornaments thereof repair'd at the discretion of the Church Warden and that a handsome New Book be provided for the Mayor for the time being, and the other Books repair'd.

December 15th. The Churchwardens are requested to have the front part of the Seat appropriated to the use of the Mayors and Aldermen's Ladies newly lined and the whole of it carefully cleaned and repaired, with new Curtains.

December 22nd. The Church-wardens are requested to have the pulpit and pews attached to it newly painted of a Norway-oak colour and the velvet Cloths of the Desks and Pulpit died of a purple colour, and the whole carefully cleaned and repaired.

1803. Mr. Edward Baker paid £20 to be excused from serving the office of Churchwarden for the year ensuing.

1804. Part of the Churchyard Wall having been defaced and torn down and the Trees in the Churchyard being hacked with an Axe by some mischievous persons. The Churchwarden is desired to have hand-bills printed offering a reward of one guinea to whoever will inform against the offenders.

1805. Mr. Benjamin Charles Collins paid a Fine of £20 to be excused serving the office of Churchwarden and Mr. George Baker was elected in his place, who also paid the like fine of £20 to be excused.

1806. May 28. It is ordered that two Gates made of Cast Iron be put up at the entrance of the Churchyard from Church Street and that Mr. Churchwarden Rumbold Mr. Churchwarden Whitmarsh and Mr. Robert Cary Corfe do see the order well executed and make any contract for the same which they shall think necessary.

1807. William Burch's Salary for cleaning the Church is increased to Fifty Shillings.

1809. Accounts signed by Thomas Davis, Rector, no Rector's name has been signed in the Vestry Book since 1796.

1809. The Churchwarden is requested to have a new Tent for the use of the Minister at Funerals.

Also to obtain estimates from Lerke, Morris and Fisher for repairs of the Bells, estimates have already been had from Bradly.

1810. Ordered that the Churchwardens put into repair the Sermon bell and the Service bell.

1811. Mr. Webb pays his fine of £20 to be excused serving the office of Churchwarden.

It is ordered that the Feoffees do grant their License and consent to enable the Assignees of the estate and effects of Mr. Burrough a bankrupt to execute an assignment of the said Lease to the said Trustees.

New Lease granted to the Trustees of the Schools established for the education of the Children of the Poor.

1813. March 31st. It is ordered that the Churchwardens provide a dry well-painted Iron Chest for the use of the Rector to contain in safety the register books of the parish.

The Churchwardens authorised to give Bounties of two Guineas each to Volunteers willing to serve in the Local Militia for this Parish.

1813. October 7. Tiling of the Church ordered to be repaired.

1816. Perambulation of the boundaries of the parish on Ascension Day & the Rector requested to attend.

1817. August 1. It is ordered that Mr. Churchwarden Cusse do cause to be put up at the North entrance to the Churchyard a New Iron railing and Gates agreeable to a plan this day produced by him to the Vestry. And also that he do cause the Walks in the Churchyard to be graveled.

November 21. The Churchwarden reported that he had executed the Order of the last Vestry by preparing New Iron Gates for the entrance of the Church Yard which it was necessary to fasten by two screws to the wall of the School house. A correspondence follows from which it appears that Daniel Eyre, Chairman of the Tontine objected to the above arrangement, but eventually consented on being assured that no injury would accrue to the School.

1818. The Churchwardens reported that the alterations at the entrance of the Churchyard were completed.

It is ordered that it is expedient that a Stove should be erected in the Church.

1819. April 12. "That it be recommended to the several Vestries of this City to appoint each one Gentleman, who with a person to be appointed by the directors, and a person appointed by the Agents of the fire offices, may regulate the Fire Engines and Firemen, and direct whatever may be necessary to render them most efficient for the protection of the City from perils of Fire."

"An application being made by the Rev[d]. Mr. Hodgson the Lecturer of Saint Thomas in this City to grant to him the use of the Church of Saint Martin for the Evening Lectures during the period that Saint Thomas Church shall be under repair." Granted.

June 5. A rate of 3[d] in the pound ordered for putting the Church in repair.

December 1st. Mr. John Pern Tinney resigns the office of Vestry Clerk and Mr. James Cobb appointed as his successor.

1820. April 3rd. "It is ordered that the Churchwarden be not allowed in future to expend the sum of £4 to defray part of the Expences of the Visitation Dinner as heretofore hath been done."

1820. Survey of Church property ordered and the Church and particularly the Tower and Steeple to be put in the best state and condition.

May 5th. The Committee report "That they have surveyed the Church with the assistance of proper workmen externally and internally and find that the repairs which require immediate attention are the thoroughly scraping cleansing and pointing the internal walls and ceiling and partly whitewashing the same, the fresh hanging and adjusting the Doors, Wainscotting, Floors and Seats of many of the Pews let out in Single Sittings: and also the pointing of the external walls, the Tower and the Steeple and taking up and relaying the Leaden Gutter on the East side of the Tower, first pointing and well preparing the stone work with Roman Cement and most effectually to secure the Tower from the beating in of heavy Rains, to put a new flushing of Lead round on all the foursides of it." The total expense is roughly estimated at £30.

1821. Application made by the School Committee to erect a Gallery in the Church for the accommodation of the Children of the National School.

1821. Sept. 19th. A meeting of the Vestry held when amongst other things it was resolved "That this Vestry protests against the assembly of any persons in vestry within this parish who are not entitled by antient usage and custom to be members of this Vestry, and earnestly requests that the Churchwardens will resist all attempts to alter affect or disturb the rights of this Vestry established by such antient usage and custom."

1822. Feoffes newly elected.

John Pern Tinney
Charles George Brodie
Thomas Cusse
Henry White
George Atkinson.
George Ambrose Baker
John Woolfryes
William Woolfryes
Joseph Saunders
Richard Sutton &

Surviving Trustees
Robert Cary Corfe
William Ghost &
William Ellis.

Trustees elected also to the various Charities

The Rev. Thos. Davis Rector
William Woolfryes Common Brewer
Charles George Brodie Wine Merchant
John Pern Tinney Esquire.
John Woolfryes Com. Brewer
Thos. Cusse Maltster
James Sutton Esquire

1822. Miss Biddlecombe elected Organist at £5 per annum and a Voluntary Subscription to be collected on 25th December & 24th June in each year. Resolved that the salary heretofore paid to Miss Smith as Organist of £5 per annum be continued to her for Life on account of her past services and advanced age.

1823. Oct. 22. Resolved that it is absolutely essential to have a New Organ.

30th. Decided to purchase an Organ of Mr. Blyth for 185 guineas.

Great Organ { Stop Diapason
Open Diapason
Principal
Twelfth
Fifteenth
Sesquailtra
Cornet &
Flute. Shifting Movement to take off the Chorus Stops. Deal Gothic Case as the Organ best suited to the limited means of the parish.

Such Organ when purchased to be erected in the Gallery at the West end of the Church now used as a public Gallery.

The Gallery in which the old Organ is now standing to be converted into a public Gallery and filled up accordingly for the use of the public in lieu of the Gallery to be appropriated to the new Organ.

Resolved. That on the opening of the New Organ a selection of Sacred Music be performed under the patronage of the Minister, Churchwardens and Vestry of St. Martins under the direction of the Organist whose offer of Twenty Guineas towards the expense of erecting the Organ be accepted.

1824. List of Subscribers to the New Organ.

Novr. 10. It is ordered that the front of the present public Gallery, the back part of Mr. Cooes and Mr. Webbs seats facing the Chancel be painted the same Colour as the front of the Organ Gallery and that Columns between the Church and the Chancel be painted and sanded.

Burial fees.

1825. Mr. Churchwarden Finley having communicated the application made to him for the purchase of the Brass Eagle, but the Vestry having some doubt as to their right of selling the same without a faculty. It was Resolv'd that the Churchwardens be requested to order the Sexton to clean the same and to place it in the Centre Aisle of the Church.

New Desks & Stools and altering the present Stools round the Communion Table £13 0s. 0d.

A new white Surplice ordered.

Resolved that the altar piece be painted the same Colour as the railing round the Communion table leaving the Glory and the Gilding in their present state, and that the Rector cause such inscription to be placed thereon as he shall think proper, with the approbation of the Dean and Chapter.

The Churchwardens ordered to forthwith cause the roof of the Church to be repaired in the best manner as in their discretion they may think fit.

Resolved that the four several monuments affixed to the pillars of the centre aisle of the Church, be taken down and affixed to the side Walls.

1826. Resolved that it is expedient that the boundaries of the parish should be perambulated according to Antient Custom on the Ascension-day.

Decr. 8th. Resolved that Miss Biddlecombes Salary as Organist be encreased from £5 to £10 in consequence of the death of Mrs. Jane Smith the late Organist who received an annuity of £5 per annum for her life such increase to commence from the 18th day of Augst last.

1827. William Henry Biddlecombe appointed Organist.

Enquiry as to Edmund Mack's Charity.

June. Frederic Parry Hodges Curate.

Hot air Stove to be erected by R. Howden & Son for £75.

Charles Henry Hodgson Officiating Minister. April.

Septr. A door covered with Green Baize ordered to be erected at the North Side of the Church.

Apology from Rev. F. P. Hodges Curate for presuming to vote in the Select Vestry.

1828. Organist's Salary increased to £15 per annum.

Gratuity to Singers increased to £10.

1828. Proceedings instituted against Mr. Coombs of Milford for refusing to pay Church Rate.

Mr. Coleridges opinion taken relative to the question as to the Church rate between this parish and Milford.

1829. Church rate of 1s. in the pound ordered to be collected.

Resolved that a communication be made from the Vestry Room into the Church provided the Cost do not exceed £5.

Resolved the Churchwardens and Vestrymen do perambulate the boundaries of this parish on Holy Thursday according to ancient custom, that the attendance of the Clergyman be requested on that occasion, and that the Churchwardens make the necessary arrangements and public notice be given thereof. The following notice was served on several of the Vestrymen, "We the undesigned do hereby severally give you notice not to enter in or upon any or either of the Lands, Coppices, Woods, Underwoods or premises or any part thereof in Milford commonly called and known as the parish of Milford in the County of Wilts for the purpose or under the pretence of perambulating the Boundaries of the Parish of Saint Martin in the County of Wilts or for any other purpose or pretence whatsoever. And if you shall hereafter be found entering upon the said lands or premises or any part thereof you will be deemed a wilful trespasser and will be proceeded with against as such by some one or all of us. Dated this 26th day of May, 1829. R[d]. & Jn[o]. Cooe, Tho[s]. Blake, Sam[l]. Whitchurch, Benj. Budd, Samuel Jones, Tho[s]. Moody, James G. Coombs, Tho[s]. Brown."

It is resolved that the perambulation be proceeded with notwithstanding such notices according to antient usage and custom.

The Rector, Churchwardens, Vestry and Inhabitants proceeded in their perambulation until they arrived at a Door way between a Garden of Wadham Wyndham Esq. in the occupation of — Butler in the district of Milford and a Rick Yard of Benjamin Budd which door they found fastened by a Padlock. A part of the Inhabitants then proceeded to the house of Mr. Budd to whom the said door belonged and desired to see him but were informed by the Servant that he was from home though the Inhabitants who attended to demand a removal of the obstruction have no doubt he was in the house at the time but would not see them—that they desired the Servant to open the door, which she said she could not do.

Resolved that as such Obstruction was no doubt purposely thrown in the way of the perambulators and as there is now an Action pending touching the rating of the Inhabitants of the parish living in the district of Milford it was thought advisable not to break open the said door, but to adjourn the perambulation and in the mean time that the Vestry Clerk should take advice of Counsel as to proceedings against the said Benjamin Budd and report the same at the next Vestry.

That as the Corn and Grass is now in a very forward state owing to the late period on which Ascension day falls this year, the proceeding in the perambulation at a more advanced season of the year would cause great injury to the Crops on the Lands over which the perambulators must necessarily pass. It is Resolved that the perambulation on that account be postponed to the next Ascension day when the Vestry and Inhabitants will again proceed therein.

1829. It is ordered to give Notice to Dr. Fowler to clean the ditch in the Field on the East side of the Church yard and open the Foot path leading from the North East end of the Church yard into the Sarum and Ealing Turnpike road.

Sep. 24. The following communication having been received by Messrs. Wheeler & Cother from Mr. Coombs relative to the pending Action commenced against him for non-payment of the Church rate, viz.: To the Churchwardens of Saint Martins parish. Gentlemen,

"In consequence of a conversation with some of the Gentlemen of your parish most interested in the settlement of the Question in dispute between us, and considering the unfortunate indecision of the Jury at the last Assizes, I thought it right to call a meeting of the Parishioners of Milford to ascertain their opinion of a compromise.

"I am authorized to say that as the evidence produced clearly exonerated us from all other obligations we consent to pay the Church rates already assessed on condition that the expences now incurred on both sides shall be paid by rates to be assessed on St. Martin's and Milford Parishes. I am Gentlemen

Your obedient Servant James G. Coombs.

23d Sepr 1829. It was Resolved that the proposition of the Inhabitants of Milford contained in such Letter be entertained in this Vestry and be acquiesced in provided the proprietors and Inhabitants in general of Milford consent to pay the past and also all future Church rates to be made by the Churchwardens and Inhabitants of the said Parish of Saint Martin on them, and that they do not object to the payment of any such rate on account of the monies to be raised thereby being applied in discharge of the expence incurred by the respective parties in the pending proceedings, and that no further steps shall be had or taken by them in the pending action. And further that the costs and expences incurred by the parties (with the exception of the costs incurred by the pltf^s. in withdrawing the record at the Spring Assizes 1829 and the costs paid to the defts thereon), be paid in equal portions out of a general fund to be raised by a rate or rates on all the Inhabitants of the parish of Saint Martin as well those within the City of New Sarum as in Milford, and that the past rates be paid by the Inhabitants of Milford forthwith.

It was further resolved that a Copy of the above resolution be sent to Mr. Coombs and be signed by the Vestry Clerk.

October 1st. A meeting of the Vestry was held to take into consideration the proposal for a compromise.

The following Letter from the Inhabitants of Milford was read: "The Resolutions of your Vestry founded on Mr. Coombs Letter having been laid before us the Inhabitants and proprietors of Milford assessed to the Rate are willing to pay it but Messrs. Cooe consider the property for which they are rated is neither in Milford nor Saint Martins and they therefore intend taking further advice before they decide on acceding to the resolutions.

"A difficulty also arises respecting the costs incurred by the plt. & defts. in withdrawing the Record at the last Spring Assizes. Mr. Coombs has proposed a settlement upon what he considers a broad and equitable basis having for its object an equal division of the expences incurred by both parties and an ultimate submission to the present and future Church rates. He does not consider the exception in your resolutions as being in accordance with his views upon the subject, nor can he consent to such an essential deviation from the terms proposed by him.

"It is hoped that upon a reconsideration of his offer your Vestry will abandon the objectionable clause when we shall be happy to congratulate the parishioners on thus effecting an amicable arrangement of the suit." Yours faithfully I. & M. Hodding.

It was resolved That the Costs incurred by the plaintiff and the defendants in withdrawing the Record in the Lent Assizes 1829 form a part of the General Costs and be included in the arrangement above entered into.

Resolved the Vestry Clerk do desist from any further proceedings in the pending Action.

Resolved that the Churchwardens immediately call on the Inhabitants of Milford for payment of the two Church rates now due.

1829. Nov. 20. Messrs. Cooe requested to give proof that the lands for which they are rated are not within the parish of Saint Martin. Dec. 3d Mr. Cooe attended and asserted that the lands in question were in Laverstock but produced no documentary evidence.

1830. Twelve forms or Stools ordered to be placed in the Aisles. The Vestry express a wish that the National School Children do not sit in the Aisles of the Church in future. Resolved that the Bells in future be chimed previous to Service on Sundays and that the Churchwardens be requested to ascertain what the expence of chiming the whole of the Bells will amount to for half an hour for the morning and afternoon services.

The final Agreement between St. Martins and Milford Mr. Cobb delivered in his Bill for conducting the Suit amounting to £993 17s. 7d.

Ordered to pay Mary Ann Safe for her services in the Choir during the past year £1 and to the other Children of the Choir £1 for their services.

Aug. 12. It is ordered that the Churchwardens do cause the Turn Stile leading into the Church yard (about which there has been much complaint on account of its inconvenience to the public) to be reduced from the bottom part upwards about halfways so as to prevent inconvenience to the public in passing through.

1831. Mr. Colborne refuses to pay his Church rate & proceedings are ordered to be taken against him in the Ecclesiastical Court to enforce the payment thereof.

1832. Mr. Coombs offers a piece of land at Milford near Laverstock bridge for the burial of those persons who may die from Cholera Morbus should the City be visited with that disease.

1837. A new twelfth stop added to the Organ. Cost nine guineas. A new Surplice ordered for the Rector, there not having been a new one for the space of 30 years.

Ordered a New Velvet Pulpit Cloth & Cloths for the Reading Desk and Clerk's Desk and a new Velvet Cushion with Silk Fringe and Tassels.

The Gold Lace on the present Pulpit Cloths and Cushions to be sold.

Resolved that Mr. Lane's estimate for whitewashing & repairing the Ceiling of the Church amounting to £35 10s. be accepted.

1837. Ordered that that part of the Roof of the Middle Aisle between the pulpit and the Chancel be repaired.

The Dean & Chapter agree to give £25 towards the proposed alteration in the Chancel, provided that their Surveyor Mr. Fisher should certify that the side walls are not likely to receive any damage by the removal of any beams upon which the present ceiling is supposed to depend.

Ordered that estimates be obtained of the Cost of taking down the present Ceiling of the Chancel and re-instating the same in its original state so as to correspond with the Ceiling of that part of the Church which immediately adjoins it, and also a separate estimate of the cost of restoring the Window at the East end thereof to its original state and repairing the same including the Glass work thereof. Estimate for the work.

	£	s.	d.
Read's estimate for Carpenter's work ...	26	11	0
Lane's Do. for plastering in the Church	16	12	0
Do. Do. in the Chancel	11	10	0
Read's Do. for erecting the Arch between the Church and Chancel	4	16	0
Osmond's Do. for Stone work ...	20	0	0
Total ...	£79	9	0

1838. Resolved that it is the opinion of the Vestry that every Gentleman serving the office of Churchwarden becomes a Vestryman of this parish and is entitled at all times thereafter to vote in the Vestry although he may not be a resident in the parish.

1839. William Martin Coates declines to serve as Ch. warden, he being a Surgeon in practice.

Lease of 40 years to the Trustees of the Tontine of the National School granted.

1840. The Tithe Commissioner holds a meeting to settle the boundary between the parish of Laverstock and Milford. (See Appendix).

The Rector proposes to have an Evening Service on Sundays. Subject deferred on account of the additional expence attending thereon.

1841. Decided to pull down and rebuild the Culver street Almshouses.

Foundations of the Tower of the Church reported to be in a dilapidated condition and require an outlay of £25.

1842. Resolved to obtain an Estimate of the cost of recasting the Bell which is cracked also of rehanging the other bells & putting the whole in repair. Also of the Cost of repairing the flooring of the Belfry & Tower.

Novr. 18. Resolved to enter into a contract with Mr. Bridgman for the repairs of the Bells for £63 with the exception of the New Bell.

Mr. Richardson elected Organist in place of Mr. Biddlecombe. To attend the Church twice on every Sunday, on the Great Festivals and 1½ hour every Thursday evening to instruct the Choir. Salary £15.

1843. Resolved to pay the Six Ringers £6 per annum.

That the Clerk's Salary be increased from £5 to £7 10s.

1846. Sexton's Salary increased to £4 per annum.

Resolved to present the Fire Engine & appliances to the Town Council if they will accept the same, as the Vestry has no Funds to defray the expenses thereof.

William Price Aylward elected Organist on same terms as last.

1847. Mr. Pothecary declined to serve as Ch.warden he being Overseer.

Reported that there was in the hands of Messrs. Brodie at the time of their failure Two sums viz. £51 7s. & £76 15s. 2d. belonging to this parish.

1848. New Lease of the Sexton's house granted by the Bishop.

George Podger elected Sexton.

1849. Church reseated. £280 raised for repairs on the estimate given by Messrs. Wyatt & Brandon.

1850. January. A Cemetery proposed, but not considered necessary.

Ordered that the Velvet Cushion be placed on the Pulpit as heretofore.

Salaries of Parish Clerks ordered to be obtained. St. Thomas £25 & fees. St. Edmunds £33 2s. 6d. & fees. St. Martin £7 10s. & fees. Now raised to £15.

Alterations made in the National School.

1851. Ordered that an estimate be obtained for erecting a Seat and Reading desk for the Clerk to be placed near the pulpit and also two Seats and Desks for the Choir close to the front of the Organ. Bells repaired by Job Dibsdell for £12 & other repairs ordered. Ordered that a Deal Cupboard be erected between the North Wall in the Vestry and the Fire place to contain a wash hand Bason and other necessary Articles for the Clergyman, that the necessary Earthenware by purchased, also a set of Fire Irons for the Vestry with a Fender.

1853. A new Surplice ordered for the Rector.

1854. Order received to close the churchyard for burials from 1st June 1855. Burial Board appointed.

1855. Cost of Cemetery about £5000. St. Thomas £2132 18s. 1d. St. Edmund £1978 6s. 8d. St. Martin £474 7s. 7d. Milford £414 7s. 8d.—on Ratable values £10,260 5s., £9516 14s., £4275 7s. & £3734 7s. 9d. respectively.

A piece of land occupied by Mr Richard Sutton selected

Cost of Land Mr. Goldwyer (Copyholder) ...	£1200
Duke of Hamilton (Lord Farmer)	200
Bishop of Salisbury (Lord of the Manor) ...	125
Tenant (Lessee under Mr. Goldwyer, Compensation)	170
	£1695

Laying out the Ground, Buildings & Wall £2500.
Conveyancing, Enfanchisement, &c. £500.

1856. Resolved that permission be given to lay down Gas pipes in the Church preparatory to lighting the same for the celebration of Evening Service, on condition that in the doing thereof no injury be done to the Fabrick, the paving, or the pews of the Church and that neither the Vestry nor the parish be put to any expense whatever in laying down such Gas pipes or consequent thereon nor for hereafter lighting the Church with Gas when such pipes are laid down, or for repairing the same, nor for any increase of Salary which may be called for in consequence of the celebration of such service.

1857. Resolved to sell the Fire Engine belonging to the parish the same being in a very dilapidated condition and quite useless.

1858. Resolved to increase the Salary of the Sexton from £5 per annum to £7 10s. in consequence of the loss of fees by the New Cemetery.

1859. Mr. Henry William Cobb appointed Vestry Clerk in place of Mr. James Cobb deceased.

1862. Sexton's Salary increased to £15.

1863. Resolved that the whole of the mounds over the Graves in the Churchyard be levelled.

1865. Mr. Thos. Hutchens surveyor reported on the state of the Arch & Piers in the Nave of the Church and it was resolved to have the Foundations of the Aisle Walls, and also the Nave Piers repaired in the most substantial way, and a proper Pipe Drain laid down on the North side of the Church so as to carry off the water falling from the roof & prevent injury to the

Foundations. Also to have the internal Walls of the Church re-coloured and the Shafts of the Pillars painted. The cost of which was £227 8s. 10d.

Mr. Thos. Cusse being the only ffeoffee surviving who was appointed in 1822, the following 13 members of the Vestry were appointed viz. William Osmond, Samuel Noke Wilmot, Henry William Cobb, John Large, William Higgins, Frederick Roe, Samuel Cusse, William Osmond, jun^r^., William Woodlands, Thomas Pay Howe and George Richardson.

1867. Is a pedigree of the Lake Family.

1868. Renewal of the Lease of the National Schools which has been held on the premises since 1812, for a term of 40 years at £25 per annum and a Fine of £270. The Garden occupied by Mr. Keynes to be converted into a playground. The fine was reduced at a subsequent meeting to £5.

Sexton's salary to be £40 per year including house.

That in future the Bells be chimed by machinery.

1870. Death of the Rev. William Wyndham Tatum, Rector.

Foundations of the Church reported to be in a bad state.

Rev. John Vodin Walters, Rector.

Church insured against Fire for £1500.

1872. Lease of School Premises extended for 62 years at £25 per annum.

Resolved that the Bells should be under Voluntary Ringers under the Control of the Rector, and that the Salary of £10 hitherto paid to the Rector be discontinued.

Moved by Mr. Wilson & seconded by Mr. Woodlands that the Lord's Table be lowered so as to prevent the obstruction of the Ten Commandments, and that the Curtain be taken down. Question put by the Chairman :—

For—		Against—	
Mr.	Wilson	Mr.	Wilmot
,,	Woodlands	,,	Howe
,,	Swyer	,,	Higgins
,,	Gerrish	,,	Cobb
,,	Holloway	,,	Walters

on which the Chairman gave a casting vote against the motion.

George Podger elected Sexton at a Salary of £20.

The Charity Trust monies to be transferred to the Official Trustee.

The foundations of the Church repaired and Alterations in the Churchyard completed at a cost of £269 17s. 9d.

Premises in Culver Street sold to Mr. C. T. Prangley for £500 and invested in 3 per cent. Consols £541 5s. 5d.

1873. Samuel W. Mangin, Rector.

1875. The Town Council build a wall at the bottom of Churchyard.

1876. Mr. Podger's Salary £25 per annum.

Sutton's Almshouses in St. Ann St. sold to Mr. H. G. Vincent for £580.

1877. Resolved that there shall be in future Quarterly Meetings of the Vestry in the first weeks in January, April, July and October.

£10 ordered to be paid to the Choir out of the Offertory.

1878. Lease of Garden 2 perch in Exeter street to Mr. Pickford expires and ordered to be let to Mr. Jones.

1879. Calcraft Neeld Wyld, Rector.

1881. Resolved to pull down the Sextons house that the road may be widened and for improving the Parsonage Site.

1882. Proposal to erect a Chapel in the Milford District.

Schedule of Fabric Property.

The Rectory of St. Martins exchanged with the Bishop for Cherhill.

Resolved that Mr. Michael Harding be appointed to receive the rents of the various properties, report thereon half yearly and carry out the necessary repairs and that he be paid an annual sum of £10 for his trouble.

The Committee reported that they had declined the offer of the piece of land at Milford offered in Mr. Kelsey's letter of the 8th March, 1882. And that the Rector agreed to purchase a piece of land in Wyndham's Park which he was willing to let for the purpose of building a Temporary Church at a rent of £6 a year.

1884. A piece of land in Milford part of the College Park 40ft. × 153 was bought by the Rev. C. N. Wyld for £120, and a Chapel of Ease thereon.

1885. Resolved that a thorough restoration of the Church is necessary.

1st July. Mr. Crickmay the architect's estimate £2850. It was resolved to sanction the expenditure of £2400, which includes permanent repairs to Roof, Walls, Flooring, Oak Seats, Improvement of the Organ, heating. The Bell framing and repairs of the Tower.

Directors of the Highways.

1830. Messrs. Giles Loder, James Ainsworth, James Cobb & John Toovey.

1831. Messrs. Joseph Saunders, James Cobb, George Atkinson & W^{m}. Hiscock.

1832. Messrs. John Toovey, James Cobb, William Wheeler & John Day Pinckney Loder.

1833. Messrs. William Prangley, Joseph Saunders, William Wheeler & John Toovey.

1834. Messrs. William Wheeler, James Cobb, John Toovey & Samuel Webb.

1835. Messrs. Henry Everett, William Wheeler, John Toovey & William Prangley.

1836. Messrs. Joseph Saunders, William Prangley, William Wheeler & Samuel Webb.

1837. Messrs. George Atkinson, Cobb, Osmund & Prangley.

1838. Messrs. George Atkinson, Osmund, James Henry Bracher & James Cobb.

The Plate Consists of

15 . A Chalice 7 inches high with its cover and a Paten bearing no hall marks. On the cover is engraved "The plate of St. Martin." The paten is quite plain $5\frac{1}{4}$ inches in diameter and is marked "St. Martin's." Round the base of the chalice is "Ex dono Gvlielmi Wickham, Episcopi Vintonia." William Wickham the second Bishop of that name was translated from Lincoln and filled the seat of Winchester for only ten weeks. He died in June, 1595.

1620. Another Paten 6in. diameter, quite plain and without hall marks; at the back is engraved a small monogram, the letters **T.R.** combined. In front is inscribed "Christopher Horte, Thomas Chiffinch, Churchwardens of St. Martin. Anno Domini 1620."

1670. A Flagon with cover, of tankard form 10 inches in height with a broad base tapering upwards. The date mark is 1669. The makers **T.L.** It is inscribed "This flaggon belongeth to the Parish Church of St. Martin in Sarum. William Antrum, William Ginaway, Churchwardens 1670."

1686. The Alms dish is a fine piece of plate, no doubt originally intended for a rose-water dish. It measures 18 inches diameter. The centre is plain, surrounded by a broad border very richly decorated with foliage, &c., in repoussé work. At some later period a large and cumbrous foot has been added to it. The hall marks indicate the year 1662, the maker's **D. R.** with a pellet above and below, within a shaped shield. In the centre is engraved a shield of arms quarterly, 1 and 4 *A chevron between three lozenges* for Hyde; 2 and 3 *On a paly of six a bend*, for Langford of Trowbridge, Wilts, charged with an inescutcheon *Cross of St. George*. The whole is surmounted by an earl's coronet, showing that it once belonged to the great Earl of Clarendon. Edward Hyde was born at Dinton, Wilts, he was made Lord Chancellor with an Earldom by Charles II. in 1661. As the hall mark shows that the dish was manufactured in the following year, it is thus one of the few remaining grandiose pieces which were so abundantly made for the court and courtiers immediately after the Restoration. This dish was presented to the parish in 1686, as appears by the following inscription, "The gift of Mrs. Alice Denham to the Parish Church of St. Martin's in the City of New Sarum. Anno Dni. 1686."

1728. A third Paten with a foot measuring $8\frac{3}{4}$ inches diameter, hall marked in the year 1728 with the maker's initials **G. S.** for Gabriel Sleath. It is inscribed with the sacred monogram, also "St. Martin's Sarum 1728."

1875. Silver gilt Chalice and Paten of 13th Century Pattern presented to the Church in 1875 by the Rev. Samuel Waring Mangin, then Rector.

A spoon, silver gilt, presented 1897.

Entries from the Churchwardens' Accounts.

1580.	For changing the pewter pott	vj[d].
1589.	for mending the tankard	viij[d].
1607.	for mendinge the Church quart pott ...	iiij[d].
1620.	pd. for a Cover for the Communion cupp & one saser weighing 8 ounces & a halfe & a drame at 6s. the ounce ...	ij[li]. xj[s]. vj[d].
1643.	Given to the Souldiers ffor bringing of the plate	16s. 0d.
1661.	To James Lake for the exchange of the fflagons	2s. 10d.
1677.	Deliv'ed to Mr. Will. Antram the new Churchwarden.	

One Silver Cupp.
One Silver flagon.

2 silver plates.
1 hollond cloth.
5 Diaper Cloths.
1 basket.

1725. Paid for a Pewter Salver 2s. 6d.

		£	s.	d.
1847—8.	Mr. Bennett Silversmith for two plates Alms plates for Sacrament	3	8	0
1884.	Bennett & Clench repairs to Alms dish ...	0	12	0
1904.	S. Rambridge, Regilding Chalice & Paten	5	7	6

Notes to the Foregoing Extracts.

Page 26.

1663. for the Act concerning fire Hearths. Fire-hearth money was a duty payable to the Crown on houses. By Statute 14, Car. II. cap. 2. "Every fire hearth and stove of every dwelling and other house within England and Wales (except such as pay not to Church and poor) shall be chargeable with 2s. per annum payable at Michaelmas and Lady Day to the King and his Heirs and Successors, which payment was called Chimney money. This tax, being much complained of as burdensome to the people, was taken off and that of windows imposed in its stead, 7 and 8 Will. III., 1696.

Page 29.

1568. The Carnis book = Book containing list of those who might eat meat during the fast.

One payer of Sersters. ? Systes = wax tapers.

ij Corprasses = Corporals, linen cloths used to cover the sacred elements.

A white deacon = a vestment worn by a Deacon.

1580. for a pound of systes. } Sises = wax tapers
1585. "ffor j[lb]. of sises." }

1588. "The tremer." ? The Streamer.

1594. "layd out to the Joyn[r] for the perryment" ?

Pages 30 & 46.

1607. }
1637. } "for one Gimell for the pewe Dore." Gimell = A jointed hinge.

Page 32.

1663. "for fower paire of snight bittles."
? s'night bittles = scent bottles.

Pages 33 & 49.

1717. "for mend 3 Sockets for the Branch of y[e] Sconce."

Sconce: "A lantern; originally a light used for sacred purposes. In the North of England the term is given to a kind of candlestick with a tin back, hung against a wall" (*Halliwell*).

"The circular tube with a brim in a candlestick into which a candle is inserted."

Pages 44 & 45.

1568. "Shyngull." Shingles are wooden tiles made of oak, used for roofs, steeples, &c.

1584. Singing bread : The wafers intended for the consecrated host in the eucharistic sacrament.

1568 to 1610. Smoke farthings = The ancient Peter's Pence.

Page 46.

1627. The plague raged in Salisbury.

Page 49.

1693. "for a grey's head. A grey = a badger.

1727. Paid for the Umbrella. Was this an umbrella for the Minister at funerals ?

1736. "For mending y^e Whoreley Gogg = a turnstile.

Page 50.

1748. "for laying 5 Orders for the Horn'd Cattle."

At this time a Cattle disease called "The Murrain" was prevalent. No doubt these Orders were restrictions issued concerning the movement of Cattle.

Page 51.

Qualification Cakes (August 12, 1819). What are they ?

Page 53.

1567. The Holy lofe.

The holy bread was ordinary leavened bread, cut into small pieces, blessed, and given to the people after mass. The distribution of the *panis benedictus* was practised in every church throughout the land. In the Constitutions of Giles de Bridport, Bishop of Salisbury, in the year 1252, it was decreed that the parishioners should provide the holy bread every Sunday.

The formula for the blessing of holy bread was, in English :—"Oh, Lord Jesus Christ, the bread of angels, the living bread of eternal life, deign to bless this bread as Thou didst bless the five loaves in the desert, that all who eat thereof may receive from thence health of body and soul."

The Holy Bread has nothing sacramental in its nature. It is used in the manner of the love feasts of the early Church as a symbol of the fellowship and brotherly love which should exist among all who are of the household of faith.

Pages 49 & 53. The Umbrella.

The Umbrella appears to have been purchased in 1727 for 22^s, & sold in 1729 to the Churchwardens of St. Edmund's for 20^s.

Page 53. Church liten wall. Litten = graveyard.

Page 57. Mr. Cooper entered on his duties as Curate of St. Martin's on The Fourth Sunday in Advent, **1903**.

Page 60. Line 20, for 1656 read 1686.

The Churchwardens appointed at the Easter Vestry, 1905, were Alfred D'Augibau & Robert Ridout Williams.

Sidesmen, Ambrose Tucker and Thomas Henry Baker.

Three ancient recumbent tombstones on the West side of the Churchyard were placed in their present positions by Rev. C. N. Wyld, who removed them from off the East wall of the Churchyard.

Since writing the foreging I have seen copies of two old wills from which the following notes have been extracted :—

1316. Robert Cheese bequeathed "To the fabric of the Church of St. Martin, of Sarum 5s."

1347. John de Shirebourne, Citizen of New Sarum, "To the fabric of the Church of St. Martin of Sarum 18d."

Page *omission page 62.*

May ye 19th 1709. At a meeting of the Vestry this present day it is order'd that the Churchwarden for the time to Come shall not Expend more than thirty shillings in goeing the preambulation of the whole bounds of the parish & in Case any Churchwarden shall Exceed that Sume no more then thirty Shillings shall be allowed him at the passing of his accounts.

Sidesmen.

1733. Walter Harris & Wm. Smith.
1735. 1736. Thos. Whale & Thomas Thomas alias Cornish.
1737. William Late & Tho. Bayman.
1738. Wm. Leate & Thos. Beamont.
1739. Thos. Beaman & Hugh Biggs.
1740. Robt. Hiscox & James Barlow.
1741. Richard ffloyd & Thos. Lake.
1742. Thos. Thomas & Thos. Bayman.
1743. Henry Cook & Thos. Bayman.
1746. Christopher Seagram & Wm. Lake.
1747. 1750. Wm. Read & Thos. Bayman
1751. 1752. George Spencer & Thos. Bayman
1755. Mr. Spencer & Mr. Rd. Lake.
1756. 1758. George Spencer & John Baden

1759. George Spencer & Rich[d]. Perrier.

1760. }
1765. } Rich[d]. Perrier & Will[m]. Hutchins.

1766. }
1767. } R[d]. Perrier & John Naish.

1768. John Naish & John Feltham.

1769. }
1770. } John Naish & Samuel Smith.

1772. Samuel Smith & Charles Othen Sen[r].

1773. }
1774. } Will[m]. Hutchence Jun[r]. & John Feltham.

1775 to 1779 } James Barlow & John Feltham.

1780 to 1784 } Rob[t]. Sutton & James Barlow.

1785 & 1786. W[m]. Kift & Robt. Woods.

1787. W[m]. Kift & W[m]. Wapshare.

1788. }
1789. } W[m]. Kift & John Webb.

1790. John Spencer & Mr. Webb.

1791. John Webb & John Compton, Maltster.

1792. Joseph Miell, Printer & John Webb.

1793. John Webb & Jos. Miell, Coachmaker.

1794. }
1795. } John Webb & W[m]. Kift.

1797. }
1798. } John Webb & G. Baker.

1799. John Webb & William Sutton.

1800. John Webb nominated by Mr. Lander & Rob[t]. Lodge by the Vestry.

1801—1803. Robert Lodge & John Mould.

1805—1806. James Mould & Robert Lodge.

1807. Tho[s]. Mould & Tho[s]. Rogers.

1811. James Bonnet & Tho[s]. Mould.

1812. Robert Sworn & Tho[s]. Mould.

1813. James Harding & Robert Sworn.

1815. Robert Sworn & W[m]. Lee.

1816—1819. Robert Sworn & Richard Sutton.

1820—1824. Robert Sworn & John Kimber.

1825. William Hayward & Robert Sworn.

1826—1833. Robert Sworn & James Simmonds.

1834. Richard Read & James George Coombs.

1836. Richard Read & John Hobbs.

1838. W[m]. Osmond.

1840. Nathaniel Lane.
1841. John Sidney Atkins.
1843. Rd. Read & George Beckingsale.
1845. George Beckingsale & Samuel Burch.
1846. Samuel Burch & James Strong.
1849. Samuel Burch & James Ponting.
1852. Robert Large & Samuel Burch.
1855. Samuel Burch & Jas. Hy. Tewkesbury.
1856. Samuel Burch & John Richardson.
1857. Samuel Noke Wilmot & Thos. Paye Howe.
1859. T. P. Howe & M. Horder.
1860. Mr. Horder & Thos. Osmond.
1862. S. N. Wilmot & Henry Foot.
1863. Thos. Osmond & H. P. Foot.
1864. Rd. Lloyd & W. H. Foot.
1866. W. H. Foot & Thos. Osmond.
1867. Thos. Osmond & S. N. Wilmot.
1868. S. N. Wilmot & Henry Finley.
1869. S. N. Wilmot & Rd. Lloyd.
1870. 1872. } John Squire & George Newman.
1873. Joseph W. Lovibond & John Squire.
1876. — Bush & George Newman.
1877. John Squire & Michael Harding.
1878. Michael Hardiug & C. H. Notley.
1881. John Harding & C. H. Notley.
1883. Rd. Lloyd & John Harding.
1884. 1892. } John Harding & John Squire.
1893. Ambrose Tucker and John Harding.
1894. Trayton Cheesman and John Harding.
1895. 1896. } Trayton Cheesman and Ambrose Tucker.
1897. Ambrose Tucker and H. Elliott Fox.
1898. H. Elliott Fox and Trayton Cheesman.
1899. Trayton Cheesman and F. W. Goodall.
1900. F. W. Goodall and Ambrose Tucker.
1901. Ambrose Tucker & Walter Goddard.
1902. Ambrose Tucker & Trayton Cheesman.
1903. Sir R. F. D. Palgrave & Ambrose Tucker.
1904. Thomas Awdry & Ambrose Tucker.
1905. Ambrose Tucker & Thos. H. Baker.

SUMMARY.

It seems highly probable that there was originally a Norman Church, traces of which may be seen on the West Wall of the South Aisle.

1217 (earliest mention on record). A perambulation was made to St. Martin's from Old Sarum on Rogation Day.

1228. Bishop Poore, founder of the Cathedral, instituted one Harvey to the Church of St. Martin with the Chapel of Stratford.

1230—40. The present Chancel built.

1268. The Provost of the College of St. Edmund appointed by the Bishop to be Rector of both St. Edmund's and St. Martin's Churches.

1318. The Tower and Spire probably built.

1546. The College of St. Edmund dissolved. St. Martin's becomes a Rectory.

The Chancel.

Classic Monument to the Swayne family, of Milford, 1748.
Curious Monument over South Door to two sons of Daniel Hales, of Highchurch, Somerset, 1645.
Piscina in South Wall.
The Pillar in North-east corner of the South Chapel shows wear by friction from the rope of the Sanctus Bell.
Three-light Lancet Window, inserted in place of Perpendicular Window, 1849.

The Nave.

Holy Water Stoup on South side of Door.
Font of Purbeck Marble, 13th Century, probably.
Pulpit, 1886, taking the place of the oak Pulpit, which is now in St. Mark's Church.
The Eagle (probably 15th Century work).
The Arch at the East end of Nave is built against previously existing pillars.

North Aisle, 1430—40.

Grotesque heads carved on the corbels.
The Chapel at the East end is now used as the Choir Vestry and Organ Loft.
Remains of a Piscina and Ambry.
Hatchments on the North Wall:
No. 1. (West). Baker, died 1794.
2. (Middle). ?
3. (East). Thomas, died 1784.
Royal Arms on West Wall, James I.

South Aisle, 1430—40.

At the West end the weather tabling of the old Norman Aisle and two fragments of stone with ornaments of the Norman period.

On South Wall the niche (15th Century restored) containing figures of the Annunciation.

Consecration Cross (13th Century).

Doorways and Staircase to Rood Loft.

Brass on South Wall, to the memory of John Sebastian Carpenter, 1632.

Piscina in Chapel at East end.

Screen, erected 1897.

Hatchments on North Wall :

No. 1. (West). Batt impaling ? 1723.
2. ? Windover quartering ?
3 and 4. Baker impaling Phipps.

Edward Baker, died 1796, Jane (Phipps) his wife, 1800.

Royal Arms, Elizabeth.

The Porch.

Tomb on the North side, inserted in a niche, belonging to some person unknown, but probably one of the 15th Century benefactors to the rebuilding of the Church ; the brasses and inscription have been abstracted.

The Chapel on the North side, dedicated to Corpus Christi, is now used as the Vestry Room.

There is a Stoup on the South side of the West Door (outside).

There was formerly a North Porch.

The Organ.

The first reference to an Organ is an item in 1567 of a payment of 8d. per annum to the organ blower.

1603. A new Organ erected, costing £3 6s. 8d., extra for painting, &c., 12s. 7d.

1869. The present Organ was erected by Messrs. Hill and Sons.

1898. The Organ was raised and the Choir Vestry was formed beneath.

The Clergy Vestry.

1897. Foundation Stone laid, July 21st, by the Mayoress, Mrs. Whitehead.

1898. Vestry opened on Palm Sunday, by the Bishop of Salisbury.

The Churchyard.

1653. The Cross was demolished and the stones sold.
1871. The remains of the Cross removed from the North side of the Churchyard and restored in the present position.

The Avenue of Limes was planted in 1792.

The Sundial on the South side of the Church was placed there 1709, for which Robert Baden was paid 30s. There is another on South side of Chancel of more ancient date.

St. Mary Magdalene (Iron Church) in Gigant Street was opened on Palm Sunday, 1880.

The Iron Church in the Park was opened November 29th, 1882, and closed when St. Mark's was dedicated.

St. Mark's Church dedicated 1894, consecrated April 30th, 1899.

St. Mark's Parish was formed by Order in Council, August, 1899.

The Iron Mission Church in the Friary was formerly a Baptist Chapel in Guilder Lane. It was bought by subscription and re-erected on land rented from Mr. Lovibond in the Friary. It was opened for service on October 6th, 1895. In 1903 the site was purchased, with the two adjoining cottages, by Rev. C. Myers, and handed over to the Board of Finance in trust for the Rector and Churchwardens. The annual income from the property, after the payment of all expenses, was to be divided thus :—£5 towards a sinking fund for repairs, £15 for the Incumbent (other than the present Incumbent), and the residue for St. Martin's Fabric Fund.

The Sidney Lear Memorial Rooms in Gigant Street, together with the caretaker's house, were presented in 1904 for the use of the Church in St. Martin's Parish by Mr. Oliver Farrer, of Binegar Hall, Wareham, the nephew of the late Mrs. Sidney Lear. The Diocesan Board of Finance hold the buildings in trust.

The electric light was introduced into St. Martin's Church, August, 1900.

NOTES BY THE REV. C. N. WYLD.

1870. Mr. Giles Loder left by will to the Trustees of St. Martin's School the sum of £1000, which was laid out in building the present Girls' School and Class Room, on the site of two cottages, then demolished, which were part of the fabric property of the parish.

Thos. Chiffinch occupied the Bell Inn at the bottom of St. Ann's Street. He led the Roman Catholic priest to the bed of Charles II. shortly before his death.

The Sexton's House stood at the entrance to the Churchyard; it extended from the iron fencing of the Churchyard in a north-westerly direction, west of the present wall of the Rectory garden, for about 15 yards. Adjoining it, at the east end, was a shed in which the fire engine was kept. The Vestry gave this property to the Rev. C. N. Wyld, on condition that he pulled it down and erected a new boundary wall to the Rectory garden.

The Tithe Barn stood at the north side of the Churchyard, extending its whole length, which, with the yard and garden adjoining, were leased to Colonel Baker by the Dean and Chapter. It then became the property of the Ecclesiastical Commissioners, who, at the expiration of the lease, sold the whole to the Rev. C. N. Wyld about 1881 for £500. An old cottage also stood here, on the site of which the present Rectory was built. A wall running through this property (the northern end of which still remains) divided the parish of St. Martin from Milford.

The Cross in the Churchyard was removed from the north side of the Church, and restored by the Rev. J. V. Walters.

The soil was removed from the walls of the Church, which it had previously buried to a depth of about 3 feet, in 1869.

The easternmost Window on the south side of the Church was renewed in 1886.

The pedestal of the Font is hollow at the top, evidently of greater age than the present basin which has been placed on it.

The Font Ewer was given by the Rev. Edgar Hoskins in 1862.

The lower part of the east wall of the Tower was wholly rebuilt in 1886. The fragments of ornamental stonework of the Norman period now exposed to view were found embedded in the old wall.

Inside the Tower, south of the doorway into the South Aisle, was discovered what appeared to be the remains of a Holy Water Stoup.

The beams over the Belfry, which support the floor above, were renewed in 1882.

The corbel in the Porch, south of the West door, was removed from the wall of the tower, where it had been inserted, east of the north doorway.

Three copper bolts were inserted as braces in the south pier of the arch at the East end of the Nave, going North and South.

The Altar was remodelled in 1871, the front legs being those of the old Jacobean Table.

The two Oak Chairs in the Chancel were the gift of an unknown donor about 1860.

The Credence Table was given by (?)

Tha Ceiling in the Chancel was painted by Clayton & Bell in 1886.

The Altar Steps were re-arranged by Mr. Walters in 1871.

The Altar in the South Chapel was the gift of the Rev. C. N. Wyld.

The Prayer Desk was given by the Guild of Holy Obedience.

1886. The whole of the plaster was cleared off the walls of the Church, when the Cross on the South wall was uncovered and the niche in which the figures of the Annunciation are placed. These were in a mutilated state, the upper portion being missing. They were restored by the Rev. C. N. Wyld. The lower parts of the figures were in their original position.

The original Parish Chest is that in the South Chapel. The large chest in the Chancel was given by the Rev. C. N. Wyld or by Mr. Whitehead. Mr. Whitehead tells me that this chest was in the "Hall of the Taylors."

The Pillars in the Nave and Aisle between Choir and Nave have scarce any foundations, consequently a good firm brick wall was built round each in 1886.

The old bench ends that were left after the restoration in 1849 were perpendicular pattern, not "Linen pattern."

The Porch. A brick and plaster wall ran straight from the doorway inside facing east to the door going into the Church facing west. This was removed, being of late construction.

Mr. Pearce says, "A wooden staircase by the Belfry led to the loft over the west porch and Vestry Room, which loft was used as a storehouse for faggots for lighting the fires."

In the North and South Aisles the seats were arranged under the walls in three tiers longitudinally, thus:—

The Mayor and Corporation Seat was the front seat the South side of the Nave.

Two of the doors of the old oak seats are now in the Old Vestry as doors to the cupboard.

The floors of the two side chapels were raised to their present level by Mr. Wyld. They were originally on the same level as the aisles and nave.

The Organ stood in the North Chapel, against the North wall after the demolition of the West Gallery.

1880. March 21st (Palm Sunday.) St. Mary Magdalen Church in Gigant St. opened. It cost about £700.

1882. An iron church was opened on Nov. 29th in College Street, and was dedicated on St. Mark's Day, 1883. This church was closed when St. Mark's Church was dedicated.

1892. April 27th. The foundation stone of St. Mark's Church was laid. On the East end is the subjoined inscription.

I. S.

TO · WHOM · COMING · AS · UNTO · A · LIVING
STONE · · · YE · ALSO · AS · LIVELY · STONES
ARE · BUILT · UP · A · SPIRITUAL · HOUSE
AN · HOLY · PRIESTHOOD · TO · OFFER · UP
SPIRITUAL · SACRIFICES · ACCEPTABLE
TO · GOD · BY · JESUS · CHRIST.

THIS · STONE · WAS · LAID · 27TH · APRIL · 1892 · BY
EDWARD · LORD · ARCHBISHOP · OF · CANTERBURY.

A. G.
ST. A.

E. J. H.

C
W.

The brass Altar Desk in the South Chapel is inscribed M. Y. 1898.
It was given by Miss Martha Young.

The Lectern in the South Aisle is inscribed on a brass plate attached

AD SACRORUM LIBRORUM LECTIONEM
IN SANCTI MARTINI ECCLESIA
A.D. MDCCCLXXXIX.
A THANK OFFERING FOR MANY MERCIES AND
IN MEMORY OF MARY LOUISA WYATT
A DEVOTED AND AFFECTIONATE WIFE.

The Credence Table. South Chapel.

ECCLES.
STI. MART.
APUD SARUM
A.D.

The Chair in South Chapel.

ST. MARTIN'S CHURCH, SARUM.
TWO THANK OFFERINGS
A.W. 1891.
A.R. 1892.

Altar in South Chapel.

ECCLES̄ SC̄T MART̄
APUD SARUM

ALTARE CAPELL̄ MERID̄.
EX DONO C.N.W. A.D. 1886.

Communion Book.

"To the honour and glory of God.
This Book
was presented for use
at the
Altar of the Side Chapel
of
St. Martin's
Salisbury
by
S. A. Sanger
Easter · 1897.

The Prayer Desk.

AN OFFERING FROM
THE GUILD OF THE
HOLY OBEDIENCE
FOR THE DAILY SERVICES
IN THE SIDE CHAPEL
S: MARTIN'S DAY, 1886.

Priest's Chair in Chancel.

FOR THE USE OF THE CLERGY OF
S. MARTIN'S CHURCH, SARUM
A THANK OFFERING FROM THE MISTRESSES
AND MANY PUPILS OF THE GODOLPHIN SCHOOL
A.D. MDCCCLXXV.—MDCCCLXXXIX.

The Prayer desk accompanying it was the Gift of the Rev. George Kent.

Sealed 28th March, 1905.

1036
5.

County—WILTS.
Parish—ST. MARTIN, SALISBURY.
Charities—Church or Fabric Estates.
Culver Street Almshouses.

Stamps { 10*s*.
10*s*.

A.
46,886

Order for—

Removal and Appointment } *of Trustees, and*
Vesting in Official Trustee of Charity Lands.

CHARITY COMMISSION.

In the Matter of the Charities called or known as The CHURCH OR FABRIC ESTATES, and the CULVER STREET ALMSHOUSES, the Parish of ST. MARTIN, in the City of SALISBURY ; and

In the Matter of "The Charitable Trusts Acts 1853 to 1894."

The Board of Charity Commissioners for England and Wales, upon an application made to them on the 9th August 1904, in writing, signed by

GEORGE RICHARDSON, of Salisbury, the Trustee of the above-mentioned Charities ; and also signed by

THOMAS HENRY BAKER, and

ALFRED D'ANGIBAU, the Churchwardens of the above-mentioned Parish of St. Martin, Salisbury ;

persons acting in the administration of the Charities ;

And it appearing that the endowments of the Charities consist of the particulars mentioned in the Schedule hereto :

And after due notice of the intention to make this Order published according to the direction of the Board by being affixed to or near a principal outer door of the Church of St. Martin, Salisbury, on the 15th September 1904, and by advertisement in the newspaper called "The Salisbury Times" on the 16th September 1904, and in the newspaper called "The Salisbury and Winchester Journal" on the 17th September 1904 (being in each case more than one calendar month before the date hereof) :

And having received no notice of any objection to the proposed Order, or suggestion for the variation thereof :

Do hereby Order as follows :—

1. The said GEORGE RICHARDSON is, at his own request, removed from being a Trustee of the Charities :

2. The CHURCHWARDENS for the time being of the Parish of St. Martin, in the City of Salisbury; are appointed to be the Trustees for the administration of the Charities :

3. The right to recover and receive all debts and other things in action due to or recoverable for the benefit of the Charities shall forthwith vest in the Trustees hereby appointed individually in trust for the Charities :

4. The lands and hereditaments specified in the Schedule hereto, and all other freehold and leasehold lands and hereditaments (if any) belonging to or held in trust for the Charities, shall forthwith vest in "The Official Trustee of Charity Lands," for all the estate and interest therein belonging to or held in trust for the Charities.

SCHEDULE OF PROPERTY.

Description.	Extent or Amount.	Tenant, Person liable, or Persons in whose Name invested.	Gross Yearly Income.
The Church or Fabric Estates.	A. R. P.		£ s. d.
Seven houses and gardens in Culver Street, Salisbury.	—	Ainsworth (weekly) ...	15 12 0
		Jeffrey (weekly) ...	13 0 0
		Tapper (weekly) ...	14 6 0
		Dear (weekly) ...	11 14 0
		Maton (weekly) ...	11 14 0
		Trimby (weekly) ...	9 2 0
		Collins (weekly) ...	9 2 0
Underground cellar in same street.	—	Wilts and Dorset Banking Company (lease 7 years from 1901).	10 0 0
House and garden in St. Martin's Church Street and buildings adjoining occupied as a National School.	—	Trustees of National School (lease 40 years from 9th December, 1868).	25 0 0
House and garden in Exeter Street, Salisbury.	—	} C. Mills (yearly) ...	16 0 0
Piece of garden ground in Bugmore.	—		
Four cottages and gardens in Culver Street, Salisbury.	—	Forward (weekly) ...	7 16 0
		Grace (weekly) ...	3 18 0
		Andrews (weekly) ...	7 3 0
		Dear (weekly) ...	5 4 0

Three pairs of houses in Culver Street, Salisbury, used as Almshouses.	—			In hand.	—		
Consols (Endowment of Robert Sutton Marsh).	129	6	6	"The Official Trustees of Charitable Funds."	3	4	8
Consols (Endowment of Robert Cooper).	688	13	4	Do. do.	17	4	4
One-half of the dividends of a sum of £123 4s. 1d. Consols, held by "The Official Trustees of Charitable Funds" (Endowment of Eleanor Walsh).							
Consols (Endowment of Edward Baker).	183	4	5	Do. do.	4	11	4
Consols (Endowment of Mary Lake).	520	0	0	Do. do.	13	0	0
Consols (Endowment of William Woodlands).	300	7	6	Do. do.	7	10	0
Proportion of income of Charity of Thomas Cooksey and Thomas Goman.							

Sealed by Order of the Board this 28th day of March 1905.

L. S.

Feoffees elected 1865.

WILLIAM OSMOND.
H. W. COBB.
W. HIGGINS.
SAMUEL CUSSE.

Wm. WOODLANDS.
GEORGE RICHARDSON.
SAMUEL NOKE WILMOT.
JOHN LARGE.

FREDERIC ROE.
Wm. OSMOND, Jr.
THOs. PAYE HOWE.

THE FABRIC PROPERTY AS DESCRIBED IN VESTRY BOOK, 1882.

Culver Street.

Freehold Premises situate in Culver Street, consisting of :—

A Dwelling House let to Inspector Ainsworth at a Rent of 6s. 3d. per week, the parish paying Rates and Taxes.

Four Cottages & Gardens in Culver Street, in the occupation of Weekly Tenants, at 6s. 6d., 6s., 5s., 3s. 6d., the parish paying Rates and Taxes.

There is a large Cellar underneath the Cottages let to Mr. Pern at a Rental of £16 a year.

The above premises were formerly in Lease to Francis White, which lease expired in 1875. A large sum has been spent in repairs.

Two Freehold Cottages & Gardens in Culver Street (adjoining White's property) in the occupations of Young and Ranger as Weekly Tenants at 3s. 9d. & 3s. 6d. per week.

This property is in good repair, the parish pay Rates & Taxes.

These premises were formerly held by Lease granted to Samuel Burch, and fell into hand in the year 1876.

Two Cottages in Culver Street, Lease granted to George Sutton, 9th August 1850.

This Lease is now vested in George Langley Young. Rent £1 10s. Lease expires 1891.

There are Four Cottages standing on this Property.

Exeter Street.

A Dwelling House & Garden in Exeter Street.

Lease granted 10th December, 1846, to Stephen Hayter for a term of 40 years at a rent of £2. Lease expires in 1886.

This property is now vested in Mr. William Hicks, and is in the occupation of Charles Mills, Chimney Sweep.

A piece of Garden ground at the back of Exeter Street, in the rear of the property now belonging to Mr. Hicks, in the occupation of Mr. Jones. Rent 6s. a year. Yearly tenancy.

This property was formerly in Lease to Mr. Pickford, under Lease granted 24th June, 1856, for 21 years, & fell into hand in June, 1877.

The property is described in the Lease as

A piece of Garden ground 28ft. long & 22ft. broad at Bugmore, bounded with the lands of Thomas Marlow on the South & East with the lands of Elizabeth Biggs on the North and the lands of the Parish Church on the West.

St. Martin's Church Street.

The National School and Garden in St. Martin's Church Street. In Lease to Trustees. Lease granted 9th December, 1868, for a term of 40 years. Rent £25. Lessee to do all repairs. Lease expires 1908.

And of a sum of Money of £541 5s. 5d., 3 per cent. annuities standing in the names of the Official Trustees of Charitable Funds purchased with the sum of £500 received on the sale of Prangley's premises at the corners of Culver Street & Milford Street sold by the authority of the Charity Commissioners. The Commissioners investing £10 annually until £800 is made up and paying the remainder of the Dividends to the Churchwardens, which difference has been carried to the Churchwardens' account annually.

	£	s.	d.	£	s.	d.
The Rents of the Property in hand amount to the sum of say				105	0	0
Insurance	13	0	0			
Repairs say	30	0	0	43	0	0
net				£62	0	0
Quit Rents. Malthouse in Milford Street (Woodlands)	5	10	0			
" 2 Messuages in Culver Street (Young) ...	1	10	0			
" House in Exeter Street (Hicks) ...	2	0	0			
Yearly Tenants. Garden Do. (Jones)	0	6	0			
" School Premises	25	0	0	34	6	0
				£96	6	0

1897.

S. MARTIN'S, SALISBURY,

AND

MILFORD WITHOUT.

NOTES AS TO CHARITIES.

Name.	Present Investments.	Annual Income. £ s. d.	Trustees.	Objects of Charity.	Remarks.
Edward Windover (1605)	Rent Charge of £1 13s. 4d. issuing out of Estates belonging to Dean and Chapter of Salisbury	1 13 4	Rector & Churchwardens of St. Martin's, Salisbury	Apprenticing Poor Boys and Girls of St. Martin's not less than 12 years old as Pupil Teachers in Salisbury, or in payment of Scholarships, or in the case of Girls for the duties of Domestic Service	Administered by the Rector and Churchwardens
Elizabeth Bath (1701)	£386 19s. 5d. Consols	10 12 8	Ditto ...	The same as the above, but limited to Girls	Ditto (see Commissioners' Scheme dated 22nd June, 1877)
Francis Newham (1807)	£1000 Consols	27 10 0	Ditto ...	For 8 Poor Housekeepers of the Parish on 12th August, "being Members of the Church of England"	Ditto Ecclesiastical Charity Blue Book, p. 436
Edmund Mack (1699)	£200 ...	...	Mr. Davis, Castle Street	Apprenticing Boys (2) "being Members of the Presbyterian Congregation and of	Ecclesiastical Charity Blue Book, p. 438

Amalgamated Charities (administered as per Sche

	£561 13s. 5d. Consols	15	8	8	Ditto ...	Ditto		See Scheme.*
Robert Sutton, No. 2 (1699)	£221 16s. 3d. Consols	6	2	0	Ditto ...	Ditto	Ditto	
Thomas Goman (1612)	£540 4s. 10d. Consols	14	17	0	Ditto ...	Ditto	Ditto	
Robert Sutton Marsh (1765)	£129 6s. 6d. Consols	3	11	0	Ditto ...	Ditto	Ditto	
Robert Cooper (1792)	£688 13s. 4d. Consols	18	18	8	Ditto ...	Ditto	Ditto	
Thomas Cooksey	£700 Consols	19	5	0	Ditto ...	£2 2s. Sunday School, 15s. Minister, 5s. each Clerk and Sexton, 21s. Churchwarden, residue for Culver Street Almshouses as below*	Ditto	
Eleanor Walsh (1830)	£123 4s. 1d. Consols	3	7	8 (One-half of Income goes to Amalgamated Charities.)	Ditto ...	For Almshouses in Exeter Street and Culver Street	Ditto	
Samuel Burch ...	£325 3s. 8d. Consols	8	18	8	Ditto ...	Administered as per scheme below*	Ditto	
Mary Lake ...	£520 Consols	14	6	0	Ditto ...	Ditto	Ditto	

* By a scheme of amalgamation dated 22nd June, 1877, Cooksey's and Goman's Charities are to be applied in paying each of the six occupants of Culver Street Almshouses such a sum as with what they are otherwise entitled to † shall make up a weekly payment of 5s., and the remaining balance applied to the out-pensions fund as noted below :—

The dividends arising from (1) proceeds of sale of Sutton's Almshouses and Baker's shop (£561 13s. 5d. Consols), (2) Rent-charge of £8 on Shapwick Farm, (3) Burch's (£325 3s. 8d. Consols), and (4) the balance of Cooksey's and Goman's referred to above, to be given as out-pensions to three poor persons, married or single, to be nominated by the Vestry; single persons receive 5s. weekly, married 7s. 6d.

† The Charities formerly devoted to paying the occupants of Almshouses were :—

	£	s.	d.
Mary Lake's	£14	6	0
Robert Cooper's ...	18	18	8
Half of Walsh's ...	1	13	10
They are also now entitled to			
Woodlands'	8	5	0
Baker's	5	0	9

so that a sum of about £27 9s. 6d. has to be taken from Cooksey's and Goman's to make the amount sufficient, leaving about £2 4s. 6d. for the out-pensions fund.

NOTES AS TO CHARITIES—(*continued*).

Name.	Present Investments.	Annual Income. £	s.	d.	Trustees.	Objects of Charity.	Remarks.
WILLIAM WOODLANDS	£300 7s. 6d. Consols	8	5	0	Rector & Churchwardens	Culver Street Almshouses (see above) *	Administered by the Rector and Churchwardens
JANE LANE (1836)	£957 18s. 11d. Consols	26	6	8	Official Trustees	Annuities for Two Poor Persons (Representatives of the Family to be preferred)	Administered by the Vestry
ELIZABETH LAKE (1836)	£790 Consols	21	14	4	Ditto	Annuities for Three Poor Persons ditto	Ditto
JOHN FRICKER (1696)	Portion of Rent of House in Queen Street	15	0	0	Ditto	Distributed in Clothing to Poor People of the Parish	To be distributed by the Minister of the Parish Blue Book, p. 442—3
JEFFERY & FRY ...	£11 6s. 2d. Consols	0	6	0	Official Trustees	Bible Charity	Administered by the Rector Ecclesiastical Charity
EDWARD BAKER (1796)	£549 Consols	15	2	4	Ditto	One-third to Sutton's Almspeople, now represented by 3 Out-pensioners (see Scheme above)* One-third to Culver Street ,, Salisbury Municipal Charity Trustees	
					Ditto	Poor generally (£3 13s. to	Administered by

						by Rector)	
Ditto	£6200 Consols	26	0	0	Ditto	5s. each per week to 2 Poor Widows	Ditto
		28	0	0	Ditto	Apprenticing a Boy annually in St. Martin's (St. Thomas' and St. Edmund's benefit by similar amounts)	Ditto
EDMUND LAMBERT (1866)	£200 G.W. Ry. Stock	10	5	0	Official Trustees	Blanket Club and Grocery Tickets at Christmas	Administered by the Rector and Churchwardens
BISHOP BURGESS	£666 13s. 4d. £$2\frac{3}{4}$ Consolidated Stock	18	6	8	The Dean The Archdeacon Rev. J. P. Greenly	One-half repair of Laverstock School One-half Prizes for Children who have for two years attended Elementary Schools in Parish of Milford in which Church of England doctrine is taught	Administered by The Dean of Salisbury The Archdeacon of Sarum Rev. J. P. Greenly (see Commissioners' Scheme, 3rd May, 1894)

THE BOUNDARIES OF ST. MARTIN'S PARISH, A.D. 1270.

"It begins with the house of Walter Das, and from thence in a straight line, ascending on the same side of the way, eastward, to the Bar."

This is the south side of Milford Street, from the corner of Brown Street.

"From the house of the said Walter, on the same side of the way, in a line to the house of Simon the tailor, and the house of Walter Cummin, situated opposite."

This comprises the eastern side of Brown Street, to St. Ann's Street.

"From the house of the said Walter, on the same side of the way, westward, to the house of Richard Blakemore, and thence to the fountain of St. Nicholas: with the parochial rights and appurtenances of all the tenants, who before were parishioners of the *Hospital of St. Nicholas*, in the same street, and the houses of all the inhabitants beyond the eastern bars of the city, as well as of Milford and Winterborn-ford."

The boundary thus traced within the city is plainly along the north part of St. Ann's Street, to the corner opposite to the gate of The Close, and from thence in the direction of Exeter Street, to the river.

The next clause is rendered obscure by its position, and by the mode in which the original document is written. In conjunction with the preceding, it however proves the previous existence of a parish, under the spiritual superintendence of the Prior of St. Nicholas.

"And whatsoever is contained within the aforesaid limits, towards the south and east, and all *the profits of that Parish, which the Prior and brethren of the Hospital of St Nicholas*, and the Rector of St. Thomas, have been hitherto accustomed to receive therein, we assign to the use of the said Provost and associated Presbyters." (*Hatcher*, page 53.)

The Church of St. Thomas with that of St. Martin, and the Chapel belonging to the Hospital of St. Nicholas, were doubtless situated in those parts where the first settlements took place.

The city continued to spread toward the north and east as the population increased. Accordingly, in 1270, Bishop de la Wyle erected a church in honour of St. Edmund of Abingdon, formerly Treasurer of the Cathedral, and then recently canonised. (*Hatcher*, page 52.)

In the year 1878 application was made to the Ecclesiastical Commissioners to increase the value of the living of St. Martin's, but nothing could be done while the population remained below 4000, and while the Presentation was in Lay hands. The Census of 1881, however, having put the first matter right, a transfer of patronage was effected, as shown below.

"The Benefice of St. Martin.

"An Order of Her Majesty in Council, dated August 18th, 1882, and taking effect immediately on the publication of the same in the *London Gazette*, sanctioned the exchange of the patronage of the living of Cherill, in the County of Wilts (having a population of 408, and gross income of £250 and a residence) in the gift of the Bishop of Salisbury, with the living of St. Martin's, Salisbury (having a population of over 4000, and gross income of £248 and no residence), in the gift of the trustees of the will of Mr. Wadham Wyndham, deceased, in accordance with a scheme prepared by the Ecclesiastical Commissioners, pursuant to the Acts of Parliament 16 & 17 Vict. chap. 50, and 23 & 24 Vict. chap. 124. This exchange of patronage has been effected to enable the Ecclesiastical Commissioners to make a grant of land and assist in the erection of a parsonage house, and the carrying out of other improvements near the Church, which they were not empowered to do while the presentation to the living of St. Martin remained in the hands of lay trustees." (*Parish Magazine.*)

The lower part of the Episcopal demesne described in Domesday as meadow was apparently the Lady Mead selected by Bishop Poore as the site of the New Cathedral and its precincts; previous to this period the ground was not unoccupied. The Lands which in Domesday the Bishop is said to have held in demesne and to have cultivated by means of his servile tenants were partly situated on Milford hill. Several documents executed during the early part of the reign of Edward III. allude to the VILLENAGE of the Bishop and to the OLD TOWN opposite to the Villenage of the Bishop, which is described as lying beyond the barrier or gate leading to St. Martin's Church.

Bishop Bingham provided for the maintenance of a Grammar School situated near the corner opposite St. Ann's Gate.

1414. Richard Spencer left the Stapel Hall and le Dragon in St. Martin's Street to be sold after the death of his widow Editha and the proceeds to be applied to works of Charity.

A building called the Abbey was situated at the corner of Endless Street and Chipper Street (*Hatcher*, page 100).

1474. Change of the name of Churchmen to Church Wardens (p. 189).

According to the original foundation, the power of presenting to the provostship of the College and the rectory of St. Edmund's was vested in the Bishop, and in case of a vacancy of the See in the

Dean and Chapter. The power remained with the Bishop unquestioned till 1543. In the following year the College was dissolved and resigned to the King. In 1547 the College house and the whole of the establishment and the advowsons of St. Edmund's and St. Martin's were granted to William St. Barbe in fee. In 1549 William and Thomas St. Barbe released the College house and the two advowsons to John Beckingham. John Beckingham sold the right of presentation to St. Martin to the Vestry of that parish, and by them the living was presented in 1606 to John Odell, on the death of Edward Clarke, by John Wendover, Esq., John and Thomas Batt, Charles Jacob, gent., John Harding and Henry Newman. At this time John Bailey, owner of Bishops Down farm, procured the grant for himself, a dispute ensued, and Bailey repaid the vestry the money which they had disbursed for the right of presentation. He employed a person named Carpenter to fulfil the duties of the Vicar as a stipendiary. On the death of Carpenter, Bishop Davenant recommended Anthony Hillary to the Lord Keeper Coventry as successor, who presented the living to Hillary as a vicarage in 1632. Soon after this the son of Bailey sued Hillary; it was submitted to Noy the Attorney General. He decided that the church was a rectory and Hillary was appointed Rector in 1635. During the civil troubles the patronage continued to be vested in Bailey, who, in 1661 presented the living to John Sedgewick. In 1664 Bailey conveyed the right of patronage to Francis Hill, Esq., of Lincoln's Inn, and he exercised it till 1687. He afterwards assigned it to Edward Hearst, Esq., of The Close, and in 1768 it finally came into the possession of the late H. P. Wyndham, Esq., in virtue of his marriage with Miss Caroline Hearst. (*Hatcher* p. 501)

1655. A gift of money from St. Martin's parish. £2 10s. was granted for the reparation of the Church and Tower of St. Edmund's.

Grant of Bishop Poor, assigning the Church of St. Martin to a certain priest named Hervey.

"Omnibus Sancte Matris ecclie filiis ad quos p^{r}sns sc'ptum p'venerit Ric'us diuina p'missione Sar' ecclie minister humilis salt'm et^{r}na in dn'o. Scire volum's vniu'sos nos intuitu caritatis contulisse dilecto mag'ro Herveo eccle'am Sci' Martini de man'io n'ro Sar' cu' Capella de St^{r}tford que ad nostram et succ' n'ror donac'oem spectare dnoscu'tr et om'es alias eccle'as et capellas constructas & construendas in Ciuit^{e} n'ra Sar' ip'mq in eisde' auct'e pontificali p'sona instituisse & in corporale possessione earu'dem' induci fecisse. Statuentes ut d'cus Herveum d'cas eccle'as & capellas habeat & possedeat toto te'pe vite sue libere et quiete honorifice et integre cu' oi'bz p'tinen suis et lib^{r}tatibus et liberis consuetudinibz ad ip'as spectantibus. Saluis com'unie eccle' n're Sar' decimis garbar et feni. Et q'd idem Hervens om'ia on'a ordinaria dictar eccl'iar sustinebit et capillar contuli'm ei decimas molendinor' n'ror p^rdicte ciuitat' Sar et om'es decimas om'n terrar' que per curtellis tenent', viz., om'n terrar' que su't infra fossata ciuitat' n're Sar'. Ita quide' qz ut omnis int^r capt'm et p^rdc'm Herveu' tollat^r contenco'is occasio solvet per oib'z d'car' terrar' decimis annuatim viginti solidos in festo Sci' Mich'is superd'ce commune. Quinetia' jurabit fidelitatem decano et capitulo Sar' ta' de dicta solutione fienda q'm de debita diligencia adhibenda qz decime capit'lo assignate de parochanis suis eis fidelit' per soluant'. Salvis et' in omnibus dignitate Sar' eccl'ie et n'ra et succ' n'ror. Quod ut p'petue firmitatis robur optineat p'ns scriptu' sigilli n'ri munimine roborauim' in testimoniu'. Dat ap'd Sct'am Brigidam Lond' septimo Kalen' Februarii Pontificatus n'ri anno vndecimo. Hiis testibus M'gro Elia de Derham et M. Henrico de Bishopston, M. Luca Will'mo de Leicest' et Thoma de S'co Martino canonicis Sar' Gilberto de Hospitali senescallo Waltero de Purl Stephano de Abel Cli'cis Andrea Camerario Alexandro Hostiario Thoma Coco, et multisaliis (1228) Liber Evidentiarum fol. 590, 591, H. (*Hatcher*, pp. 730, 731.)

"Know ye, that we, by the impulse of charity, have conferred on our beloved Master Hervey, the church of St. Martin, of our manor of Sarum, with the Chapel of Stratford, which are in our gift, and those of our successors. We also grant to him all other churches or chapels, built or to be built, in our city of New Sarum, ordering that the said Hervey shall hold and possess, for the term of his life, the said churches and chapels, with all their appurtenances, saving to the commons of our Church of Sarum the tithe of corn and hay. And that the said Harvey may fulfill the duties attached to such churches and chapels, we give him the tithe of our mills in Sarum, and the tithe of all the lands within the ditch of our City of Sarum. In order also to obviate all cause of contention between the Chapter and the said Harvey, he shall pay for the tithes of the said lands yearly the sum of twenty shillings, to the Commons at the feast of St. Michael. He shall also swear to the Dean and Chapter, to use due diligence, in procuring from the parishioners the payment of the tithes assigned to them. This we grant, saving the rights, authority and dignity of the Church of Sarum, and those of ourself and our successors."

(Carta Ricardi Ep'i apud St. Brigidam Lond. 7 Kal. Feb. anno Pont. 11° Liber Evidentiarum B.H.)

We have given the substance of the institution of St. Martin's by Bishop Poore in 1228. By that document the bishop seems to have vested the Rectory in the dean and chapter, and appropriated the tithes of corn and hay to their commons; they, perhaps as was usual in such cases, being bound to provide for the spiritual wants of the parish, by the appointment of a vicar, in the ancient and strict sense of the word. Still however, the prelate, as a temporary arrangement, took from the rectory such a provision as was expedient for the person who was to superintend the religious concerns of a population rapidly increasing, reserving, at the same time, a rent, as well as requiring ecclesiastical obedience from him to the dean and chapter. When Bishop de la Wyle divided the city into parishes, the consent of the dean and chapter, of the prior and brethren of St. Nicholas, and of the rector of St. Thomas, is expressly mentioned, as confirmatory of this arrangement; but no allusion is made to an incumbent of St. Martin's. In fact, thenceforward, under the character of a vicarage, the care of that church was annexed to the Provostship of St. Edmund's. It was probably in consequence of this transfer, that we find "the houses of all the dwellers beyond the eastern bars of the city with Milford and Winterborne ford, and whatsoever is contained within the said limits, towards the south and east, and all the profits of the said parish, which the prior of St. Nicholas and the rector of St. Thomas had been accustomed to receive" assigned to the provost and presbyters. Between this period and the Reformation, the duties of the Church of St. Martin appear to have been performed by the parochial chaplains, or other members of the College of St. Edmund; for, in the interval, no record occurs, in the Episcopal Registers, of the institution of any minister to that church.

Between 1441 and 1446 William Spaldyngton, Provost of St. Edmund, made an attempt to increase the profits derived from the parish, by instituting a suit against the dean and chapter, for certain tithes to which he laid claim. The question was submitted to arbitration, and the result so precisely defines the character of the provost, as vicar of St. Martin's, that the principal stipulations are here subjoined.

Some discord has lately arisen, between the Reverend Adam Moleyns, Dean of the cathedral church of Sarum, and the chapter of the same, as *Rectors* and *Impropriators* of the parochial church of St. Martin, on one side, and Mr. William Spaldyngton, provost of the collegiate church of St. Edmund, on the other, to which collegiate church the *vicarage of the church* of St. Martin is united and annexed, with regard to the perception of the great and small tithes, and especially the tithes of the hay of a certain meadow, newly brought back to pasture, in the field surrounded with hedges, and commonly called the new mead, under Larkstock, the tithe of which, the said William, as vicar of the church of St. Martin, demands and claims, as belonging to his vicarage. The said dean and chapter, on the other hand, maintain that the great tithes of the church of St. Martin belong to them, as rectors and impropriators. At length the aforesaid parties unanimously and indifferently confided to us, John Pedwell, sub-dean of the cathedral of Sarum; William Berwyck, sub-chanter; Simon Huchyns, and John Sypherwest, bachelor of laws; and chose us, as arbitrators and amicable composers of the aforesaid controversy, binding themselves, under a penalty of forty pounds, to abide our arbitrement. We therefore, for the sake of peace, after making diligent inquiry, and examining evidence, have found that the dean and chapter aforesaid, rectors of the church of St. Martin, are endowed with all the great tithes, namely, of grain and hay, and the provost aforesaid, as vicar, in right of his vicarage, is endowed with all the small tithes, for instance, personal tithes, those of wool, lambs, and gardens, in which grow herbs, cardoons, hemp and flax. Wherefore we decree and award in this manner, and concerning the perception of the tithes of gardens and other places within the boundaries and limits of the parish of St. Martin's, where of old, houses and tenements were built, in which gardens and places any grain is sown, and in which soever any hay now grows.

By this decision, the question concerning tithes, and the relation of the provost towards the dean and chapter, was set at rest, and the two benefices continued united, until the dissolution. At that period they were both conveyed to William St. Barbe, together with the other lands, possessions, and privileges belonging to the college of St. Edmund. (*Hatcher* pp. 242—243).

Population of Salisbury at different periods

1675.	Parish of	St. Edmund's	1456	Dissenters	44	Recusants
	,,	St. Thomas	1092	,,	3	5
	,,	St. Martin's	788	,,	9	3
	,,	Fisherton Anger	273	,,	7	
		Total	3609		63	8
1695.	,,	St. Thomas's	2665			
	,,	St. Edmund's	2742			
	,,	St. Martin's	1569			
		Total	6976			
1775.	Total	...	6856			

1821.	"	St. Thomas	2230	Inhabited houses ...		390
	"	St. Edmund's	3912	"	"	707
	"	St. Martin's	2104	"	"	423
	"	The Close	517	"	"	85
		Total	8763			1605
1831.	"	St. Thomas's	2364	"	"	421
	"	St. Edmund's	4612	"	"	907
	"	St. Martin's	2362	"	"	457
	"	The Close	538	"	"	86
		Total	9876			1871

Fisherton Anger

1801. 865 ; 1811, 893 ; 1821, 1253 ; 1831, 1496.

Grant by John de Opere, son of Robert de Opere, to masters William de La Riuere and Richard de Nogent, clerks, of a tenement in the street leading from the canon's close to the church of St. Martin, to be held of the church of St. Mary the Virgin of Salisbury. Et ad maiorem huius rei securitatem liberaui predictis magistris Willelmo et Ricardo una cum presenti carta omnia instrumenta que penes me habui de predicto tenemento. Witnesses: Master Ralph of York, chancellor ; sir William of Braybrock, and Stephen of Remmesburi, canons ; master Walter Hervy, clerk ; master William of Schyrebourn', sir John of Winchester, William of Wokyngham, William of Stok', Ralph of Stevenbache, vicars in the church aforesaid ; Roger of Stok', bailiff ; Reginald of Todeworth mayor ; John le Stut and Philip Aubyn, coroners ; Adam Leyrenmanggere and Alan of Canygges, reeves ; and others named. Thursday before the Nativity of St. John Baptist [21 June, 1302] 30, Edw. I. Seal.

(Hist. M. S. Com. Vol I. p. 346.)

From the record of a visitation of the parochial churches by Bishop Waltham in 1394, we find the following statement of the number of members belonging to each. To the church of *St. Thomas*, the rector, one parochial chaplain, and fourteen chaplains celebrating in chantries. To *St. Edmund's*, the rector, one parochial chaplain, and eight chaplains attached to chantries. To *St. Martin's*, of which the dean and chapter were rectors, the vicar, one parochial chaplain and three chantry chaplains. One chaplain belonged to the hospital of the Trinity ; and to St. Peter's, at Old Sarum, a rector and a chaplain. (*Hatcher*, p. 191).

APPENDIX.

In the parish chest are many documents of interest, which have not hitherto been published. Copies of the most important are here given.

Aug. 28, 1734. I was instituted & inducted to the Rectory of St. Martin's. (Rev. John Lumby).

The Terrier of St. Martin's in the Bishop's office dated 1705 sets forth that the Tythe of Corn & Hay belongs to the Dean & Chapter of Sarum or to their Tenant. And all other Tythes, Dues, Obventions, Oblations, customary Payments from Marriages, & Burials whatsoever, & Church-Yard belong to the Incumbent for the Time being.

There is in the Chest in the Vestry a Copy of an Act of Chapter by which the Dean & Chapter oblige themselves to keep the Chancel constantly in Repair.

Some particulars relating to the Parish of St. Martin taken from a Paper of Anthony Hilary, Rector. "There is an ancient Record in or belonging to the Cathedral shewing that the then Rector of St. Martin (upon the Motion of the then L[d]. Bishop) yielded that the Tythe of Corn & Hay yearly growing within the Parish of St. Martin Should be for ever alienated from the Rectory & appropriated unto the Dean & Chapter of New Sarum (then newly incorporated) towards the Maintenance of their Commons. There is also an ancient Record showing that when the Church & College of St. Edmunds was founded the then Bishop, willing to make the Church of St. Edmunds both a Collegiate & Parochial Church, prevail'd with the then Rectors of St. Martin & St. Thomas to yield that a Portion of Houses within the aforesaid City should be taken out of each of their Parishes & annexed to the Church of St. Edmund, which was accordingly done & the 3 Parishes distinctly bounded.

There is also an ancient Record shewing that the then Bishop ordain'd that the Provost of the College of St. Edmund's & his Successors, should be Rector of both St. Edmunds & St. Martin's & discharge the ministerial Duties of both Parishes by himself & his Collegiate Priests.

There is also an ancient Record, showing that the Provost of St. Edmunds stiling himself (but erroneously) Vicar of St. Martin commenc'd a Suit ag[t] the Dean & Chapter for the Tythe of some Lands w[ch] being formerly pasture were newly turn'd into Tillage w[ch] Suit by Arbitrators was determin'd as follows. That (notwithstanding such alteration of the Nature of Lands) the Dean & Chapter should thenceforth quietly enjoy the Tythe of all Corn & Hay wheresoever growing within the said Parish; and that the Provost & his Successors, as Vicars (but erroneously so stiled) should quietly enjoy all other kinds of Tythes whatsoever growing within the said Parish.

There is also a Record in the Augmentation Office in Westminster shewing that when the College of St. Edmunds was dissolv'd Harry the 8th sold the said College House of St. Edmund's with Demeanes belonging thereto & in Particular the Patronage of the aforesaid Parish Churches of St. Edmunds & St. Martins, unto William St. Barbe Esqr. one of his Majesties Bedchamber but with this express Proviso & Ordinance that the said Churches should remain presentative for ever as formerly they had been, & that the said St. Barbe as rightful Patron should forthwith sue out a Commission for the rating of them distinctly in order to the Payment of the first Fruits & Tenths wch (as appears upon Record in the first Fruits Office) was accordingly done.

The right of Patronage of both the Churches came in Length of Time into the hands of one Mr. Beckingham who sold his right of Patronage of St. Edmunds to the Vestry of St. Edmunds & his Right of Patronage of St. Martins to the Vestry of St. Martins. A principal Member of St. Martin's Vestry was one Mr. Iohn Bayly owner of Bishopdown Farm, where Tythe of Wool & Lamb being a great Part of the lesser Tythes belonging to St. Martins & he by the Vestry being entrusted to purchase a Patent for them to invest them with a right in the lesser Tythes (as being told that they were a Lay Fee in the Power of the King to grant unto whom he pleas'd) He the said Bayly went to London & purchas'd a Patent thereof as of a Lay fee to himself; and at wch the Vestry were highly incens'd, but by the Mediation of Friends, the Matter was compos'd & Baily paid them the Money they had formerly disburs'd for the Patronage of the Church. And thus Baily having in his Hands both the Right of Patronage & a Patent for the lesser Tythes he conceal'd his Right of Patronage & without opposition receiving the lesser Tythes as a Lay-Fee he employ'd one Carpenter* to serve the Cure as a stipendiary under him wch Carpenter continued thus under him for twenty-two years. Upon his Death the then Bp. Davenant (being inform'd that the Church of St. Martin was & ought to be presentative) recommended Mr. Hilary to Ld. Keeper Coventry, who upon perusal of Records (wch Hilary deliver'd from the Bishop to him) gave the said Hilary his Presentation, who was accordingly instituted and inducted into it under the Title of a Vicaridge. Soon after the Son of Baily sues Hilary, who applied to Ld. Coventry, who advis'd him to remove his Suit into the Exchequer & procur'd Attorney General Noy to be his Advocate. Hilary did so; & Bayly's Counsel mov'd that the full determining of the Cause might be referr'd to Noy himself. Noy upon opening & pleading

* "formerly a R. Catholic but newly converted."
The above is struck out.

of the Cause by Council on both sides deliver'd his Judgment as followeth: that St. Martin's was undoubtedly a Rectory that the Tythes of Corn and Hay only were alienated from the s^d Church and y^t all other Tythes, Oblations &c. still continued due solely to the presented Incumbent: That as to the claim to those lesser Tythes & as to a Lay-Fee purchas'd by Patent from K. James, he judged it to be of no Validity, the King having no Right to grant it: Only for the Patronage, he conceived it to be in the Heirs of Bayly who purchas'd it of the Vestry; & therefore he gave his final Determination y^t Hilary sh^d resign his Presentation to St. Martins as unto a Vicarage & that the Heirs of Bayly sh^d forthwith present the s^d Hilary unto it anew as unto a Rectory: Ordering that this his Determination sh^d by the Council on both sides be drawn up, & deliver'd into the Exchequer to be confirmed. But as soon as y^s Determination was drawn and ready to be deliver'd Noy fell sick, Bayly's Council took this advantage & instead of joyning with Hilary's Council in the said Delivery made a Motion in Court (while Hilary's Council were absent) that the Cause might be made a Law Case & determined by all the Judges of England. Upon this Hilary petitions the King, who referr'd it to 3 of ye L^{ds} of his privy Council. They gave y^r Judgment as Noy had done & Hilary was anew presented by Bayly & anew instituted & inducted into St. Martin's not as it was before erroneously stil'd a Vicarage but a Rectory. After this the better to settle the Church as a presentative Rectory for ever, Hilary went up to compound for the First Fruits, & finding them to be great in the King's Books he obtain'd the Taking off 8 ^{li}. charg'd for annual oblations at the Altar of Corpus Christi, wch s^d Altar was plac'd in a little Chappel on the left Hand of the Porch of the church. As to the Glebe belonging to this Rectory of St. Martin's, Hilary [in the above mentioned (letter) ?] says that in his Time it was reported, & upon no weak Grounds, that the Ground near the Church (now in Possession of the Dean & Chapter or y^r Lessee) was the Plat where the Houseing belonging to the Rectory stood & that in his own remembrance there remayn'd some decay'd Building commonly call'd the Parsonage-House wch in his Remembrance also was burnt down. This mov'd him to make Suit to the Dean & Chapter to restore to him that part of the said Plat wch was turn'd into an Orchard on wch he promised to build a little Parsonage-House for himself & Successors. Dr. Barnestone assur'd him his kinsman (the Dean & Chapter's Lessee) sh^d restore him the Platt, but he refus'd to perform w^t his Uncle had engag'd for & w^n the Dean & Chapter seem'd to assent to. Whereupon Hilary desisted from stirring any more about that Part of the Glebe or some other Parts of Glebe wch some ancient Men then living told him lay in Bugmore & elsewhere.

An Account of the Profits arising Annually from the Rectory of St. Martin's, 1744.

Names of Lands.		Occupiers.	What they Pay. £	s.	d.
The Churchyard		Mr. Rolleston ...	3	0	0
Gardens in Church Street ...	1	Russell ...	0	1	0
	2	Newman ...	0	4	0
Gardens in Tanner Street	1	Mrs. Hancock ...	0	5	0
	2	Mrs. Head ...	0	2	0
	3	Mr. Stoddart ...	0	8	0
	4	Mr. Maton ...	0	2	0
Gardens in Bugmore ...		Mr. Safe ...	0	2	0
		Mr. Gillow ...	0	1	0
		Mr. Davis ...		—	
		Mr. Martin ...	0	4	0
		Mr. Presly ...	0	2	6
		Mr. Hall ...	0	2	6
		Mr. Davis ...	0	1	0
		Mr. Kimber ...	0	2	6
Grounds at the Bottom of D. Street		Mr. Harris ...	0	4	0
		Mr. Keen ...	0	6	0
Farms, Gardens, Grounds, &c., in Milford.					
Bayley's Garden		Mr. Bayley ...	0	1	6
Taylor's Garden		Mr. Taylor ...	0	0	6
Floyd's Paddock		Mr. Thorp ...	0	2	0
Nursery		Mr. Swayne ...	0	2	0
Brown's Garden		Brown ...	0	1	0
J. Swayne's Garden ...		J. Swayne ...	0	1	0
Wyndham's lesser Garden ...		Horsy ...	0	3	0
Safe's Garden		Safe ...	0	1	0
Hy. Ayer's Garden		Hy. Ayer ...	0	1	0
Ben. Chant's Garden ...		Chant ...		—	
Gardens behind the Mill	1	Knight ...	0	2	6
	2	Willoughby ...	0	2	6
	3	Hinxman ...	0	2	0
	4	Bennet ...	0	2	0
	5	Clerk ...	0	2	0

Names of Lands.		Occupiers.		What they Pay.			Acres.	Sheep.
				£	s.	d.		
Swayne's Y[d]. Lands	...	Westcoat	...	0	15	0	7½	200
Powell's Y[d]. Lands	...	Robbins	..	0	16	6	4½	
Wentworth's Y[d]. Lands	...	Coster	...	0	6	6	1½	112
Blackhead's Y[d]. Lands	...	Robbins	...	0	7	0	3½	
Burrough's Y[d]. Lands	...	Swayne	...	0	4	0	4	160
Floyd's Y[d]. Lands	...	Swayne	...	0	2	0	1	80
Harriss's Y[d]. Lands	...	Swayne	...	0	1	0	0½	40
Gamber's Y[d]. Lands	...	Goodbee	...	0	3	0	1	60
Stagg's Y[d]. Lands	...	Robbins	...	0	2	4	1	
Batt's Y[d]. Lands	...	Robbins	...	0	1	0	0½	
Goldwyer's Y. Lands	...	Robbins	...	0	2	0	1	
Cotton's Y. Lands	...	Westcoat	...	0	2	0	1	
Wheeler's Y[d]. Lands	...	Westcoat	...	0	1	0	0½	

These are call'd Yard Lands. Each Y[d]. Land contains about 20 Acres, and pays an acknowledgm[t]. to the Minister of 2 Shillings p[r]. Yard Land. These Lands have a Right of Sheep Lease; Two Sheep are allotted to an Acre, and each Sheep pays one farthing a month to the Minister as long as they are fed.

Copied by T.H.B. from a Loose Sheet.

Quere L(ad)y Mead.
Pest house Mead in 1701 p[d]. 6s. in 1702 10s.
Black bear Mead in 1701 p[d]. 6s.
Causeway Mead in 1701 p[d]. 7s.
Milford Bridge Mead in 1702 p[d]. 6s.
Waterman's Mead in 1703 p[d]. 4s. 6d.
Edmund's Farm in 1703 p[d]. 10s.
Bullpit, I. Brown, of Stratford, 2 acres that have a Right of 60 Sheep.
Rec[d] but one Year's Tythes of Shergold's Mead since the year 1737.
Quere the B[ps]. Mead.
Quere the Fryers.
Winterborne Mead after-feed in 1700 p[d] 4s.
Freeman's Mead in 1700 p[d]. 16s. for y[e] Afterfeed.
Whitebear Mead in 1700 p[d]. 8s. for the Afterfeed.
Swayne's Sheep Lease in 1741 rented by Burrough.
Edmund's Farm in 1700 p[d]. 10s.
Grove's Ground in 1700 &c. p[d] 15s.
Eyre's Mead in 1700 after feed p[d].
Freeman's Mead in 1700 for aft. Feed p[d]. 16.

Bell-Mead after feed 1701 pd. 4s.
Gorges' Mead in 1701 aft. feed pd. 5s. 1703—5s.
Masters Pesthouse Mead half fed in 1702 pd. 2s.

Mem. Mr. Skates paid me Oct. 11, 1755, 18 shillings in full for Tythe to Mich. last, viz., twice 6s. for white bear mead & 6 shillings for Gorges.

A LETTER.

Freshford, April 19th, 1810.

DEAR SIR,—I herewith send you the Books & Documents originally delivered to me concerning the Rectory of St. Martin's. In addition to which I have extracted from old Account Books some further particulars relative to the Tythes I received about Thirty years since I gave several Tythe Tenants Notice to set out their Tythes in Order to make some little Advance. I began with Mr. Westcott the then Occupier of Bishop Down Farm. He resisted and as Mr. Tinney did not seem confident of success in the farther Prosecution of my Claims I dropped the matter. But tho I thus consented to accept a Composition from Mr. Westcott and others, such Acceptance could by no means so far operate against the Rector as to establish a Modus. Soon after this I agreed with Mr. Combes for a certain annual Sum to be paid me & tho' the advance was very trifling, I was released from the Trouble of receiving Payment from so many Hands. I have detailed on the other side the particular Sums I received & when they were due. The sum paid me by Mr. Gifford who lived in St. Ann's Street in the house lately inhabited by Mr. Collins was Tythe I imagine for Lands in Bugmore. I beg my Compliments to Mrs. Davis & remain Dear Sir, your most obedient Servant,

JOHN BAKER.

From Bishop Down Farm
due St. Mark's Day.

For late Swayne paid by Mr. Westcott	8 1	6 17	8 5
From Mr. Brownjohn for Gardens in St. Edmond's Church & on St. Thomas Day	1	10	0
Mr. Gifford	1	1	0
Small Tythes collected by the Clerk exclusive of 8s. paid for collecting ...	8	14	0
	£21	9	1

To
The Revd. Mr. Davis
Rector of St. Martin's, Sarum.

1749.

Names of Lands.		Occupiers.	Sum. £	s.	d.	
The Church-yard ...		Mr. Collis ...	2	10	0	This is all due at Mich. tho' some of these being subscribers, the Tythe is seldom demanded.
Gardens in Church-Street	1	Robt. Summers	0	1	0	
	2	Widow Russell	0	1	0	
	3	World's End ...	0	4	0	
Gardens in Tanner Street	1	Mr. Brander ...	0	8	0	
	2	Mr. Best ...	0	2	0	
	3	Mr. Gowan ...	0	8	0	
	4	Mr. Maton ...	0	1	0	
	5	Mr. Barman ...	0	1	0	
	6	Mr. Blanchet ...	0	2	0	
Gardens in Bugmore	1	Marsh ...	0	2	0	
	2	Gillow ...	0	1	0	
	3					
	4	Martin ...	0	4	0	
	5	Griffen ...	0	2	6	
	6	Half ...	0	1	6	
	7	Roberts ...	0	1	0	
	8	Jay ..	0	0	6	
	9					
	10					
Grounds at the Bottom of Dragon Street	1	Mr. Keen ...	0	6	0	
	2	Mrs. Harris ...	0	4	0	
Farms, Grounds & Gardens in Milford.						
Black Swan Garden ...		... ...	0	2	0	
Sutton's Ground ...		... ...	0	2	6	
Staple's Garden ...		... ...	0	0	6	
Floyd's Paddock ...		... ...	0	2	0	
Nursery		Thrasher ...	0	2	6	
Brown's Garden ...		Wastcoat ...	0	1	0	
Royal Oak Garden ...		.. ...	0	1	6	
Red Lyon Orchard ...		... ...	0	1	6	
Swayne's Great Garden		Brownjohn ...	1	10	0	
Swayne's House Garden		Mr. Clerk ...	0	7	0	
Wyndham's little Garden		Horsy ...	0	3	0	
Grove's Ground ...		Thorp ...	0	15	0	
Safe's Garden ...		.. ...	0	1	0	
Hyllyers Garden ...		... ...	0	1	0	
Blackheads Garden ...		... ...	0	2	0	
Chant's Garden						

Names of Lands.		Occupiers.	Sum. £ s. d.	
Gardens behind the Mills ...	1	Knight	0 2 6	The Great Tithes are paid to Laverstock Parish alternately, but not the After Feed.
	2	Willoughbee ...	0 2 6	
	3	Powell	0 2 0	
	4	Hinxman	0 2 0	
	5	Bennet	0 2 0	

1749

When Alternate.		Names of Meads.	Acres.	What they at any time have paid.	
	1	Witebear ...	8 0 0	In 1700 pd. for after feed 8s.	
	2	Lambslease ...			
The odd years	3	Rankins ...	4 Acres 4 Lug		*Note by T. H. B.*
The odd years	4	William Freemans	7 2 5	1700 16s. after feed	Similar Accounts to these on pages 8 and 9 are entered every year up to 1753.
	5	Soper's 18s. always paid	13 0 14		
The odd years	6	Gorges ...	14 2 5	In 1701 & 1703 paid 5s.	
	7	Duck ...	18 1 0		
	8	Winterborn ...	18 0 24	£0 4s. 0d. in 1700	Mem: Mr. Cooper has paid 30s. for Milford Farm to Mich. 1755.
	9	Bathurst's ...	4 0 10		
	10	Eyre's ...	—	£0 15s. 0d. in 1700	
	11	Bell ...	—	£0 4s. 0d. in 1703	
	12	Picked			

Shoulder of Mutton	Wastcoat ...	0 3 0
Collyer's Mead ...	—	0 2 0
Cannigare ...	—	0 2 6
Blake's Living ...	Blake ...	0 12 0
Grey's Living ...	—	0 5 0
Ash Close ...	—	0 2 0

Yard Lands.	
Swayne's ...	
Powels ...	Wastcoat
Wentworth ...	Robins
Blackhead ...	Costar
Burrough ...	White
Floyd ...	
Harris ...	
Goodbee ...	
Stagg ...	
Goldwyer ...	
Cotton ...	Wastcoat
Wheeler ...	Westcoat
Robins ...	Robins

Nov. 1757. I was instituted & inducted to ye Rectory of S^t. Martin's.

S^t. Thos. JAMES LEWIS

Subscription Collection.

		£	s.	d.			£	s.	d.
Mr. Brander	...	0	5	0	Mrs. Newman	...	0	2	6
Mr. Smith	...	0	1	6	Mr. Dennis	...	0	5	6
Mr. Willis	...	0	2	6	Mr. Marsh	...	0	2	6
Mr. Collis	...	0	1	0	Mr. Goodfellow	...	0	2	0
Mr. Baily	...	0	2	6	Mrs. Floyd	...	0	2	6
Mr. Bayment	...	0	0	6	Mr. Staite	...	0	5	0
Mr. Spratt	...	0	2	0	Mr. Floyd	...	0	5	0
Mr. Bartlett	...	0	5	0	Mr. Othen	...	0	0	6
Mrs. Maton	...	0	2	0	Mr. Cooper	...	0	5	0
Mr. Gawin	...	0	2	6	Mrs. Rooke	...	0	1	0
Mr. Froome	..	0	5	0	Mr. Lake	...	0	5	0
Mr. Swanton	...	0	5	0	Mr. Spencer	...	0	0	6
Mr. Seaward	..	0	1	0	Mr. Rolfe	...	0	5	0
Mrs. White	...	0	2	6	Mr. Whitchurch	...	0	1	0
Mrs. Waters	...	0	2	6	Mr. Payne	...	0	10	6
Mrs. Marsh	...	0	2	6	Mr. Thorpe	...	0	10	6
Mr. White	...	0	1	6	Mr. Perrier	...	0	1	6
Mr. Robbets	...	0	0	6	Mrs. Smith	...	0	1	0
Mr. Spaggs	...	0	1	0	Mr. Hall	...	0	2	6
Mr. Safe	...	0	1	0					
Mr. Wheeler	...	0	1	0	Rec^d.		£5	14	0
Mrs. Thomas	...	0	2	6					

Lady Day Subs^n. 58.

The Subscribers are almost identical with the above list, with the addition of Mr. Rowland, £0 2s. 6d., and the withdrawal of

Mr. White
Mrs. Waters
Mrs. Marsh

			£	s.	d.
1758.	Oct. 18.	Quarteridge Collections for ye whole year last past amounted to	23	2	6
		Surplice fees to ab^t	7	10	0
		Easter Dues	4	0	0
		Rec^d. of Mr. Blake at Midsummer last Due Mark's Day for Tythe of Bishop Down Farm	8	6	8
	Oct. 12.	Rec^d. of Mr. Costard for Wentworth's farm including			
	,, 13.	Yard Lands & Sheep as had been Customary paid	0	6	6

According to Mr. Wascoat's account Groves ground was once lett from ye farm to Mr. Thorpe for w'ch being fed Mr. Thorpe readily paid 15 Shillings & ye farm p'd the same customary tythe to ye Minister as if it had not *been let off.* *Quære if Truth.*

		£	s.	d.
Oct. 14.	Rec^{d}. of Mr. R. White for Blackheads ...	0	7	0
	,, ,, ,, for Harris's ...	0	1	0
	,, ,, ,, for Stags ...	0	2	4
	Rec^{d}. of Mr. Waistcoat Due St. Mark's Day last for Tythe of Swaynes Farm Milford including Groves Ground	1	18	5
	Rec^{d}. of Mr. Cooper for Milford Farm ...	1	10	0
	of Brownjohn for Last St. Thos. Day part of wch was Mrs. Lumbys Due, & his deducting for 13 trees bought my part is nothing (p^{d}. again for ye year 1758)	1	10	0
	of Mr. Skaytes wch I agree to take yearly ... alias it would be 12^{s}. one year & but 6^{s}. ye next year.	0	9	0
	of Mr. Lenton for ye Rack Close ...	0	8	0
	Rec^{d}. of Andr. Chapman for Tythe of his Garden	1	0	0
	p^{d}. him for 6 Trees 6s. out of y^{e} £1 0s. 0d.			
	of Rogers for Wentworths Garden ...	0	8	0
	Behind ye Mills: Mrs. Knight 2 6; ,, Willoughbee 2 6; ,, Papps 2 0; ,, Hinxman 2 0; ,, Moore 2 0 — some names altered lately	0	11	0
	Mr. Morris for Powels next year is to be 2s.	0	2	0
	Bath Blue Boar Mead	0	4	0
	Mr. Still	0	4	0
	Mr. Smith of Milford for Swaynes great Garden	0	7	0
	The Griffin	0	2	6
	Goodfellows Garden	0	1	6
	Mr. Cush for ye Conigar at Ford	0	2	6
	Mr. Blake for his own at Ford	0	12	0
	Mr. Sutton for Bugmore Gardens only ...	0	9	0
	Mrs. Hussy for her Garden at Milford ...	0	2	0
	Mr. Safe w^{d} pay no more than (16s. due)	0	10	6
		52	15	5
	Let the Ch. Yard to Sam. Smith ...	2	0	0
		54	15	5

Mich'mas 1764

		£	s.	d.
	Quarterly Subscription amounted to ...	7	0	6
	Easter Dues for ye year sixty five amounted to	6	6	9
1763.	Of Mr. Goldwyer his Farm at Milford ...	0	2	0

Name of Lands.	Occupiers.	What they pay			
		£	s.	d.	
Church y[d]. ...	George George & Rich[d]. Forhead	0	1	0	This is all due at Michalmas
	Sam[l]. Smith ...	0	1	0	
	Worlds End ...	0	4	0	
Gardens in St. Ann's Street	Mr. Ro[t]. Cooper	0	8	4	
	Pellican ...	0	2	0	
	Mr. Stoddart ...	0	8	0	
	Mr. Stoddart late Maton ...	0	2	0	
	Mr. Baily ...	0	6	0	
Gardens in Bugmore (10)	... ...	1	6	0	
Grounds at Bottom of Drag[l]. Street ...	... ...	0	10	0	

Farms, Grounds, Meads, &c., in Milford.

Bishops Down farm	Mr. Wescott J[r].	8	6	8	This is paid att Midsummer
Millford farm ...	Mr. Wescott Sen[r].	1	10	0	Due St. Marks Day
Swaynes Great Garden	Brownjohn ...	8	10	0	

A List of the Subscribers to the Rector of St. Martins from St. Tho[s]. Day 1767 to Lady Day 1768.

	£	s.	d.		£	s.	d.
Mrs. Rook ...	0	1	0	Mr. Corfe ...	0	2	6
Mrs. Husey ...	0	5	0	Mr. Bayman ...	0	0	6
Mr. Smith ...	0	1	0	Mr. Spratt ...	0	2	0
Mr. Roger White ...	0	1	6	Mrs. Thratle ...	0	2	6
Mr. Hopgood ...	0	1	0	Ja[s]. Bartlett, Esq[r].	0	10	6
Mr. Reynolds ...	0	10	6	Mr. Price ...	0	2	6
Mr. Rob[t]. Cooper Junior ...	0	10	6	Mr. Gawin ...	0	2	6
				Mr. Keins ...	0	2	0
Mr. Feltham ...	0	1	0	Mr. Frome ...	0	5	3
Mrs. Collis ...	0	1	0	Mrs. Thomas ...	0	2	6
Mrs. Willis ...	0	5	0	Mr. Wheeler ...	0	1	0
Mr. Stoddart ...	0	2	0	Mr. Jn[o]. Rolfe ...	0	5	0
Mr. Baily ...	0	2	6	Mr. Whitchurch ...	0	2	6

	£	s.	d.
Mrs. Safe ...	0	1	0
Mr. Gillo ...	0	1	0
Mr. Spaggs ...	0	1	0
Mrs. Cary ...	0	2	6
Mr. Ed. White ...	0	2	6
Mr. Read ...	0	5	0
Mr. Woodberry ...	0	0	6
Mr. Naish ...	0	0	6
Mr. Dennis ...	0	5	0
Mr. Jno. Goodfellow	0	2	6
Mr. Matt. Goodfellow	0	2	0
Mrs. Scott ...	0	2	0
Mr. Floyd ...	0	5	0
Mr. Harbidge ...	0	2	6
Jno. Thorpe, Esq....	0	10	6

	£	s.	d.
Mr. Baden ...	0	1	0
Mr. Dew ...	0	2	6
Mr. Staite ...	0	5	0
Mr. Othen ...	0	0	6
Mr. R^{t}. Cooper ...	0	10	6
Mr. Cooksey ...	0	2	0
Mr. Lake ...	0	5	0
Mr. Newman ...	0	1	0
Mr. Diaper ...	0	1	0
Mrs. Bryant ...	0	1	0
Mr. Jos. Rolfe ...	0	2	6
Mr. Befford ...	0	1	0
Mr. Boucher ...	0	2	6
Mr. Bayman ...	0	0	6.

1775.	£	s.	d.
Mr. Lewis for Gorges mead ...	0	9	0
Mr. Barter for 3 meads	0	14	6
Mr. Stephens for Worlds End ...	0	2	0
Mr. Smith for his farm	0	10	6
Mr. Goodfellow ...	0	1	6
Mr. Sillwood ...	0	2	0
Mr. Biddlecombe Bowling Green ...	0	8	0
Mr. Geary ...	1	0	0
Mr. Hinxman ...	0	2	0
Mr. Whitmarsh ...	0	2	6
Mr. Merri ...	0	14	6
S^{r}. Alex^{r}. Powell ...	0	2	6
Mr. Brown Serjeant	0	2	0
Mr. Brown Harnam	0	5	0
Mr. Still ...	0	4	0
Mr. Collins ...	0	7	6
Mr. Marks ...	0	1	0
Mr. Mundy ...	0	2	0
Mr. Cusse ...	0	7	6
Mr. Blake ...	0	12	0
Mr. Lewis Milford Farm ...	1	10	0
Mr. Coombs ...	0	10	4
Dr. Herrington ...	0	4	0
Mr. Goldwyer ...	0	2	0
	£8	12	4

	£	s.	d.
Recev^{d} of Mr. Hibberd for Winterburn and Bathurst Mead, 1779 ...	0	5	6
Mr. Cooe for Millford Farm ...	1	10	0
Do. for three meads	0	18	0
Mr. Skates ...	0	2	0
Mr. Marks ...	0	1	0
Mr. Coombs ...	0	10	4
Mr. Goodfellow ...	0	1	6
Mr. Brown, Harnam	0	5	0
Mr. Still ...	0	4	0
Mr. Collins ...	0	7	6
Ogden ...	0	2	6
Mr. Merris ...	0	14	6
Mr. Hinxman ...	0	2	0
Mr. Brown, Serjant	0	2	0
Dr. Harrington ...	0	4	0
Mr. Geary ...	1	0	0
Mr. Ody ...	0	2	0
Mr. Smith ...	0	10	6
Do. for Bowling Green ...	0	8	0
Mr. Blake ...	0	12	0
Mr. Cusse ...	0	7	6
Mr. Munday ...	0	2	0
Mr. Newman ...	0	2	6
	£8	14	4

1777.

	£	s.	d.	
Mr. Foyle ...	0	14	6	for 4 meads 2 of them pay only every other year
Mr. Cox for George Mead	0	9	0	Pays every other year
Ditto the farm for Mr. Cooper ...	1	10	0	Millford farm
Mr. Smith ...	0	10	6	the farm call'd Powells
Mr. Hutchence ...	0	2	0	Worlds End Garden
Mr. Goodfellow ...	0	1	6	A Garden
Mr. Brown Harnam	0	5	0	A Meadow in Dragal Street
Mr. Still ...	0	4	0	A Meadow in Dragal Street
Mr. Collins ...	0	7	6	A Garden Call'd Swayne's house Garden
Mr. Brown Serjant	0	2	0	A Garden behind the Mills
Mr. Newnan, for Sr Alex ...	0	2	6	A Garden behind the Mills
Mr. Merris ...	0	14	6	for his farm and Rack Close
Mr. Whitmarsh ...	0	2	6	A Garden behind the Mills
Mr. Hinxman ...	0	2	0	A Garden behind the Mills
Dr. Harunton ...	0	4	0	Blue Boar Mead
Mr. Boyter ...	0	8	0	Bowling Green Garden
Mr. Marks ...	0	1	0	A mead Belonging to Goodbees farm
Mr. Coombs ...	0	10	4	for Blackheads Harris & Stags
Mr. Skates ...	0	2	0	for Goodbees farm or Burroughs
Mr. Goldwyer ...	0	2	0	for his farm now Lett to Mr. Ody
Mr. Geary ...	1	0	0	for his Garden Call'd Wyndhams Great Garden
Mr. Blake ..	0	12	0	for his farm at Ford
Mr. Cusse ...	0	7	6	for a farm call'd Grays and a mead call'd Coniger
Mr. Mundy ...	0	2	0	for Ash Close near Winterburne
	8	16	4	

Mr. Gifford for Bugmore 0 9 6

This paper, written 8 Hen. VII. (A.D. 1492), appears to be the opinion given by some lawyer as to the application of certain rents of houses originally left, as it seems, by one Richard Vesey to maintain his Obit, then to certain poor people, and the remainder to the Priest of the Holy Ghost in St. Martin's parish.

8 H. 7 iiij tents in Culver Strete Ass(ured) to the Churche Wardens by
3s. 4d. the executors of Richard V.

to certen persons of St. M'tyns in Sarum to bestowe yerely thereof
iij^{s} iiij^{d}
uppon an Obbit 8 H. 7
Note y^{t} y^{d} apperethe not by that dede that the
lands weare gevyn to kepe that obbyt for ever
& therefore not within the Statute of i. E. 6
H. 7 Of the iiij tents' next the Churche yarde of St. Martyns
5s. ther is orderyd to be bestowed of the rents therof yerely for
ever v^{s} for an obbytt &c. / & the rest of the rents
thereof after the quit rent & reparac'ons payed, shalbe
yerely delyvered to the vse of the exhibyc'on of the Holy Gost
prest there prayeng dayly & yerely for the donor for ever
vt patet per cart' de 2 H. 7
by thys yt apprethe that the Kyng is intitled
to the v^{s} & to the rest of the old rent thereof
after the reparacons of the tenements as the rent
was at the tyme of the grant / but I thynke
that yf the ffeffees can nowe ymprove
the lands thorowe theyer charges there to be done
that the Kyng shal have no more but
the v^{s} & so muche of the rest of the rent as the prest was
wont to have after reparacons done yf the
obbyt weare kept within v yeres of the Act
& otherwyse not
The corner tenement with th'appurtenances given by Mr. Vesey
in i. E. 4.
to Mr Bat & others the ffeffees owght to fynd his obbyt
& to expend therupon viij^{s} of the profytts of the land viz.
for the prests & clarks xx^{d} for massyng / for the
pore people wch came to the mas xx^{d} for bred
oile & chese & grete bel iiij^{s} 8^{d} and for the ffeffees
labors yerely ij^{s} / And for too lamps iij^{s} iiij^{d}
And for the v tents' parcel of the sayde corner tent' they are
to be kept for v pore people & the ffeffees to repayer
them / And the overplus of the rent of the sayde
corner tenement after al reparacons thereof & of the
fyve almeshouses done to remayne to the Holy Gost
prest of that paryshe. but saythe not to his successors
nor yet for ever / & therfore of that overplus rent I thynke
the Kynge shal (have nothynge) therof for that yt ys not
lymytted to (have any claym) thereof contynued
And for the viij^{s} for the obbyt / I thynke the
xd. Kynge shal hereof have that but the xx^{d}
lymytted for the prest & clarke for mas. /
& the Kyng shal also have the
4d. iij^{s} iiij^{d} for the too lampes yf those never

weare ymployed w^thin the v yeres of the sayde . . . . / And that the ffeffees shall styl hold the lands by their ffeffem^t

A note in the Parish Chest
Augmentation Office—Chantry Certificate. Co. of Wilts
No. 91 St. Martin's Sarum.
Thomas Vesye's Obit founded Michaelmas of Edw. III. out of a tenement in Winchester Street,'

A.D. (1465). Sciant p'sent' et futuri qd' Ego Willi'us Wotton tradidi Dimisi hac p'sente carta mea confirmaui Edwardo Chitterne Rob'to Chandeler Joh'i leyed Joh'i ffrannces Thome leker Joh'i Hamersmyth Thome Gleber Nicho' Stote Thome Blakker Joh'i Jacob Joh'i Brydmer, Rob'to Newe & Henrico Wotton illa Dno Cotagia mea cum gardinis & alijs suis p'tin connecti' sit' in Noua Sar' in Culver strete int' Cotagia nup Ricardi Barwe ex parte austral' & Cotagia Thome Knoyle ex parte boriali que quid'm cotagia cu' gardinis & alijs eius p'tin' nup' hui' simul cu' Gill'mo Cokkys Gill'mo Halstede Joh'i Cleve Brewer, Gilli' Prydy & Thome Saundre de Ciuitate Noue Sar' iam defunct' exdono & feoffamento Edithe que fuit uxor Willi' Caumbrigge nup civis london' Joh'is Caumel nup de Noua Sar' p'dict' iam defunct' Thome Gabayn Willi' Merwe & Roberti Smyth de london sub certis condicoibus pront patet in quad'm carta indentata cuius Dat' est Apud Nouam Sar' die mercurie p'x post festu' Assumpcoi's b'te marie virgi's Anno regni Regis Henrici Sexti post conquestum Decimo nono inde confect plenius apparet Hend' & tenend' p'dict' duo cotagia cum gardinis & alijs suis ptin' vt supradict' est p'fatis Edwardo Joh'i Joh'i Thome Joh'i Thome Nicho' Thome Joh'i Joh'i Rob'to & Henrico hereds & Assignat' & inpp'm De capital' Dno' ciuitatis p'dict p' reddit & suic' inde det in & De re consuet' sub condenis & intencoe' Ad per impend & tenend' omes illas conuencaes & condicoes' vt patet in p'd'ca carta indentata prout Ego ipe' p'dcus Will'us Wotton simul cum p'dict' Will'mo Cokkys Will'mo Halstede Joh'i Glebe Will'mo Prydy & Thome Saundre Astrict cum & ligatis virtute & rat'one p'dic' carta indentata In cuius Rei testimoniu' huic p'senta carte mee Sigillum meu' Apposui Et quia Sigillum meu' pluribus est incognitu' Sigillu hoc vna cu' sigillo officii maioritatis ciuitatis noue Sar' Apponi procurani hijs testibus Will'mo Wotton tunc maiore Sar' Joh'i Whittokesmede tunc ballino ib'm Rob'to Geve tunc coronatore ib'm Henrico ffrende & Hugone ffitzrichard tunc p'positio ibm Thome ffreeman . . . . Hore sen. Will'mo Swayne Johe' Syse Edmundo Penston & Johe' Craswell tunc thesaurario ? & multis alijs Dat apud Novam Sar' p'd'cam quinto decimo die mensis Septembris Anno regni Regis Edwardi quarti post Conquestum Angle. quarto.

Robert Sowbride of Abbotsbury Co. Dorset conveys to Wm. Ludlow of Ludgershall & John Wyse of New Sarum, Four Cottages with a dovecote in New Sarum, near the Cemetery of St. Martins Witness Robert Long Esq. Bailiff of New Sarum, Richard Payne Mayor, and others.

Noui'nt Vniv'si per p'sentes me Ricardum Gage de Noua Sar' remisisse relaxasse & omio' pro me & hereds meis imp'pm' p' met' clamasse Radulpho Pakker hereds & Assigns suis totum jus meum & clam' que heo' seu quouismodo in futur he'r' pot'o in illis duobz cotagiis cu' gardino columbari et omibz aliis pt'en' que sit' sunt in Noua Sar' inxta Cimet'um ecc'ie Sci' Martini ib'm ex p'te orientali & ten' nup'r Ioh'is Dogskyn ex p'te occidentali Quoquidum' cotagia cu' gardino columbari et aliis omnibus p'tin' suis nup'r hu'i communi' cu' Joh'e Dudlegh & Will'mo Godmanston ex dono et ffeoffamento Rob'i Haras Ita q'd nec ego p'dict' Ricu's nc hereds mei nc aliquis Alius noin'e meo aliquid juri seu clamei' in p'dict' cotagiis cu' gardino columbar' & alijs ptin' suis nec in aliq' pte cord'm nec in D— nec inde neqz sui'cio erga p'dict' Radulphum hereds seu assignt' suis de tot's exigs seu vendicare pot'ims in fut'um Sz' Ab omi'bz accoi'bz iuribz . . . . udis quit . . . . a'qz simul exclusi imp'pm' G— p'deu's Ricu's hereds me p'dict' Duo' cotagia ad gardino columbar & alijs p'tin' suis p'dict' Radulpho hereds et assign' suis omc's gentes Warantizabims imp'pm' In cuius rei testiom p'sentibz Sigillu' meu' Apposui Et Sigillu' c' vna cu' Sigillo maioritatis Ciuitatis p'dm' similit' Apponi p'curaui Hijs testibz Robto' Long tunc Ballino Ciuitat' p'dict' Joh'e Wyet tu'c maiore ibm' Robto Cove & Willmo Halsted tunc Coronator ib'm Thoma Somse & Willmo Olyver tu'c ib'm p'poitz Willm'o Wardeyk Rob'to Warmwell Henrico Man Thoma ffrenuch Joh'e Aport (?) & multis alijs Dat ap'd Nouam Sar' In festo sc'i Nichi Epi' Anno regni Regis Henrici sexti post conques vicesimo.

An extract from the Will of Edward Windover, who in 1605 left a yearly Rent Charge of £1 13s. 4d. to apprentice boys. This was formerly paid by the Dean & Chapter, but now by the Ecclesiastical Commissioners.

In the name of God Amen. The . . . and
yeare of or lorde god One thousand six hund-
of the Cittie of newe Sarum in the Countie of (Wilts) . . . .
and p'fecte memorye thankes be given to Almightie(God) . . .
my last will and testament in manner and forme fol(lowing I) .
bequeathe towards the Repacons of the Churche of St. M. . . .
shillinges fower pence. Item I doe (bequeath) and devise unto th
pish Church of St. Martyns aforesaid and to theire successors for

ever One Rente/ of Thirtie three shillinges fower pence by the yeare wch I purchast of Mr. Henrye/ Ashleye to be Received yearlie of the Chapiter of the Cathedrall Churche of Saru/ and to be bestowed yearlie for ever towards such poore Children's premises as have moste neede and are like to Chardge the pishe of S^t. Martyns aforesaid as to the discrec'on/ of the Churchwardens and the Rest of those who have byn Churchwardens of the parish/ aforesaid or the moste parte of them from time to time shall seeme meete.

(10) Henry VI. to 1444. Culver Street Cottages.

Sciant p'sentes & futuri qd. ego Joh'es Clyne Brewer dedi concessi & hac p'senti carta mea confirmaui Rico' Hogge de Ciuitate Noue Sar' Carpenter illa sex cotagia cu' suis p'tin' con'iunctum Sit^o in Ciuitate p'dica in Coluerstrete int' cotagia Rob'ti Knoell ex p'te Australi & cotag' Joh'is Pope ex p'te Boriali Que quidem cotagia cu' suis p'tin' nup hui' ex dono & feoffamento p'dicti Rici' Hogge pront in quadam carta inde michi per ipm' Ricu' confect' plenius Apparet hend & tenend p'dict' sex cotagia cu' suis p'tin' p'fat' Rico' Hogge heredibz & assign' suis de capitali dno' Ciuitatis p'dice per Seruicia inde debit' & de jure consuet' imp'pm' per p'sentes In cuiz rei testiom' huic p'senti' carte mee Sigillu' meu' apposui Et Sigillu' coe' vna cu Sigillo maioritatis Ciuitatis p'dce' similit' apponi procuravi hiis testibz Rob'to longe Armigo tunc ballio' Ciuitatis p'dce Willo' Hore tunc maiori eiusd'm Ciuitatis Willmo Halstede & Rob'to Cove tunc Coronator ib'm Thoma Silke & Thoma Benet Helyer tunc p'poi'tis ib'm Robto' Warnwell Willo Wardeyk Willo' Pakyn Joh'e Wyet Thoma ffreman Joh'e Hampton Pho' Morgan Thos & Alijs Dat' Apud Nova Sar' die dn'ica in festo Omnin' Scor' Anno regni Regis Henrici sexti post conqui' Anglie vicesimo tertio.

James 1. 1610.

THIS INDENTURE made the Third daye of Aprill in the yeare of the Reigne of o^r Sonor'aigne lord James by the grace of god of England france and Ireland King Defender of the faithe Seaventh and of Scotland the two and ffiftie **Betweene** John Batt of Milford in the Countie of Wilts Yeoman, James Newman als' Evered of the Cittie of New Sarum in the countie aforesaid yeoman. Charles Jacobb of the Cittie of newe Sarum in the Countie aforesaid Tanner ffeoffees in trust of the lands belonginge to the p'ishe Church of Sainte M'tynes within the Cittie of newe Sarum in the countye aforesaid of the one p'tye. And Edmund Burges of the Cittye and countye aforesaid of the other p'tie **Wittnesseth** that the said John Batt James Newman alias Evered and Charles Jacobb as well for and in consid'a'con of the Som'e of Thirty poundes of Curraunte Englishe moneye vnto them at and before thensealinge hereof by the said

Edmunde Burges in the name of . . . . hand well and truely contented and . . . . hereof and . . . . . . acknowledge themselves to be well and truelie satisfied contented and payed and therof and of everye p'te and p'cell therof clearelye acquitte and discharge . . . . Edmund Burges his executors administrators and assignes thies p'sents as well for & in consideracon of the rents and Covenants in these p'sents reserved Haue demised graunted and to farme letten and by thies p'sents for the doe demise graunte and to ferme let vnto the said Edmunde Burges his executo[rs] administrators and Assignes All that their Corner Messuage and Tenement with th' app'ten'nes therof all and all manner of grounde there vnto belonginge or in any wise apperteyninge set lyinge and beinge w[t]hin the Cittye of newe Sarum there commonlye call'd Milford Streete of William Lack Deceased or of his Assignee or Assignes and now are in the tennure use or occupacon of the said Edmund Burges . . . . his Assignee or Assigns ex of this p'sent graunte all wayes reserved one little Tenn[t] being p'cell of the said Corner Messuage or Tenn[t] lyinge betweene the five almshouses on the . . . . . side and by the yeate house belonginge to the said Messuage or Tenum't on the Southside and nowe in the vse and occupac'on of Annis Johnsoune Widowe **To have or to** all and singuler the same Corner messuage or Tenn[t] wth Thapp'tennes house . . . e backeside and garden grounde aforesaid excepte before excepted vnto the said Edmund Burges his executors administrators and Assignes from the Daye of Birthe of o[r] lord god lo . . . . . st before the date hereof for by and Duringe and vnto the full end and tearme of Seaven and twentye yeares from thence nexte following and fullye to be Compleate and ended **yealdinge** and payinge therefore yearlie duringe the said tearme vnto the saide John Batt James Newman als' Evered and Charles Jacobb their heires & Assignes or to the Churchwardens of the p'ishe of Sainte m'tynes aforesaid for the tyme beinge the yearlie rente or some of Three poundes of Curraunte Englishe money at ffower seu'all ffeastes or tearmes in the yeare . . . vsuall. That is to say at the feast of Thannunciacon of o[r] Ladye Sainte Marye the Virgine, at the Natyvitye of S[t]. John Baptist, the feast of Saint Mychaell Tharchangell, and at the birth of o[r] lord God by even and equall porc'ons **And** the said Edmunde Burges for himselfe his execut[rs] administrato[rs] and Assignes doth Coven'nte promise and graunte to and with the said John Batt, James Newman als' Evered and Charles Jacobb theire heires and Assignes by these p[r]sents. That he the said Edmund Burges his executors administrato[rs] and Assignes shall and will at his or their owne proper costes & charges from tyme to tyme and at all tymes duringe the saide terme of Seaven and Twenty Yeares when and as often as need shall require well and sufficientlye repayer uphould sustayne maynteyne and fence all and singuler the sayd Corner messuage or tenne't with Thapp'tennes He roome backside and garden ground in all and all manner of needful and necessarye repacon's whatsoeu' and the same soe well and sufficientlye repayred upheld susteyned mayntayned and fenced in the end of the said tearme shall and will leave and yeald upp. And the said Edmund Burges for himself his Executors administrators and Assignes. Coven'nteth . . . . and graunt to and with the said John Batt James Newman als' Evered and Charles Jacobb their heires executors administrators and Assignes by thies p'sents That he the said Edmund Burges his executors administrators and assignes duringe the tearme aforesaide shall not alter Translate nor divide nor cause to be altered Translated nor divided the Message and Tennemte be . . . . to make thereof Tennements more then Two at the most and what buildinge else shall happen to be erected, sett up and annexed vnto the messuage and Tennen't aforesaid shall not be moved in the end and expirac'on of the saide tearme to be left and yealded up undefaced. **Provided** all wayes that it may and shalbe lawfull to and for the said John Batt James Newman als' Evered and Charles Jacobb or anye or eyther of them their heires executors administrators and Assignes att all tyme and tymes heerafter to hane ffree ingresse egresse and regresse into and from the said messuage and Tenn't with Thapp'tennces and all other the p'misses before demised and eu'ye p'te and p'cell therof for the vewinge or surveying of the Decayes estate or . . . . of the said Messuage or Tenn't with Thapp'tenn'ces and all other the p'misses before demised **And yf it happen** the saide yearelie rente of Three poundes or any p'te or p'cell thereof to be behinde and unpayed in p'te or in all by the space of ffifteene Dayes nexte after anye of the saide ffeastes and tearmes of paymente aforesaid in wh^ch^ as aforesaid ought to be payed and hane bine lawfullie asked and Demanded and not payed **Or yf** the said Edmunde Burges his executors administrators and Assignes or anye of them shall not within one . . . eare nexte after Warninge given by the said John Batt James Newman als' Evered and Charles Jacobb or anye or one of them their heires executors administrators and Assignes at the messuage or Tenn'et aforesaid sufficiently amend repayre, erecte and sett up all such faultes and Decayes as they or eyther of them shall publishe and give notice or Warninge of without Coven frande Deceipte or further Delaye, accordinge to the trewe intente and meaninge of thies p'sents. That then and att all tymes after this p'sente Indenture Demise, Lease and graunte shall utterlie cease

Determyne and be voyde, and at everye tyme after it shalbe lawfull to and for the said John Batt James Newman als' Evered and Charles Jacobb or any or eyther of them their heires executors administrators and Assignes into the said messuage or Tenne't and all other the p'mised p'misses wholye to Reenter reposses and enjoye as in his or their former estate or estates and the said Edmund Burges his executors administrators and Assignes out of and from the said messuage and Tenn't wth Thapp'tenances utterlie to expell amove and putt out anye thinge in thies p'sente Indentures contayned to the Contrarye thereof in any wise notwithstandinge. **And** the said John Batt James Newman als' Evered and Charles Jacobe for them their heires executors administrators and Assignes Doth Covenaunte promise and graunte to and with the said Edmunde Burges his executors and Assignes by thies p'sents That he the said Edmunde Burges his executors administrators and Assignes for and under the yearlie rente aforesaide and under p'formance of the Covenants herein specified shall and may peaceablie and quietlie haue hould Occupie posses and enjoye the land messuage or Tenne't wth all and singular Thapp'tennces heerby graunted W'hout the lawfull let Deniall molestac'on eviction or Disturbance of the said John Batt James Newman als' Evered and Charles Jacobe their heires executors administrators or Assignes or of anye p'son or p'sonnes lawfullie Clayminge through them or anye of them. **In witnes whereof** the parties abovesaide to thies p'sente Indentures interchangeablie haue putte their handes and seales yeoven the day and yeare before . . . .

5) pril. abeth faced) ng the ate of Gheast, 1577.

Omnibus x'pe fidelibz ad quos hoc p'sens Scriptu' Indent' p'uen'it Thom's Jacob de Ciuitate Nove Sar' com' Wiltes Tann' Nichn's Storie de civitat' p'dc in Com' p'dc Tann' et Joh'es Ockford de East harnam in com' p'de tallow chandler Slt'm in d^{o} no' Sempit'nam **Sciatis** nos p'fat Thomam Jacob Nich'm Storie . . . in Edertas pro et in considerat' cuiusd'm pecuniar' sim' bone et legali monete Anglicane sigillaco'em p'sentim vobis p'manibus solut' per Henric' Euered senior Joh'em Tayler Joh'em Jervis Dani'em Kyffyn Charo(lum. Jacob) Rob'tum Bundye, Ric'um Emory, xpoferum Player ffranciscu' Davys Robtu' Crede Rog'u . . . Jacobu' Euered Henric' Euered Junior Joh'em Batt (?) Thomam Batt Charo'lm Jacob Junr Jo(hannem) Crede et Anthonin' Crede unde fatemur nos plenar' fore satisfact' et content' pro puteo **Dedisse** concessisse et hoc p'sent' scripto n'ro confirmasse p'fat' Henrico Euered senior' Joh'i Tayler Joh'i Jervys Dan' Kyffyn Charolo Jacob senior xpo'fero Batt, Rob'to Bundye Ri'co Emerye xfo'fero Player ffrancisco Davys Rob'to Crede Rogero Euered Jacobo Euered Henrico Euered Junior Joh'i Batt, Thome Batt Charolo Jacob Jun' Joh'i Crede et

Anthonio Crede totum illud Angular Tenement siue messuag' et gardin' n'rm cum ptin' et quinqz p'na tent' nr'a vocat Almeshouses cum p'tin' Scituat iacent et existen' conjunct in ciuitat' Noue Sar' p'd in duobus vias ib'm voc' Milforde Streat inter terr' quondam Jacobi Andrewes ex p'te occident' via ibm' exp'tibus orient' et boriali et ter' quond'm Rob'ti Walker ex p'te australli **Necnon** quatnor tenement' siue messuag' ac quatuor gardin' n'ra cu' p'tin' scitnat' . . . in Ciuitat p'd in p'dico' vico ib'm voc' Culner Streat inter ter' quond'm pd'ce Robti Walker ex Boriali p'te ter' Joh' Baylie ex australi p'te Regia via ex orient' p'te et ter quond'm Joh'is Coriet gen'os defunct' ac ter' quond'm Joh'is Abyn' gentes defunct ex occident p'te Ac vnu' aliud tenement siue messuag' ex gardin' n'rm . . . in ciuitate p'd in p'dco' vico ibm' voc' Culu' streat inter ter' Joh'is Baylie ex boriale p'te et ter' quond'm Thome Cater Defunct' ex australi p'te ac Regia' via' ex orient' p'te et ter' Joh'is Coles ex occident' p'te Ac . . . quatnor alia tenta' sine messuag' ac quatuor gardin' nr'a cu'p'tin' scitnat' et existen' coniunct in Ciuitate p'd . . . ib'm vocat St. Martyns Streat int' Regiam viam ibm' ducent' ad Eccl'iam St[1] Martini ex boriali . . . queddm p'tu' vocat Prato Bugmore reu'endi in x'po p'ris Edmundi Epi' Sar' ex anstrali p'te . . . yson ex occident pte et Cimet'm ecc'lie p'ochali St[i] Martini p'de' ex orient' p'te A ten'tm sine mesuag' et gardin' nrm' cu' p'tin' Scitnat' iacent' et existen' in Ciuitate Nove Sar' . . . vico ibm' vocat' Dragons Streate inter ter' Anne Coriett vidue ex boriali p'te nup' (Willi Holmes ?) . . . de Sendlo defunct' ex australi p'te ter p'da Willi'm Holmes ex orient' p'te et Regia via ducent' a ciuitat' p'dict usqz ad Harnam bridge ex occident' p'te Necnon

Hend' et tenend' om'ia et singla' per messuag' sine tent' ter' tent' Ca . . n' . . ceta' p'missa omnia' et singla cum omibz et singlis suis p'rem' quibus cunqz p'fat.' Henrico Euered Senior Joh'i Bayley Joh'i Tayler Danielo Kyffyn Carolo Jacob sen' Xpofero Batt Rob'to Bundye Rico' Em'ye Xpofero Player ffrancisco Davys Rob'to Crede Rog'o Euered Jacobo Enered Henrico Euered Jun' (Joh'i Batt Carolo Jacob Jun' Joh'i Crede et Anthonio Crede heredibus et assign' suis imp'pm' ad solimodo opus et ru' ip'or' Henric' Enered Joh'is Tayler &c. . . . . Tenend de capitalib Dn feod . . . . debit et de iure consnet' Ac non vero p'dic Thoms Jacob Nich'us Storie et Joh'is om'ia et singla p'd. messuagia ten't ter' gardin' . . . . singl . . . . Henrico Enered &c. heredibz et assignatis suis contra nos et heredes n'ros Warantizabimz acquietabimuz et imp'p'm defendimz . . . Insuper . . nos p'fat' . . . Jacob Nich'm Storie et Joh'em fecisse ordinam constitnisse nris Dil'cis nobis in x'po

Thoman Seynt barbe et. Will'm Holmes gen'os n'ros voces et loquitur . . . . quat Comment. & Comisrs pro mois vice et in . . . n'ris in p'dc tenement' messuag' ter' gardin' et cor'a pmis' omnia' et singla' cu' omibz et singlis'

. . . .

vice et in no'ibus . . . (here follows the 17 names above) . . . . . n're desup. confect

Datum secundo die Ap'lis Anno regni Dne n're Elizabeth. Dei gra' Anglie ffrancie et . . . . . .

(Indorsed with Certificate of the said Attornies that possession had been given.)

Grovely & Clarendon.

Graueling foresta Custod' : medietat' : eiusdem vizt. :
le Northbayley sicut Grymesditch diuidit de
feod' et profic' : p'tinen et redd' exeunt Escaet'.
25 Ed. 3 post mortem Willi' Ruintyn nº : 6j.
p'tinet ad Manerium de Wycheford et debet
habere housbote &c. : et pastur : pro animalibz.
Robertus Brent tenet Manerium de Wycheford de
Domino Rege vt de Ducatu suo Lancastr' : in
Socagio per quod seruiciu' ignorant Esc' 9. H. 5. Nº. 25.
Will'us Ruyntyn tenet die quo obit. j mes' : et
LX acr' terre iij acr' : prat : et 8s redd' : in
Wycheford magna de domino Rege in Capite
per Serjanciane ad essend' fforestar' Domini
Regis in Gronele et per seruiciu' ijs per annu'
soluend' ad Castrum Sar' : Esc : 15 : Ed. 3. Nº. 17.

at. 6 H. 4. s. j. m. 8.

Rex concessit Joh'i Comiti Som'set Custodiam
foreste et parci nostroru' de Clarendon
et forestarum de Grouele Melchet et
Bukholt habend' ad totam vitam ipsius Comitis
cu' omnibus feodis et proficuis &c.

at. ii. H. 4. s. 1 m. 2 Hum'fro fil' Regis.

Rex omnibus &c. de gra' n'ra spali' concessimus
carissimo fil' n'ro Hum'fro Custodiam foreste et
parci n'ror de Clarendon : ac forestar' n'rar' de
Grouele Melchet et Bukholte haben'd' ad
terminu' vite sue cu' omnibus feodis &c. adeo
integre sicut Carissimus frater noster Joh'es
nuper Comes Somerset' defunctus percepit &c.
Grouele, Melchet Exemplificacio ampla et optima
Et custod' eiusdem p'tinen' ad quasdam terr' in

at. 3 R. 2. s. 3 m. 26.

villa de Bereford Sci' Martini et de proficuis
Et aduantagiis eidem vndequaque p'tinen'
Et de Balliua ibidem vocat Le North bayley
Et proficuis &c. p'tinen'. Escaet : 7. H. 5.
post mortem Elisabethe Stubbere.

Escaet. 25 Ed. 3 No. 61.

Will'us Ruyntyn de Wychford tenuit in d'nico
suo vt de feodo die q° obijt vnu' mesuagiu'
vnam hidam terre decem solidatas redditus
cum p'tinen' in Wichford pr'dict' de
D'no Rege in Capite per Serjantiam ad
Custodiend' medietatem foreste de
Grauelynge vizt. la North baillie sicut
Grymmesdich diuidit et per seruicium 22^{s}
per annu' vizt. D'no Regi ad Castrum Sar'
ij^{s} Et Priori et Conventui de Maydene bradley
xx^{s}.

Rot. 19 Inter pl'ita Cheminor'. 29 Ed. 3 Tully office.

fin ijs.

Nich'us de Bonham clam' cursu' cujusdam aque voc' Wily cum / piscar' in eadem currente sup' solu' ipius' Nich'i infra meditat' / M'ij de Magna Wichford simul cu' attachianca et amers / in eadz &c. : Et quia cump'tum est q'd Idem Nich'us et Antecess'rs / sui seisit fuer lib'tat et pro fic predictis in aqua p'd'ca ideo inde / het alloca'coem jure Dni' Rg in oib'z semp' saluo &c.

alloc.

The above is copied from an old document written on paper in the Parish Chest of St. Martin's, Salisbury. (T.H.B., 1904.)

The last 7 lines are written in a different hand. (T.H.B.)

37 Hen. VIII. An extract in Modern Writing in Parish Chest.

Chantry Certificates Wilts Roll 59
Certificate of College Chantries see for
Commissioners Dated 14 Feby 37. Hen. VIII.
Collegium Sci' Edmundi Sarum valet in
Redd'us sive firma Recor'ie Sci' Martini existensis et
includis in d'ca ciuitate Nove Sar' cum omi'bz decimis
oblationibz aliis qz pro ficiis eodem Recor'ie p'tinen'
quam Henricus Jeneno cap^{uus} tenet & occupat
que Recor'ia estimat' esse in valoris xli.

The Boundary between Laverstock and Milford.

This is to Certify that I James Jerwood Esquire an Assistant Tithe Commissioner have on the date hereof made and published my Award concerning the Boundaries of the Parish of Laverstock in the County of Wilts and particularly concerning that portion of the Boundary between the said Parish of Laverstock and the Parish of Milford a District within the Rectory Parish of Saint Martin in the said County of Wilts and that I have thereby found adjudged and determined that the said Boundary Line extends from the point at the end of Laverstock Lane where the North West Angle of the Close numbered thirty four in the Map to my said Award annexed meets the South East Fence of the said Laverstock Lane being the point marked with the Letter A in the said Map and continues along the Northern Fence of the said Close numbered thirty four as aforesaid to the extremity thereof thence along the East Fence of the said Close to the extremity thereof thence along by the Deer Leap in the same Close to the South West Angle thereof (the said Close numbered thirty four as aforesaid is called Milford Piece and is part of Milford Farm belonging to the Right Honorable The Earl of Ilchester and Messieurs Richard and John Cooe his Lessees for Lives and occupied by the said Richard and John Cooe) thence along in the same direction to the middle of Laverstock Lane aforesaid thence along the middle of the said Laverstock Lane to the point which is seventeen yards or thereabouts distant from the North West Angle of the Wall of a Malthouse the property and in the occupation of the said Richard and John Cooe thence along the Middle of a Lane leading from the Farm Yard of the said Richard and John Cooe to Petersfinger Turnpike Gate to a point which is four yards or thereabouts distant from an Elm Tree growing in the Northern Fence of the said Lane, and three yards or thereabouts distant from the North West Angle of the Brick Wall adjoining the said Malthouse thence along to the said North West Angle of the said Brick Wall forming the point marked with the letter B in the said Map to my said Award annexed thence along the North West side of the said Brick Wall to the extremity thereof thence along the North West Fence of the Close formerly called St. Looe's Meadow to the extremity thereof (the said land formerly called Saint Looes Meadow is part of Laverstock Farm belonging to Wadham Wyndham Esquire and now occupied by the said Richard and John Cooe) thence along in the same direction across the Watercourse to the South West bank thereof thence along the said South West bank of the said Watercourse to the North West Angle of the Bridge nearest to the Petersfinger Turnpike Gate thence along the West side of the said Bridge to the point where the South West Angle thereof adjoins a piece of waste Land being the point marked with the letter C in the said Map thence along the said Waste Land in a straight line extending thirty four yards or thereabouts to the North East end of the Drain in the Close numbered seven in the said Map (The said Waste Land is part of Lands belonging to the Trustees of the Sarum and Ealing Turnpike Road) thence along the Middle of the said Drain through the Closes numbered seven and eight in the said Map to the point where the said Drain meets the River Avon being the point marked with the letter D in the said Map to my said Award annexed (The said Closes numbered seven and eight as aforesaid are called Saint Nicholas Meads and are part of the possessions of the Master and Brothers of Saint Nicholas Hospital and now occupied by the said Richard and

John Cooe) And I do hereby certify that the dotted Line in the said Map to my said Award annexed is the Boundary Line which I have set out and described and which I have found adjudged and determined to be the true Boundary Line of the said Parishes of Laverstock and Milford a district within the Rectory Parish of Saint Martin as aforesaid between the aforesaid several points respectively. In witness whereof I the said James Jerwood have hereunto set my hand this thirty first day of October one thousand eight hundred and forty.

JAMES JERWOOD.

(16) An Agreement for the Sale of 7 houses, &c., in New Sarum.

Hac est finalis Concordia f'at in Cur' d'ni Regis apud Westm' in crastino Ascencionis D'ni Anno regnor' Jacobi sed'i Dei gra' Anglz Scocie ffranc' & Hibine Regis fidei defen's etc a Conqu' quarto Coram Edwardo Herbert Thoma Street Edw' lnt Wich & Cristofero Milton Justic' & alijs dni Regis fidelibz tunc ibi p'sentibz Int' Johem Staples & Johem West quer'et' Henr' Gauntlett & Vrsulam vxem eius deforc' de septem mesuagijs & Septem gardinis cum p'tin in Civitate Nova Sar' vnde Plit'm Conuencoi's suus' fuit int' eos in eadem Cur Scilt' qd' p'dei Henric & Vrsula retogu' p'dic't'ten cum'ptm esse ius' ipius' Joh'es Staples Ve illijque ijdem Johes & Johes West hent de dono p'dicor Henric & Vrsule Et ill pmesor' & quietilani dede ipis Henric & Vrsula & hereds suis p'dict' Joh'i & Joh'i & hereds ipius' Johis Staples imp'pm Et p'tot' ijdem Henr' & Vrsula concesser pro se & hereds ip'ius Henr' q'd ipi Sarau't p'deis' Joh'i & Joh'i & hered' ipius Johis Staples p'dea' ten'tum p'tin contr p'deos' Henr' & Vrsulam & hered' ipius Henr' imp'pm Et pro hacretogu' remissione quietilani' Warant fins & concordia ijdem Johes & Johes deder p'deis' Henr' & Vrsule trescentas librs sterlingor' :

(17) 1609. Thomas Goman.

This document, almost illegible, apparently from damp, is a Final Agreement for purchase of two messuages and gardens in the City of New Sarum by Thomas Goman from Edmund Uvedale for £80.

" Hac est finalis Concordia fact'in Cur D'ni Regis apud Westm' die pasche in quindecimo Anno regni Jacobi Regis Angl' ffranc Scotic hibni Regis fidei defensor &c. Angl ffranc Hibn' tricesimo octavo coram Edmundo Anderson Thoma Walingston Roggro Kingsnight Petro Edgburton & Will'o Daniell Justic & alijs d'ni Regis fidelibz tunc ibi p'sentibz Int' Thomam Goman quer' et Edmundum Vuedalle deforc' de duobz mesuagiis & duobz gardinis cum p'tin' in Ciuitate Nove Sar' vnde Plit'm conuenicoe's sum' fuit' int' eos in eadem Cur' Scilt' q'd p'd'cus Edmundus retogu' p'd'ct ten' cum p'tin ipius' Thomæ vt ille que idem Thomas he't de dono p'd'ci Edmundi . . . . primisibz quit'ni de se & hereds suis p'de's Thoma & hereds suis Imp'pm' Et p'tota idem Edmundus concessit pro se & hereds suis q'd ipi' p'dc'o Thome & hereds suis p'dc'a ten tent[u] p'dc'm Edmundum & hereds suos Imp'pm' Et pro hoc recogn p'missione lain' warant' fine & toucq, dic idem Thomas dedit p'dc'o Edmundo octoginta libras sterlingor'.

(18) 21 Aug., 1643. THIS INDENTURE made the one & Twentieth day of August & in the Nineteenth yeare of the reigne of our Sou'aigne Lord Charles by the grace of God Kinge of England Scotland ffrance & Ireland, defender of the faith &c. Between Thomas Chiffinch of the City of Newe Sarum in the County of Wilts Inholder & Xp'ofer Horte of the same City Mercer ffeoffees in trust of the lands of the p'ish Church of St. Martin's w'thin the said City of Newe Sarum in the said County of Wiltes George Antram of the same City Parchm[t]. maker & John Windover of the said City gent'. Churchwardens of the p'ish Church of St. Martins aforesaid of thone p'te and Henry ffricker of the City and County aforesaid yeoman of thother p'te. **Witnesseth** that the said Thomas Chiffinch Xp'ofer Horte George Antram & John Windover ffor and in Consideracon of the rente & Coven'nts hereafter in and by theis p[r]sents reserved & menconed on the p'te & behalf of the said Henry ffricker his executo[rs] administrato[rs] & assignes to be yealden don paid & p'formed **have** demised granted & to ferme letten and by theis p[r]sents doe demise graunt & to ferme let vnto the said Henry ffricker **All** that Corner Messuage or Tenem[t]. and garden w[th] the appurten'nes as it is nowe devided situate lyinge & beinge w'thin the City aforesaid in a certaine streete called Milford streete bounded w'th the said streete Called Milford streete on the North a certaine street called Culver street on the West lands of one John Grey on the East by the lands of the holy Trinity w'thin the said City of newe Sarum on the South And now in the tenure or occupac'on of the said Henry ffricker or of his assignee or assignes **To have** and to hold the said Corner Messuage or Tenem[t] & garden here by demised & eu'y p'te & p'cell thereof wth thappurten'es vnto the said Henry ffricker his executo[rs] administrato[rs] & assignes from the ffeast of S[t]. Michaell the Archangell next ensuinge the date hereof ffor by and dureinge & vnto the full end & tearme of one & thirty yeares from thence next ensuinge & fully to be Compleat & ended **yealding** and payeinge therefor yearely dureinge the said tearme vnto the said Thomas Chiffinch Xpo'fer Horte George Antram & John Windover theire heires and assignes the yearlye rente or sume of ffive pounds & Tenne shillings of currant English money At ffower ffeasts or tearmes in the yeare most usuall that is to say The ffeasts of

the Birth of our Lord and the Annunca'con of the blessed Virgin St. Mary the Nativity of St. John the Baptist & St. Michaell the Archangell by even and (equal porc'ons) **and** the said Henry ffricker for himselfe his executo^rs^ administrato^rs^ & assignes Doth Coven'nte p'mise & graunte to and wi^th^ the said Thomas Chiffinch Xpo'fer Horte George Antram & John Windover theire heires and assignes by theis p^r^sents that he the said Henry ffricker his executo^rs^ administrato^rs^ & assignes or some or one of of them at his & theire or some or one of theire owne proper Coste & chardge shall & will from tyme to tyme and at all tymes hereafter when and . . . . shall require dureinge the tearme hereby gr'unted well and sufficiently repaire uphold sustaine hedge fence keepe amend & maintaine the said p^r^misses hereby demised & eu'y p'te & p'cell thereof wth the appurten'nes in all manner of needful & necessary rep'acons & fenceings And the same & eu'y p'te thereof beinge soe well and sufficiently repaired upheld sustained hedged fenced kepte amended and maintained in the end expirac'on or other Determinac'on of the tearme hereby gr'unted shall & will (peaceably) and quietly leave and yeald upp unto the said Thomas Chiffinch Xpo'fer Horte George Antram & John Windover theire heires & assignes **And alsoe** that it shall & may be lawfull to and for the said Thomas Chiffinch Xpo'fer Horte George Antram & John Windover theire heires and assignes at all Convenient tyme & tymes dureinge the said Tearme to haue free lib'ty of ingresse egresse & regresse into and from the said demised p^r^misses & eu'y p'te & p'cell thereof & the apperten'nes to viewe see & search the decayes & lacke of rep'ac'on thereof & to give notice or warneinge for the repairinge and amendinge of the same if need shall require w^t^hout the lett deniall molestac'on or interrupc'on of the said Henry ffricker his executo^rs^ administrators or assignes **And if** it shall happen the said yearely rente or sum'e of ffive pounds & Tenne shillings or any p'te thereof to be behind & vnpaid in p'te or in all by the space of ffifteene dayes next after any or either of the said ffeasts or Dayes of paim^t^ on wch as aforesaid the su'me ought to be paid & beinge lawfully asked or demaunded & not paid **Or if** the said Messuage or Tenem^t^ & garden & eu'ry p'te thereof w^t^h the appurten'nces be not from tyme to tyme dureinge the said tearme of one & thirty yeares well and sufficiently repaired upheld sustained hedged fenced kept amended & maintained w^t^hin Six monethes next after notice or warneinge for the doeinge thereof shalbe given by the said Thomas Chiffinch Xpo'fer Horte George Antram & John Windover their heires & assignes vnto the said Henry ffricker his executo^rs^ administrato^rs^ & assignes or any of them at any tyme dureinge the tearme hereby gr'unted **Or if** if the said Henry ffricker . . . . . of them doe or shall at any tyme or tymes dureinge the said tearme bargaine sell lett assigne or sett over the said p[r]misses hereby demised or any p'te thereof to any p'son or p'sons whatsoever . . . . . . goodwill licence or Consente of the said Thomas Chiffinch Xpo'fer Horte George Antram & John Windover their heires and assignes in writeinge thereunto under theire hands & seales first . . . . thenceforth . . . this p[r]sent Indenture & eu'y thinge herein Conteyned shall cease determine & be utterly void And that then and from thencefourth and at all tymes after it shall & may be lawfull to and for the said Thomas Chiffinch Xpo'fer Horte George Antram & John Windover theire heires & assignes into the said Messuage or Tenem[t] & p[r]misses & eu'y p'te thereof w[th] the appurten'nes wholy to reenter & the same to haue againe repossesse & enioy as in theire any . . . . former estate or estates this Indenture or any thinge herein Conteyned to the contrary thereof in any wise notw[th]standinge **In witnes** whereof the said p'ties to theis p[r]sents haue hereunto Interchangeably sett theire hands & seales . . . . the day & yeare first aboue-written Annoqz Dom' 1643.

Without date. "Sold the Estate at Shapwicke to Mr. James Lambert of Shapwicke who lives upon the Estate, who is to pay the Quit Rent or Annuity from Michaellmas next when becomes Due, you may Direct to him to Shapwicke near Blandford by post."

xiiij[o] die novemb[r] a[o] regni Dnæ' Elizabeth
Regine decimo Octavo Etc'.

Receavyd the daye and yere abovesayde of Xpo'ffer player Churche warden of S[t]. martens the sum' of viij[s] and is for one hole yeres rent Dewe vnto the Quen's Matie endyd at the feaste of S[t]. mychaells tharchangell laste paste out of a corn' ten't in Wynchester Strete per me Thoma Eyre. } viij[s].

1448. Die Veneris xxi Junij xxxxxxxx

Placuit eisdem etiam tunc tempore quod magister Robertus Langrygge Communarius et Dominus Ricardus Trovy traderent ad firmam ecclesiam parochialem Sancti Martini alicui pistori in civitate sicquod ipse qui sic recipit ad firmam solvet firmam suam in panibus et elemosinis per manus communarij distribuendis et supra isto dederunt licentiam dictis Langrygge et Trovy quod mitterent pro Will'o Baker qui diu huiusmodi panes elemosinarios fecit ad computandum etc. an velit firmam illo modo capere quod si noluerit attemptarent alium pistorem.

(Burgh Register fo. 16 D & C of Salisbury Records).

Terra Ep'i Sarisberiensis Ep'atus Sar'
Hatcher p. 807.

Mylford

Reddit' assis' ib'm per annu'	xxiiii	ii	v
Terr' d'nic' per annu'	xxv	iiii	viii
Fin' he'itt coi'bz annis	—	lxx	—
Reddit' cert' ib'm annuatim	—	xlvi	—
	lv	iii	i

Unde

In feod' Ric'i Lobbe collect' reddit ib'm per annu'	—	xix	xi	ob
In feod' Willi' Londh subsenescalli man'iorum Sar' Wodford et Milford per ann'...	vi	—	—	
	lxii	iii	—	ob

Corp'acio Cano' Eccl'ie Cath' Sar'

R'coria S'ci Martini Civitatis Nove Sar' per annu'	xx	—	—

Milford P^at^.

In redd'n prati p'pe Milford voc' o^r^ Lady Mede per annu'	—	liii	iiii

Valor Ecclesiasticus vol. ii. p. 69.

A case reported in the subdecanal visitation
In the Church of St. Martin's 17 Aug. 1477.

Defamation.

In quada' cau' defamac'ois p'tens' int' Elizabet' Edward' p'och' Sci' Thome p'tem actricem et Jacobum Wryghtington famulu' Joh'is Ringewood p'och' Sc'i Martini ejusd' civitat' p'te' ream pretens' comparuerunt p'tes et q'z p'posita per actrice' negantur a reo datur term' ad p'ponend' in forma ju'. (*Hatcher*, p. 761).

Laudum sive arbitrium int' Decanum et Capitulu' Sar' et p'positu' eccl'ie Sc'i Edmundi sup' p'ceptione decimar' infra p'ochias eccliar' Scor' Martini et Edmundi Sar' 1400.

In Dei nomine Amen. Cum nuper orta erat discordia inter venerabiles viros Mg'rum Adam' Moleyns Decanum Eccl'ie Cath' Sar' et ejusd' Eccl'ie Capitulum ut rectores, et per pietarios eccli'e Parochialis Sc'i Martini Sarum ex una parte ac Mag'rum Will'm Spaldyngton p'positu' eccl'ie Collegiate Sc'i Edmundi Sar' cui quidem Eccl'ie Collegiate vicaria Sc'i Martini p'dict' est unita et annexa ex parte altera sup' p'ceptione decimarum maior' et minor' et p'sertim sup' p'ceptione decimarum feni cujusdam prati de novo redacti a pastura in pratum sepibus circumseptum vulgarit' vocatum "The newe mede under Larstock" cujus prati decima' dictus Magist' Will'imus ut vicarius Eccl'ie Sc'i Martini petit et vendicabat et ad vicaria' sua' p'tinere debere asserebat: Dictis Decano et Capitulo in contrarium opinantibus per p'terea quod maiores decime eccl'ie Sc'i Martini ad ipsos ut rectores et appropriétarios p'tiner' demonstrant'. Tandem partes p'dicte ad pacis concordiam convolantes coi't et concordit' ac unanimit' et indifferent' compromiserunt in Nos Johannem Pedwell subdecanum Eccl'ie Cath' Sar' Will'm Berwyck ejusd' Eccl'ie succentor' Simone' Houchyns et Johanne' Sypherwest in legibus baccalarios et elegerunt nos in arbitros arbitratores laudatores seu amicabiles compositores super controversia' p'dicta' p'mittentes se ratu' et gratu' atque firmu' habitur' ac nostro stare laudo et arbitrio sub pena quadraginta librar' prout patet in scriptis obligatoriis hinc inde confectis totum et quicquid nos conj'ti' laudaverimus et arbitramus vel maior pars nostru' laudaverit et arbitrata fuerit in p'missis. Nos igitur omnes hujusmodi compromissi in nos suscipientes pro bono pacis et concordie utrumqz part' p'dict' super om'ibus et singulis decimis p'missis ad quem seu ad quos p'tinere debent diligentius fecimus inquisitione' et habita per nos diligenti super hiis testimon' examinatione quor' dicta et testimonia in registro p'fator' decani et capituli inscriptis redigunt' ad p'petuam rei memoriam: Invenimus quod p'fati decanus et capitulum eccl'ie cathedral' p'dict' Rectores Sc'i Martini sunt dotati in omnibus decimis maioribus videlicet granor' et feni et p'fatus prepositus vicarius eccl'ie Sc'i Martini p'dict' ratione Vicarie sue est dotatus in minoribus decimis ut puta in decimis personalibus lane agnor' et ortor', in quibus crescunt olera cardones linum et cannabium. Quam ob rem nos p'fati Joh'es Pedwell Will'mus Berwyck Simon' Houchyns et Joh'es Sypherwest arbitri arbitratores sive amicabiles compositatores ut p'mittit' elect' ducimus firmamus laudamus et arbitramus ac pronunciamus laudum et arbitrium nostrum ad hunc modum; In primis Xti nomine primitus advocato et deu' p'oculis nostris habentes decernimus atque ordinamus quod predicti decanus et capitulum eccl'ie Sar' percipient' decimam omn' granorum et feni ubi ab antiquo percipere consueverunt infra fines et limites dicte Parochie Sc'i Martini ac eciam decimam feni sup'dicti prati vulgarit' vocat' Newe Mede integraliter et indistincte. Item decernimus ac ordinamus ut sup^{a} quod p'fatus p'positus et vicarius Sci Martini decimam agnorum et lane et omnium aliarum decimar' minor' provenienciu' infra fines et limites p'fate parochie Sc'i Martini integraliter et in solidum et quod p'cipiet decimam omn' ortor' sive gardinor' in quibus ab antiquo olera crescebant licet modo redacti sunt ad p'tum (pratum) sive agriculturam et de quibus vicarii Sc'i Martini qui protempore fu'int olim percipere consueverant. Et quantum ad ortos existentes super ripariam molendini Epi' non sumus informati nec aliqui testes sunt examinati quare ad presens nolumus laudare super illa materia (*Hatcher* pp. 755, 756) Bishops Records, Reg. Rub. Huchyns Register, Chapter Records. H.

The dispute was afterwards renewed, and a new composition took place.

St. Martin's (*Hatcher*, page 703).

In page 242 it is observed that Bishop Poor, in the institution of St. Martin's, "vested the Rectory in the Dean and Chapter, and appropriated the tithes of corn and hay to their commons, they perhaps, as was usual in such cases, being bound to provide for the spiritual wants of the parish, by the appointment of a Vicar' in the antient and strict sense of the term." This supposition must, however, be acknowledged to be erroneous altogether. In the deed of institution of St. Martin's the Bishop vests no new right in the Dean and Chapter; but on the contrary, expressly reserves the rights which they had previously possessed, apparently in virtue of the grant of the tithes of the church of Sarum, contained in the charter of Bishop Osmund. The vicarage of St. Martin's was united with the provostship of St. Edmund's at some early period, now unknown, and continued united with that office till it was abolished at the Dissolution. In all subsequent documents also the Dean and Chapter are expressly mentioned as Rectors of St. Martin's, and no record of the appointment of a Vicar to that church occurs till after the Reformation.

Fielding Fielding, the novelist, having lived in this parish some years, anything relating to him must be of interest.

Fielding, the novelist, married a lady of Salisbury named Craddock. He first occupied the house in the Close, on the South side of St. Anne's Gate. He afterwards removed to that in St. Ann's Street, next to the Friary (now a School), and finally established himself in the mansion at the foot of Milford Hill where he wrote a considerable part of his "Tom Jones." *Thwackum* is said to have been drawn for Mr. Hele, master of the Close School. *Square*, the philosopher, for Chubb, the Deist. *Dowling*, the lawyer, for a person named Stillingfleet, who exercised that profession. *The Golden Lion*, where the ghost was acted, was at the corner of the Market place and Winchester Street, and the person who sustained this part was *Doughty*, one of the serjeants at mace.

Humphry Beckham. Humphry Beckham, born 1588. Died 1671. Was apprenticed to Mr. Rosgrave, a painter and gilder, of this city.

William Dodsworth. William Dodsworth was a natural son of Captain Dodsworth. He was born in Salisbury, 1760. Apprenticed to a tailor, and at an early age was appointed one of the vergers of the Cathedral. He died 1826.

o Barracks. The Barracks in Brown Street was the mansion of the family of Hussey. In 1574 it was sold by John Hussey and Margaret his wife to John Gifford. The garden then extended to Catherine Street. It then passed to Dodington, then to Dowce. 1657, it was the property of Edward Edwards, Ambassador to the Low Countries. In 1724 it passed to Richard Mortimer, then to Walter Sheppard. In 1790 to William Benson Earle, who bequeathed it to the late Rev. E. Benson and Edward Earle Benson as joint tenants, then to his son, the Recorder. Mr. Hicks afterwards purchased it and pulled it down.

1651. The Landlord of the King's Arms was named Huet or Hewett.

ohn Tobin. John Tobin, solicitor, was born in Endless Street, in the house now (1840) occupied by Mr. Foot, solicitor. His mother was daughter of Mr. Webb, of the Manor House, Stratford, an opulent West Indian merchant.

rtin's Croft. Martin's Croft in 1428 is described as being opposite the cemetery of St. Edmund.

1398. The Workhouse in Brown Street.

1230. The Grey Friars. 1335, the Blackfriars at Fisherton are mentioned.

John Pern Tinney. John Pern Tinney was baptised at St. Martin's Church 17 July, 1779, having been born at Gillingham, Dorset, November 24, 1777. The family was anciently settled at South Barrow, Somerset, and a freehold estate for many generations belonged, and still belongs, to them. His mother, an heiress, whose maiden name was Pern, was descended from Dr. Andrew Pern, Master of St. Peter's College, and Dean of Ely in the 16th century, who was selected by Archbishop Parker to translate from the Hebrew a portion of the Bible, commonly called the Bishop's Bible. His (J. P. Tinney's) mother was great grand-daughter of Bishop Stillingfleet. He (J. P. T.) was educated at the School of the Canons, in the Close, then under Dr. Skinner. He entered as Commoner of Edmund Hall, Oxford, being then designed for the Church. He was articled to his father, a solicitor, who died 1801, leaving a widow and ten children, before he proceeded to Oxford. He quitted Oxford on the death of his father, and established himself in Salisbury in his father's profession, and thus aided in the support of his family. He married in the year 1822 Charlotte, the widow of the Rev. Arthur May, by whom he had an only daughter, who died in her infancy. He died January 24, 1832, and was buried in the family vault on the south side of the chancel of St. Martin's Church.

Godolphin School. In 1720 a bequest was made by Dr. Henry Godolphin, Dean of St. Paul's and Provost of Eton, of certain monies then vested in foreign funds, to be applied to the care and education of eight young gentlewomen "so born," whose parents were of the Church of England and whose fortunes did not exceed £300. Their friends were to provide them with decent apparel, and they were not to be admitted before the age of eight nor remain after that of 19. They were to be brought up in the City of New Sarum, or at some town in the county of Wilts, under a prudent governess, who was herself a communicant of the Church of England. By the will of his relict, Eliza, dated in July, 1724, it appears that the money had been remitted to England, to the amount of £3359, and that by an addition subsequently made she had increased it to £5000, to be invested in the purchase of lands. She made also some modifications in the original arrangement of her husband, especially in directing that the young ladies should be boarded with the governess, and taught to dance, work, read, write, and cast accounts, and be instructed in the business of housewifery; and that their portions should not respectively exceed £400. She farther committed the fulfilment of this bequest to her nephew, William Godolphin, and his heirs, to whom she assigned the nomination of the governess and the management of the charity, directing them, in case of difficulty, to recur to the Court of Chancery. By a codicil, dated July 2nd, 1725, she had disposed of the money in the purchase of annuities, arising out of lands in Somersetshire, viz., £120 out of the estate of Thos. Nichols, £40 out of that of Thomas Burgess, and £20 out of that of Hannah Burgess.

1780. Since the year 1734 no steps had been taken towards the establishment of the Godolphin School. The matter had been referred to the decision of the Court of Chancery, and the property had for many years remained under its control. Mr. Edwards, of Salisbury, had received the rents till Christmas, 1776; that Mr. Simon Wetherall had been appointed receiver by the Court since that period, and had remitted the rents till Christmas, 1779; that £300 was to be paid into the bank where the other arrears had been deposited. Mr. Wetherall had lately died, but his executors had remitted his accounts to Mr. Nicholls, of the Six Clerks office, for settlement, and the payment of the balance. Lastly, on 22nd May, the Court ordered a receiver to be appointed (*Hatcher* p.p, 516 and 533).

In 1788 the School was in Rosemary Lane, Miss Gifford being mistress.

Miss Gifford was succeeded by Mrs. Davis, who in 1815 was followed by Miss Anna Maria Alford; on her resignation Miss Emly became governess, and continued till her death in 1832.

Miss Bazley succeeded Miss Emly. Miss Bazley lived in the Close, in the King's House (now the Training College), whence she removed to the house in Milford Grove where Mr. Fulton now lives. Miss Bazley was followed by Miss Polhill in the same house, whence she removed to Elm Grove, now Fawcett House.*

* Miss Polhill was succeeded by her sister, Miss Emma Polhill.

Then Miss Andrews became mistress. Since the reconstruction in 1886 Miss Douglas has been Principal.

The endowment :—

	A.	R.	P.		Per annum. £	s.	d.
Wick Farm, Glastonbury ...	114	1	5,	value	155	9	0
Laurence House, Glastonbury ...	2	3	33	,,	248	6	0
Lawrence Farm, Glastonbury ...	48	1	24	,,	107	1	5
Sand Hole	0	3	20	,,	22	0	0

Two rent charges in West Pennard of £40 and £20 per annum.

The following inscription is taken from a monument in the cloister of Westminster Abbey :—

"Here rest in hopes of a blessed resurrection, Charles Godolphin, Esq. (brother to the Right Hon. Sidney, Earl of Godolphin, Lord High Treasurer of Great Britain), who died July the 10th, 1720, aged 69, and Mrs. Godolphin, his wife, who died July the 29th, 1726, aged 63, whose excellent qualities and endowments can never be forgotten; particularly the public spirited zeal with which he served his country in Parliament, and indefatigable application, great skill and nice integrity, with which he discharged the trust of a Commissioner of the Customs many years. Nor was she less eminent for her ingenuity, wit, sincere love of her friends, and constancy in religious worship. But as charity and benevolence were the distinguishing parts of their characters, so were they most conspicuously displayed by the last act of their lives: a pious and charitable institution by him designed and ordered, and by her compleated to the glory of God, and for a bright example to mankind, the endowment whereof is a rent-charge of one hundred and eighty pounds a year, issuing out of lands in Somersetshire and of which one hundred and sixty pounds a year are to be for ever applied from the 24th of June, 1726, to the educating eight young Gentlewomen, who are so born, and whose parents are of the Church of England, and whose fortunes do not exceed three hundred pounds, and whose parents or friends undertake to provide them with decent apparel; and after the death of the said Mrs. Godolphin and William Godolphin, Esq., her Nephew, such as have neither Father or Mother, which same young Gentlewomen are not to be admitted before they are eight years old, nor to be continued after the age of nineteen, and are to be brought up at the city of New Sarum, or some other town in the county of Wilts, under the care of some prudent Governess, or Schoolmistress, a Communicant of the Church of England, and the overplus, after an allowance of five pounds a year, for collecting the said rent-charge, is to be applied to the binding out one or more poor children apprentices whose parents are of the Church of England. In perpetual memory whereof Mrs. Frances Hall, executrix to her aunt Mrs. Godolphin, has, according to her will, and by her order, caused this inscription to be engraved on their monument. 1727."

(*S. & W. J.*, Nov. 28, 1768.)

1395. Visitation held in the Church of St. Thomas.

Adam Charles, Vicar of St. Martin.

Adam Teffont, Thomas Eyr, William Hull, Stephen Edyngton, John Marye, Thomas Touner, John Hogeman, William Raynold, John Corpe, John Feror, webber, Peter Wotton, Robert Durant, parishioners, were cited to appear.

William Caundell, Chaplain of the Hospital of the Trinity.

1613. Receaued the eyght daye of April An°. D'ni 1613 Anoqz regni D'ni Jacobi Regis undecimo of Mr. Will'm Bennett, Gent. the sum of fiev pounds thyrtene shillings & foure pence being rent due unto the Deane & Chapter of Saru' f & for the personage of St. Martyns adioyning to the Cyttye of Saru' fiev pounds & thyrtene shillings and foure pence being rent due for certeyne meads neare Saru' called oure Ladyes meades for one quarter ended att the feast of the Annunciation of the blessed Virgin Marye last past before the date hereof. Receved I saye

by me Thomas Paynter Co'moner to The Deane & Chapter of Saru'.

Burials in Gigant Street at the Friends' Meeting House.

1772. April 26th. Died at Bath Miss Moore, daughter of Mr. James Moore, of this city, and the Sunday following her corpse was interred in the Quakers' burying ground at the meeting house in Gigant street. (*S. & W. J.*, May, 11, 1772.)

On Thursday morning died in childbed Mrs. Riley, wife of Mr. Riley, shopkeeper at Wilton, and the next day her corpse was interred in the burial ground belonging to the Quakers' meeting in this city. (*S. & W. J.*, Nov. 23, 1772.)

1778. Oct. 17th, died in an advanced age, at his house at Grenton, near Glastonbury, Mr. James Moore, of this city, a retired clothier. A sensible, honest Quaker, a man of fortune and good character, much esteemed and respected by all who knew him. We hear he is to be interred at the Quakers' meeting in this city, on Wednesday next. (*S. & W. J.*, Oct. 26, 1778.)

1784. On 2nd inst. died Miss Mary Moore, in the Oatmeal Row, and one of the people called Quakers. And on Wednesday last her remains were attended by many of those respectable people to the place of interment in Jigging street, where they were deposited in very decent solemnity. (*S. & W. J.*, July 8, 1784.)

1769. Lately departed this life Mrs. Rachel Philips, wife of Mr. Philips the Baptist Minister in this city. She was buried on Lord's day afternoon, 29th January, 1769, at the Baptist Meeting in Brown Street. (*S. & W. J.*, Feb. 6, 1769.)

1784. On 19th inst. died Mrs. Philips, wife of Mr. Philips, Baptist Minister of this city, who was very exemplary in the Christian temper and life. (*S. & W. J.*, Nov. 27, 1784.) Late Mrs. Evans, married Mr. P. 1776, Feb.

Nathaniel Spinckes, Rector of St. Martin's, 1687.

Nathaniel Spinckes, Preb. of Sarum, Rector of St. Martin's, Salisbury, Nonjuring Bishop, was born at Castor, in Northants, where his father was Rector, and educated under a neighbouring rector, Samuel Morton, of Haddon, until he went to Trinity College, Cambridge, in 1670. In 1673, he migrated to Jesus, where he was elected scholar on the Rustat foundation. Having received Holy Orders, he acted as chaplain, first to Sir Richard Edgecombe, at Mount Edgecombe, and then to the Duke of Lauderdale, at Petersham. On the duke's death, in 1682, he became curate and lecturer at St. Stephen's, Walbrook. In 1685, he was presented by the Dean and Chapter of Peterborough to the rectory of Peakirk-cum-Glinton, where he married; and in 1687 he became a prebendary and rector of St. Martin's at Salisbury. Of course, he lost all his preferments when he refused the oaths, and he was for a time in straitened circumstances. He is an instance of a Nonjuror who had recourse to literary activity when practical activity was denied him. He published nothing before the Revolution, but after that event his pen was very busy till his death. Beneath his portrait, inserted in the fourth edition of his "Sick Man Visited," is this inscription :—"'The Rev. Mr. Spinckes.' This very eminent divine was venerable of aspect, orthodox in truth, his adversaries being judges. He had uncommon learning and superior judgment. His patience was great, his self-denial greater, his charity still greater; his temper sweet and unmoveable beyond comparison. It is said that he never made a personal enemy." The following epitaph in the burial ground of St. Faith's, on the north side of St. Paul's, where he was interred, really seems to say no more than the truth. His wife survived him only seven days :—

Depositum
Viri plane reverendi
NATHANAELIS SPINCKES, A.M.
Ortu Northamptoniensis
Academia Cantabrigiensis
Ecclesiæ Anglicanæ Pr. dignissimi,
Amicis, patriæ, erudito orbi,
XVIII. Jul. MDCCXXVII.
Abrepti.
Erat ille ingenio miti,
Vultu placidissimo :
Rem Christianam
Scriptis tuebatur luculentis,
Luculentiori ornabat exemplo.
Crederes antiquorum Patrum
Et mores et doctrinam
In nostrum Theologum,
Nupero quasi miraculo,
Transfusos
Moritur
Anno ætatis Septuagesimo Quarto,
Iniqua fortuna non diuturnior
Sed major.
Proximam huic terram occupat Dorothea conjux.

He was essentially a learned man, and a man of varied accomplishments, and he was by no means disinclined to enter the lists of controversy. He wrote five separate treatises on the Roman Controversy of a strongly anti-Roman character ; one against the French Prophets, a set of fanatics who made a great sensation in England in the early part of the 18th century ; one against that very able latitudinarian, Benjamin Hoadly, and several against "the Usagers." He was an accomplished linguist, being a proficient in Greek, Latin, Anglo-Saxon, and French, and having some knowledge of the Oriental languages. His brother Nonjurors had so great confidence in him as a Grecian that they engaged him to translate into Greek the proposals of union which they sent to the Greek Church ; and he had so high a reputation for general knowledge that he is said to have been called in to assist in the writing of such different kinds of works as Grabe's "Septuagint," Newcourt's "Repertorium," Laurence Howell's "Synopsis Canonum," Archbishop Potter's "Clemens Alexandrinus," and Walker's "Sufferings of the Clergy." But he was even better known by his contemporaries for his goodness than for his erudition, and he is chiefly remembered by posterity for his devotional works. Spinckes was always, and rightly, regarded as one of the chief saints of the Nonjuring community. He was consecrated a bishop at large of the Catholic Church on Ascension Day, June 3, 1713, together with Jeremy Collier and Samuel Hawes, without any titular see. (*The Nonjurors*, by Canon Overton.)

In "A History of the Nonjurors," by Thomas Lathbury, M.A., page 161, it is stated :—"Spinkes was permitted to serve his parish by a curate."

Within the church are some monuments; the altar piece and other parts of the Church are "beautified," as the churchwardens commonly term it, with painted panels, scroll work, and carving from the Cathedral. *(Beauties of Wiltshire, by John Britton, 1813.)*

John Thornborough

Was born in St. Martin's parish, Sarum, and educated in the free-school in that City. In 1570 he became Demy of Magdalen College, Oxon, at the age of 18. After he had taken a Degree in Arts he was ordained and constituted Chaplain to the Earl of Pembroke, who, after some time, conferred on him the Rectory of Chilmark, Wilts. The same Patron had him nominated one of the Chaplains in ordinary to Queen Elizabeth, whereby he got another benefice in Yorkshire,

Being now on the road to preferment, on the promotion of Dr. Matthew Hutton to the See of Durham he was advanced to the Deanery of York, October 28, 1589, and soon after installed. In 1593 he was made Bishop of Limerick, in Ireland, where, performing many singular services to the Government, he was translated to the See of Bristol in 1603, with liberty to hold the Deanery of York in Commendam. Feb. 17, 1616, he was removed to Worcester, where he continued to his death.

Thornborough was esteemed as a man of wisdom, learning, and courage. He was particularly skilled in Chemistry.

He published :—

1. "The joyful and blessed re-uniting the two mighty and famous Kingdoms of England and Scotland, into their antient name of Great Britain, 1605."
2. "A Treatise on the same subject in 1604."
3. "Λιθοθεωρικος: sive nihil, aliquid, omnia ingratiam, eorum, qui artem Auriferam physico-chemice & pie profitentur. Oxon, 1621."
4. "The last will and testament of Jesus Christ, touching the blessed Sacrament of his body and blood. Oxon, 1630."
5. "A Discourse shewing the great happiness that hath, and that may still accrue to his Majesty's Kingdom of

England and Scotland, by re-uniting them in one Great Britain. In two parts. London, 1641."

"Pax vobis. Concerning the unity and peace of the Church."

He departed this life the 9th day of July, 1641, at Hartleborough, in Worcestershire, and was buried in his own Cathedral, near a fair Alabaster Monument which 14 years before he had erected to himself, with his Statue in Episcopal Robes, curiously carved, lying thereon. *(Antiquitates Sarisburiensis.)*

The Registers.

The Earliest book is handsomely bound in Calf. On the cover is inscribed Saint Martin's/parish register/1559 to 1650/.

This is somewhat misleading. The entries are neatly written from November 1559 to December 1604 (Baptisms). Marriages from September 1559 to Aprill 1607.

Buryalls from August 1559 to March $16\frac{04}{05}$. From this period there is a blank in each case till 1630.

On the first leaf is, in Old English characters, "This Booke of Records for/Christeninges, Mariages/and Buryalles Belongeth/to saynte Martin's Church/of Sarum written by me/Thomas Smythe parishe/Clarke in the yeare/of our lord God 1599; and/in the XLI yeare of the Raigne/of our soueraigne Ladye/Queene Elizabeth and in/Tyme of Lancelott Dauys/ and Maister John./*

1634. Churchwardens Iohn Windover & Christopher New (Register).

Notes on the Rectors.

1604. Dec. 20. John Odell was appointed as Prebendary of Gillingham Minor alias Axford. He died in 1628.

1660. Aug. 26. Francis Horton was appointed Prebendary of Alton Borealis and

Sept. 9 to Bedminster and Redcliffe. Canon Resident Vicar of Melksham 1686.

He was successively incumbent of St. Martin and St. Thomas.

In 1683 he was "locum tenens" for the Dean.

He wrote "Reasons why the Bishop of Sarum's visitation should not extend *ultra annum*." "His reply to the Bishop's plea with the rejoinder," a letter from him to Archb. Sancroft (1685). There is also a letter to the Archbishop from R. Woodward, Canon of Salisbury, on "The proceedings against Francis Horton in

* Maister John is John Baylie, who, with Lancelott Davys, was Churchwarden that year.

the Consistory Court for disrespectful language to the Judge of that Court, and an account of such conduct" (Jones' Fasti, p. 354).

1661. Aug. 17. Thomas Henchman was appointed as Prebendary of Netherbury in Ecclesia. He was Archdeacon of Wiltshire 1663.

1679. Feb. 7. Timothy Morton was appointed Prebendary of Yatesbury.

Sept. 18. Of Major pars Altaris.

1687. July 25. Nathaniel Spinks was appointed as Prebendary of Major pars Altaris. Deprived 1689; non-juring Bishop.

1694. June 28. Peter Terry was appointed as Prebendary of Major pars Altaris. Succentor 1703, May 24.

1751. July 3. John Lumby was appointed as Prebendary of Minor pars Altaris and

1756. March 6 to Alton Australis. He died in 1757.

1905. Dec. 21. St. Thomas's Day the Rev. Charles Myers, M.A., was installed as Prebendary of Durnford in Salisbury Cathedral.

Notes.

1310. December 10, Richard Pynock gave by his will to the fabric of the Church of St. Martin xij^{s}.

1346. John de Homington gave to the Church of St. Martin, Sarum, by his will dated on the day of the Sabbath on the feast of St. Matthias the Apostle vj^{d}. (25th February.)

1348. Henry Baudrie, of New Sarum, left by his last will to the fabric of St. Martin's Sarum iij^{s}. iiij^{d}.

1406. John Chaundler senior by his will dated 10th May gave to the Church of St. Martin xx^{s}.

1605. "I geve to my brother William Bennett of Norton Bavent my lease of the parsonadge of Saint Martin's in Sarum."

(From the Will of Thomas Bennett of Westburye under the plaine dated 3d daye of maye 1605.)

(From "Conforming Clergy under the Directory of Public Worship and Intruded Ministers and Preachers" by Rev. Chr. Wordsworth, M.A.)

Gower Stanley. Appointed to St. Martin's Salisbury about 1649 (Shaw II. 546).

Eyre W., M.A., son of Giles Eyre, of Whiteparish in Wilts, became a rigid Calvanist, and in 1654 assistant commissioner for ejecting "scandalous" ministers and schoolmasters, some of them his former friends or acquaintances (Wood, Ath. II. 458). He appears to have ministered at St. Martin's, Salisbury, in 1649 as successor to Stanley Gower (Shaw II. 546).

Mr. Eyres appears as minister at "St. Martin's in Milford," Salisbury. W. Eyre. Battler or commoner and subsequently tutor of Magd. Hall, Oxon., 1629. R. of Compton Bassett 1641, sequestrated to Odstock. R. Minister of St. Edmund's, Sarum. Died at Melksham 1670, where he had an estate—Mentioned as "Pastor of St. Thomas in Sarum in August 1655" (Peck, Desid. Cur. II. 493). There in 1658—9 (Wilts Mag. Vol. xxxiv. p. 179).

Hillary, or Ellary Antony, son of J. Ellary, of Salisbury, pleb. B.A. Ch. Ch. Minister at Winterbourne Gunner. He had been Vicar of St. Martin's, Salisbury, in 1632—45.

Troughton, William, son of W. Troughton, of Waberthwayt, Cumberland, sacerd. Queen's Coll., Oxon. Chaplain to Col. Hammond, I. of Wight 1647. St. Martin's, Salisbury, about 1658—9* (Shaw II. 397, Calamy II. 756). "Preach'd often in private after he was silenced at Salisbury; and he did the like afterwards at Bristol. He wrote an Exposition of Ps. 45."

In St. Martin's Register are also the following entries:—

1654. Aug. 5. Charles son of Nathaniell ffoster, Minister (Buried).

1656. May 7. Alice daughter of John Willson a Minister (Baptized).

Nathanael Spinkes only signs the Register once as Rector, viz. 1688.

Peter Terry signs as Rector in 1689 and the succeeding years.

Translation of the Foregoing Latin Documents in St. Martin's Parish Chest.

Page 132. A.D. 1465. Be it known to all present and to come that I, William Wotton have delivered demised and by this my present charter have confirmed to Edward Chitterne, Robert Chandeler, John leyed, John Frances, Thomas leker, John Hamersmyth, Thomas Gleber, Nicholas Stote, Thomas Blakker, John Jacob, John Brydmer, Robert Newe & Henry Wotton those my two Cottages with their gardens and other appurtenances situate together in New Sarum, in Culver Street, between the Cottages late of Richard Barwe on the south part, & the Cottages of Thomas Knoyle on the north part, which same cottages with their gardens and other appur-

* His name is mentioned in St. Martin's Register in 1653 as follows:—

1653. Oct. 14. Martha daughter of Mr. William Troaten, Minister (Baptized).

Jan. 30. William Troaten son of Mr. William Troaten, Minister (Buried).

tenances I lately had together with William Cokkys, William Halsted, John Cleve, Brewer, William Prydy & Thomas Saundre of the City of New Sarum now deceased by the gift & feoffment of Edith who was wife of William Caunbrigge late citizen of London, John Caumel late of New Sarum aforesaid now deceased, Thomas Gabayn, William Merwe & Robert Smyth of London under certain conditions as more fully appears in a certain indenture thereof made, dated at New Sarum on the Wednesday next after the feast of the Assumption of the blessed virgin Mary, in the nineteenth year of the reign of King Henry VI. after the conquest. To have and to hold the aforesaid two cottages with their gardens and other appurtenances as is above mentioned by the beforenamed Edward, John, John, Thomas, John, Thomas, Nicholas, Thomas, John, John, Robert & Henry their heirs & assigns for ever of the chief Lord of the city aforesaid by rents & services thence due and of right accustomed under the condition & intention of Observing and holding all those agreements & conditions as it is declared in the aforesaid indenture as I myself the aforesaid William Wotton together with the aforesaid William Cokkys, William Halstede, John Glebe, William Prydy & Thomas Saundre am tied & bound by virtue & reason of the aforesaid Indenture In Witness whereof I have affixed my seal to this my present charter. And because my Seal is unknown to many I have procured this seal together with the seal of the office of the mayoralty of the city of New Sarum to be affixed, these being witnesses: William Wotton then Mayor of Sarum, John Whittokesmede, then bailiff there, Robert Geve, then coroner there, Henry ffrende & Hugh Fitzrichard, then provosts there, Thomas Freeman . . . . Hore sen^r^., William Swayne, John Syse, Edmund Penston & John Craswell, then treasurer, and many others. Dated at New Sarum aforesaid the fifteenth day of the month of September. In the year of the reign of King Edward the fourth after the Conquest of England, the fourth.

[...]e 133. [...]I., 1442. Know all men by these presents that I Richard Gage of New Sarum have remitted released & wholly for me & my heirs for ever quit claimed to Radulph Pakker his heirs & Assigns all my right & claim which I have or in any manner in future may have in those two cottages with garden, dovecot and all other appurtenances which are situated in New Sarum adjoining the Graveyard of the Church of St. Martin there on the east part & the tenement late of John Dogskyn on the west part, which same cottages with garden, dovecot & all other their appurtenances I lately had in common with John Dudlegh & William Godmanston by the gift and feoffment of Robert Haras. So that neither I the said Richard nor my heirs, nor anyone else in my name may wholly in future be able to exact or claim any right or claim in the aforesaid cottages with garden, dovecot and their other appurtenances nor in any part of the same nor in . . . . nor thence nor by service towards the aforesaid Radulph his heirs or assigns. But from all actions, rights . . . . customs quit claims be for ever excluded [and I] the aforesaid Richard my heirs will warrant for ever the aforesaid two cottages with garden, dovecot and all other their appurtenances to the aforesaid Radulph his heirs and assigns against all men. In witness whereof to these presents I have affixed my Seal & the Common Seal with the Seal of the Mayoralty of the City aforesaid I have in like manner procured to be affixed. These being witnesses Robert Long then Bailiff of the City aforesaid, John Wyet then Mayor there, Robert Cove & William Halsted then Coroners there, Thomas Somse and William Olyver then prepositi there, William Wardeyk, Robert Warmwell, Henry Man, Thomas ffrennch, John Aport & many others. Dated at New Sarum. In the feast of St. Nicholas the bishop. In the year of the reign of Henry the sixth after the conquest the twentieth. (1442).

Page 134. 1445. Be it known to all present & to come that I John Clyve. Brewer, have given, granted and by this my present charter have confirmed to Richard Hogge of the City of New Sarum, Carpenter, those six cottages with their appurtenances together situate in the City aforesaid in Culverstreet between the cottages of Robert Knoell on the south part & the cottage of John Pope on the north part which same cottages with their appurtenances I lately had by the gift & feoffment of the aforesaid Richard Hogge as in a certain charter thereof to me made by Richard himself more fully appears to have & to hold the aforesaid six cottages with their appurtenances to the beforementioned Richard Hogge his heirs & assigns of the chief lord of the City aforesaid by services thence owing and of right accustomed for ever by these presents. In witness whereof to this my present charter I nave affixed my seal. And the Common Seal together with the Seal of the Mayoralty of the City aforesaid I have procured to be similarly affixed these being witnesses Robert longe, Esquire, then bailiff of the City aforesaid, William Hore then mayor of the same City, William Halstede & Robert Cove then Coroners there, Thomas Silke & Thomas Benet, Helyer, then prepositi at the same place, Robert Warmwell, William Wardeyk, William Pakyn, John Wyet, Thomas ffreman John Hampton, Philip Morgan, Thos. & others. Dated at New Sarum on Sunday in the feast of All Saints in the year of the reign of King Henry the Sixth after the conquest of England the twenty third.

Page 137.
2d April,
zabeth (year
ced, but dur-
the Episco-
of Edmund
Gheast),
71—1577.

To all the faithful in Christ to whom this present writing Indented shall come Thomas Jacob of the City of New Sarum in the county of Wilts Tanner, Nicholas Storie of the city aforesaid in the County aforesaid Tanner and John Ockford of East harnham in the county aforesaid tallow chandler Greeting in the Lord everlasting. **Know ye** that we the beforenamed Thomas Jacob, Nicholas Storie . . . Edertas for and in consideration of a certain sum of good and lawful money of England before the sealing of these presents in hand paid by Henry Evered senior, John Taylor, John Jervis, Daniel Kyffyn, Charles Jacob, Robert Bundye, Richard Emory, Christopher Player, Francis Davys, Robert Crede, Roger . . . James Evered, Henry Evered Junior, John Batt, Thomas Batt, Charles Jacob Junr, John Crede and Anthony Crede whereby we acknowledge ourselves fully satisfied and contented by these presents **Have given**, granted, and by this our present writing have confirmed to the beforenamed Henry Evered senior, John Tayler, John Jervys, Daniel Kyffyn, Charles Jacob senior, Christopher Batt, Robert Bundye, Richard Emerye, Christopher Player, Francis Davys, Robert Crede, Roger Evered, James Evered, Henry Evered Junior, John Batt, Thomas Batt, Charles Jacob Junr, John Crede and Anthony Crede all that our Corner Tenement or messuage and our garden with appurtenances and our five little tenements called Almshouses with appurtenances, Situate, lying and being together in the City of New Sarum aforesaid in two ways there called Milford Streat between the land of a certain James Andrewes on the west part; the way there on the east and north, and the land of a certain Robert Walker on the south part. **Moreover** four tenements or messuages and our four gardens with appurtenances situate . . . in the City aforesaid in the aforesaid street called Culver Streat between land formerly of the aforesaid Robert Walker on the north part, the land of John Baylie on the south part, the King's way on the east part and land formerly of John Coriet, gent., deceased and land formerly of John Abyn, gent., deceased on the west part. And one other tenement or messuage and our garden . . . in the city aforesaid in a street there called Culver streat between land of John Baylie on the north part and land formerly of Thomas Cater, Deceased, on the south part and the King's way on the east part and land of John Coles on the west part. And . . . four other tenements or messuages and our four gardens with appurtenances situate and being together in the City . . . aforesaid . . . there called St. Martyns Streat between the King's way there leading to the Church of St. Martyn on the north . . . a certain meadow of the reverend father in Christ Edmund Bishop of Salisbury called Bugmore meadow on the south part . . . ison on the west part and the Graveyard of the parish church of St. Martin aforesaid on the east part. [And also] our tenement or message and garden with appurtenances Situate, lying and being in the City of New Sarum . . . in a street there called Dragon's Streate, between the land of Ann Coriett widow on the north part, late of William Holmes . . . of Sendlo deceased on the south part, the land of the aforesaid William Holmes on the east part and the King's way leading from the city aforesaid as far as to Harnam bridge on the west part (Moreover) . . . To have and to hold all and singular the aforesaid messuages or tenements, lands, tenements . . . the other premises all and singular with all and singular their appurtenances whatsoever to the aforesaid Henry Evered Senior, John Bayley, John Tayler, Daniel Kyffyn, Charles Jacob senior, Christopher Batt, Robert Bundye, Richard Emery, Christopher Player, Francis Davys, Robert Crede, Roger Evered, James Evered, Henry Evered Junior, John Batt, Charles Jacob Junr, John Crede and Anthony Crede their heirs and assigns for ever to the sole behoof and use of them, Henry Evered, John Taylor, &c. [To have and] to hold of the chief Lords [of that] fee [by rents and services] due and of right accustomed. And we indeed the aforesaid Thomas Jacob, Nicholas Storie and John . . . all and singular the aforesaid messuages, tenements, lands, gardens . . . . singular . . . . to Henry Evered &c. their heirs and assigns against us and our heirs will warrant, acquit and for ever defend. . . . Furthermore [know ye that] we the beforenamed (Thomas) Jacob, Nicholas Storie and John (Ockford) have ordained constituted . . . by our . . . our beloved in Christ Thomas Seynt barbe and William Holmes gentlemen our true and lawful attorneys . . . and Commisioners for us and in our [place and names] into the aforesaid tenements, messuages, lands, gardens and all and singular the other appurtenances with all and singular . . . . in the place and in the names of the aforesaid Henry Evered Senior, John Bayley, John Tayler, Daniel Kyffyn, Charles Jacob senior, Christopher Batt, Robert Bundye, Richard Emery, Christopher Player, Francis Davys, Robert Crede, Roger Evered, James Evered, Henry Evered Junr, John Batt, Charles Jacob Junr, John Crede and Anthony Crede.

Dated the second day of April, In the year of the reign of our Lady Elizabeth, by the grace of God of England, France and Ireland. Date missing, but as it was in the time of Edmund, Bishop of Sarum, it must have been during the Episcopate of Edmund Gheast, 1571—1577.

Page 139. Grovely & Clarendon. Grovely forest The Custody of a moiety of the same, viz.
The North bayley as Grymes ditch divides from
The fee and profits : The appurtenances and rents issuing from
Escheat
25 Edward III. after the death of William Ruintyn No. 61.
belongs to the Manor of Wycheford and ought
to have housbote & : and pasturage for animals
Robert Brent holds the Manor of Wycheford from
The Lord the King as of his Duchy of Lancaster; in
Socage by what service they know not. Esc. 9. H. 5., No. 25.
William Ruyntyn holds on the day of his death, one messuage and
lx. acres of land 3 acres of meadow and 8 shillings rent in
Wycheford Magna from the lord the King in Capite
by Serjeanty to be forester of the Lord
the King in Grovely and by the service of two shillings per annum
to be paid at the Castle of Sarum : Escheat, 15 Edward III.,
No. 17.

at. 6, H. 4, j. m. 8. The King hath granted to John Earl of Somerset the Custody
of our forest and park of Clarendon.
and of the forests of Grovely Melchet and
Bukholt to hold for the whole life of the Earl himself
with all fees and profits &c.

'at. ii.H. 4. p. 8, 1 m. 2 Hum.'fro fil' Regis. The King to all, &c., of our special grace we have granted
to our very dear son Humfry the Custody of our forest
and park of Clarendon ; and of our forests of
Grovely Melchet and Bukholte to hold for
the time of his life with all fees &c. as
fully as our very dear brother John
late Earl Somerset deceased received &c.
Groveley, Melchet. Full and best exemplification.
and the custody of the same pertaining to certain lands in

Pat. 3 R. 2 . s. 3 m, 26. the vill. of Bereford St. Martin and of the profits
and advantages to the same whencesoever pertaining
and of the Bailywick there called Le North bayley
and the profits &c. pertaining. Escaet 7. H. 5.
after the death of Elizabeth Stubbere.

Escaet. 75 d. 3 No. 61. William Ruyntun of Wycheford held in his demesne
as of fee on the day on which he died one messuage
one hide of land ten shillings rent
with appurtenances in Wichford aforesaid of
the Lord the King in capite by Serjeanty to
take charge of the moiety of the forest of
Grauelynge vizt the North baillie as
Grymmesdich divides it and by the service of 22 shillings
per annum vizt To the Lord the King at the Castle of Sarum
2 shillings and to the Prior and Convent of Mayden bradley
20 shillings

Roll 19. Amongst the pleas of Ways. 29 Ed. III. Tully office.

Nicholas de Bonham claims the course of a certain water called Wiley with the fishing in the same running over the soil of Nicholas within the moiety of the Manor of Great Wishford together with the attachments and amerciaments in the same &c. : And because it is ascertained that the same Nicholas and his Ancestors were seised [of] the liberties and profits aforesaid in the aforesaid water therefore he has therein allowance by the right of the Lord the King in all things, always saving &c.

Page 140. 1605.

The College of Saint Edmund of Sarum is worth in
Rents or farm of the Rectory of St. Martin existing and
included in the said city of New Sarum with all tithes
oblations and other profits to the same Rectory belonging
which Henry Jeneno the chaplain holds & occupies
which Rectory is estimated to be in value x. pounds

Page 142. 1689. Thomas Goman.

This is the final Concord made in the Court of the Lord the King at Westminster on the morrow of the Ascension of the Lord in the year of the reign of James the second by the grace of God, King of England Scotland, France & Ireland, defender of the faith &c. after the Conquest the fourth, Before Edward Herbert, Thomas Street, Edward Lutwich & Christopher Milton Justices & other faithful subjects of the Lord the King then there present, Between John Staples & John West plaintiffs and Henry Gauntlett & Ursula his wife deforciants concerning seven messuages & seven gardens with appurtenances in the City of New Sarum. Whereas a plea of convention was summoned between them in the same Court, that is to say that the aforesaid Henry & Ursula acknowledged the aforesaid tenements with appurtenances to be the right of John Staples as they the same John & John West have of the gift of the aforesaid Henry & Ursula, And those tenements they promise quit claim for them the said Henry & Ursula and their heirs to the aforesaid John & John & the heirs of him the said John Staples for ever And moreover the same Henry and Ursula have granted for them & the heirs of Henry himself that they will warrant to the aforesaid John & John & the heirs of the said John Staples the aforesaid tenements with appertenances against the aforesaid Henry & Ursula & the heirs of the said Henry for ever. And for this acknowledgement, remission quit claim, warranty fine and agreement the same John & John have given to the aforesaid Henry & Ursula three hundred pounds sterling.

605. Goman. This is the final Concord made in the Court of the Lord the King at Westminster on Easter day to the fifteenth day* in the year of the reign of James King of England, France, Scotland Ireland defender of the faith &c. of England ffrance, Ireland the second and of Scotland the thirty eighth before Edmund Anderson, Thomas Walingston, Roger Kingsnight, Peter Edgburton & William Daniell, Justices & other faithful subjects of the Lord the King then there present. Between Thomas Goman plaintiff and Edmund Uvedale . . . . deforciant concerning two messuages & two gardens with appurtenances in the City of New Sarum, whence a plea of convention was summoned between them in the same Court. That is to say that the aforesaid Edmund acknowledges the aforesaid tenements with appurtenances to be the right of the said Thomas those which he the same Thomas had of the gift of the aforesaid Edmund . . . . . they promise quit claim for themselves & their heirs to the aforesaid Thomas & his heirs for ever. And moreover the same Edmund granted for himself & his heirs that they (shall warrant) to the aforesaid Thomas & his heirs the aforesaid tenements . . . . against the aforesaid Edmund & his heirs for ever. And for this acknowledgment, remission [quit claim] warranty fine & concord the same Thomas gave to the aforesaid Edmund eighty pounds sterling.

"1448. Friday 21 June.

ge 145. "It pleased the same also at that time that Master Robert Langrygge Communarius and Sir Richard Trovy should to farm let the parish church of St. Martin to any baker in the city on condition that he who thus receives it to farm should pay his farm in loaves and alms, to be distributed by the hands of the communarius and upon that they have given leave to the said Langrygge and Trovy to send for William Baker who for a long while has made alms-loaves of this kind to account &c. whether he will undertake the farm in that manner, which if he be unwilling to do, to try another baker."

(Burgh Register fo. 16. D. & C. of Salisbury Records.)

* The usual translation is "In the quinzime of Easter."

The Vestments.

A letter, dated October 25th, 1886, and signed by some twenty members of the congregation and friends of St. Martin's, was sent to the Rev. C. N. Wyld, with a set of linen vestments. It ran thus:—"We, whose names follow, believing that the use of a distinct vestment at Celebrations of the Holy Eucharist in St. Martin's Church would tend to produce among the worshippers a greater feeling of reverence towards that holy Sacrament, with little or no ill effects, have subscribed and bought a plain linen vestment, which we now present to you, in the hope and with the earnest desire that you will accept and allow such to be worn."

In 1895 a set of white silk vestments, with burse and veil, was given by a number of communicants connected with St. Martin's, the majority of subscribers being males. It was worn for the first time on St. Martin's Day. In 1896 a set of red silk vestments, with burse and veil, was given by communicants and worn on Whit-Sunday; and in the same year a set of purple vestments, with burse and veil.

In 1897 a very fine set of red silk vestments, with burse and veil, was given by about 100 subscribers; and in 1898 a very fine set of white silk vestments, with burse and veil, was given by subscription, and worn for the first time on Easter Day.

The Church, therefore, possesses five sets—two white, two red, and one purple—and they were all made by the Sisters of Bethany, 6, Lloyd Street, London, W.C. The best red frontal, which was a gift to the Church at Whitsuntide, 1897, and the best white frontal, which was presented by a number of subscribers at Easter, 1903, were both worked by the Sisters of Bethany. A purple frontal, the gift of Mrs. Lister and Miss Palgrave in memory of their mother, Lady Palgrave, and worked by Miss Palgrave, Miss F. Awdry, and Miss Cripps, was given in 1906.

It would be impossible to give a list, with dates and donors, of all the dossals, hangings, linen, &c., which have been given from time to time to the Church, but some of the early work was done by Mrs. Sidney Lear, who for many years was an active worker in the parish.

The Altar rails, of polished oak and metal work, in the Side Chapel, were made by Messrs. Barkentin, of London, and were the gift of Miss Wade.

The Altar rails in the Chancel were given by the Ecclesiastical Commissioners in 1906.

Note to Page 54.

On the North side of the Tower is the following inscription, now almost illegible :—

"This Spire was repaired in
the year of our Lord 1791.

T. ADAMS }
J. YOUNG } Churchwardens."

Note to Page 99.

The Altar of St. Martin's Church is partly formed out of a screen erected in Salisbury Cathedral by Sir Christopher Wren. (From a note of Mr. Fisher's, late Clerk of the Works at the Cathedral.)

Note to Page 116.

	1811. Population.	Inhabited Houses.
St. Thomas	2579 ...	417
St. Edmund	3252 ...	868
St. Martin	1888 ...	365

In the autumn of 1904 a crack was observed at the East end, in each corner of the Chancel wall. This fact having been reported to the Ecclesiastical Commissioners, in the following summer they caused the whole of the parts affected to be underpinned, which work was carried out by Mr. Kite, and in the succeeding spring they replaced the old Altar Rails by new ones of oak, and remodelled the Steps around the Altar by laying Hopton Wood stone, white marble and glass mosaic tiling in place of the previous red tiles.

ERRATA.

Page 5, line 22, for *east* read *west*.
„ 15, 1698. Peter Terry, Rector, should be 1689.
„ 60, Del. 1632.
„ 130, "This paper, written 8 Hen. VII. (A.D. 1492)," which is indorsed on it in a later hand, is evidently wrong, as it treats of matters after 1 Ed. VI. (1547). (*T.H.B.*)
„ 132, line 31, for *de re* read *de jure*
„ „ „ — for *condenis* read *condicon'e*.
„ „ „ 32, for *conuencaes* read *conuencoes*.
„ „ „ 35, for *cum* read *sum*.
„ „ „ 36, for *carta indentata* read *carte indentate*.
„ „ „ — for *p'senta* read *p'sente*.
„ „ „ 42, for *p'positio* read *p'positis*.
„ 133, line 7, for *p'met'* read *quiete*.
„ „ „ 21, for *simul* read *simus*.
„ „ „ 22, for *ad* read *cum*.
„ „ „ 23, for *suis ome's* read *suis contra om'es*.
„ „ „ 25, for *p'dm'* read *p'd'ce*.
„ 137, line 34, for *sim'* read *sum*.
„ „ „ 41, for *pro puteo* read *per p'ntes*.
„ 138, line 13, for *ex* read *et*.
„ „ „ 32, for *p'rem'* read *p'tin'*.
„ „ „ 38, for *rn'* read *usu*.
„ „ „ 40, for *non* read *nos*.
„ „ „ 41, for *Joh'is* read *Joh'es*.
„ „ „ 46, for *ordinam* read *ordinaui*.
„ 139, line 1, for *voces* read *veros*.
„ „ „ 2, for *loquitur* read *legales*.
„ „ „ — for *mois* read *nobis*.
„ „ „ 3, for *cor'a* read *cet'a*.
„ „ „ 23, for *Serjauciane* read *Serjanciam*.
„ 142, line 19, for *suus'* read *sum*.
„ „ „ 20, for *retogu* read *recogn'*.
„ „ „ 21, for *Ve illijque* read *Vt illaque*.
„ „ „ 22, for *Et ill*, &c., read *Et illa p'misor*, &c., *quietilam de se*.
„ „ „ 24, for *p'tot* read *p'ter*.
„ „ „ 25, for *Sarau't* read *Warant'*.
„ „ „ 26, for *ten'tum* read *ten't cum*.
„ „ „ 28, for *retogu* read *recogn'*.
„ „ „ — for *fins* read *fine*.
„ „ „ — for *quietilani'* read *quietclam*.
„ „ line 2 from bottom, for *conuenicoe's* read *conuencionis*.
„ „ bottom line, for *retogu' p'd'ctt* read *recogn' p'd'ct*. In the blank space insert [*esse jus*].
„ „ margin, for *1609* read *1605*.
„ 143, line 2, for *primisibz quit'ni* read *p'miserunt quiet'm*.
„ „ „ 3, for *p'tota* read *p'terea*.
„ „ „ 6, for *toucq. die* read *concordia*.
„ „ „ — for *p'missione . . . lain'* read *remissione quietclam*.

www.ingramcontent.com/pod-product-compliance
Lightning Source LLC
LaVergne TN
LVHW060451051026
849518LV00002B/729